THE LEARNING STRATEGIES HANDBOOK

Anna Uhl Chamot
Sarah Barnhardt
Pamela Beard El-Dinary
Jill Robbins

Longman

This book is dedicated to our children: Geoffroy Alain Chamot,
Paul Barnhardt Streett, Aaron Ashruf El-Dinary, and Andrew and Katie Robbins.

May strategies give them the motivation to be lifelong learners!

The Learning Strategies Handbook

© 1999 by Addison Wesley Longman, Inc.

Pearson Education, 10 Bank Street, White Plains, NY 10606

Editorial director: Louise Jennewine
Acquisition editor: Anne Stribling
Development editor: Elise Pritchard
Director of design and production: Rhea Banker
Production supervisor: Liza Pleva
Managing editor: Linda Moser
Associate production editor: Martin Yu
Senior manufacturing manager: Patrice Fraccio
Manufacturing supervisor: Edith Pullman
Cover design: Rhea Banker
Text design: Helene Berinsky
Text art: Publication Services, Inc.
Text composition: Publication Services, Inc.

Library of Congress Cataloging-in-Publication Data

The learning strategies handbook / Anna Uhl Chamot . . . [et al.].
    p. cm.
  Includes bibliographical references and index.
  ISBN 0-201-38548-1
  1. Language and languages—Study and teaching. I. Chamot, Anna Uhl.
P51.L53 1999   99-13597
418' .007—dc21   CIP

5 6 7 8 9 10–BW–04 03

Contents

PART THREE: *From Theory through Practice*

List of Figures

PART ONE

Helping Students Learn

Chapter

INTRODUCTION

This book is for teachers who believe that all students can learn. It is for teachers who believe that they can help students become more successful learners. And it is for teachers who want their students to become more independent learners. Although the guidelines and sample lessons presented in this book focus on helping students learn a second or foreign language, they can be applied to any subject or curriculum content.

In this book, we describe learning strategies that can help students learn both language and content, and we provide a practical approach to learning strategies instruction. Learning strategies are procedures or techniques that learners can use to facilitate a learning task. While some learning strategies, such as *taking notes* or *making graphic organizers*, are observable, most strategies are mental processes that are not directly observable. Teachers can gain insight into their students' mental processes by discussing with students their approaches to specific learning tasks and any special techniques or tricks they have for understanding, remembering, and using information and skills. These discussions not only help teachers better understand their students' learning strategies. They also help students better understand themselves as learners.

Metacognition, or reflecting on one's own thinking and learning, is the hallmark of the successful learner. The goal of learning strategies instruction is to assist students in developing awareness of their own metacognition and thus control of their own learning. Learners who are aware of their own learning processes, strategies, and preferences are able to regulate their learning endeavors to meet their own goals. In other words, they become increasingly independent and self-regulated learners.

We have worked for a number of years with language learners and their teachers to identify, describe, and develop learning strategies. This book is the result of our own research and that of others as we have explored practical applications of learning strategies to many different types of classrooms. Our intent is to share what we have learned through research and practice with teachers interested in applying learning strategies instruction in their own classrooms. We believe that learning strategies instruction can assist teachers in implementing a number of important current educational trends, including national curriculum standards, content-based second language and foreign language instruction, portfolio assessment, and a social-cognitive model of teaching.

National Curriculum Standards

The establishment of national curriculum standards is seen as an essential component in educational reform. Educators in the United States and in many other countries are calling for curriculum standards that clearly state what elementary school and secondary school students should know and be able to do in different subject areas at particular grade levels or ages. A review of content standards advocated by professional educational organizations in the United States and by national education systems in other countries clearly shows that the standards reflect the high expectations held for all students, including students learning a second language. To meet these high expectations and attain national, state, and local standards, students need to know how to learn as well as what to learn.

The English as a Second Language (ESL) Standards for Pre-Kindergarten through Grade 12 students identify three major goal areas (Teachers of English to Speakers of Other Languages [TESOL], 1997):

1. Using English for communication in social settings
2. Using English to learn subject matter content
3. Using English in culturally appropriate ways

Each of these three ESL goals is accompanied by three standards that identify the types of knowledge and skills needed to reach that goal.

Thus standards for Goal 1 (communication in social settings) include using English for personal expression and enjoyment. Standards for Goal 2 (academic achievement in content subjects) include both classroom interaction and learning subject matter through English, and standards for Goal 3 (sociolinguistic and cultural competence) include using different aspects of language in culturally and socially appropriate ways. The third standard for each goal specifies the use of learning strategies in achieving the goal, as follows (TESOL, 1997, pp. 9–10):

- Goal 1, Standard 3: "Use appropriate learning strategies to extend communicative competence."

- Goal 2, Standard 3: "Use appropriate learning strategies to construct and apply academic knowledge."

- Goal 3, Standard 3: "Use appropriate learning strategies to extend sociolinguistic and sociocultural competence."

The ESL Standards document also provides descriptors that identify both mental and observable behaviors that characterize each standard. Sample progress indicators for different grade levels are identified in the ESL Standards as well. Descriptors of each standard list strategies designed to assist students in reaching the goals, as well as sample progress indicators that describe how students within a range of grade levels (Pre-K–3, 4–8, or 9–12) should apply the learning strategies. Finally, the ESL Standards document provides classroom vignettes illustrating appropriate instruction for each grade-level range.

The learning strategies identified in the ESL Standards are among those described in the metacognitive framework of Chapter 2 of this book. In Chapters 3 to 8, we explain how teachers can assist their students to develop skills to use these learning strategies independently, and in subsequent chapters, we provide lesson plans for teaching these learning strategies.

The standards for foreign language learning also recognize the importance of strategies use in language learning (National Standards in Foreign Language Education Project, 1996). Both learning strategies and communication strategies are identified as strands woven into the foreign language curricular elements. Strategies support all five of the standards: Communication, Cultures, Connections, Comparisons, and Communities. These standards are often referred to as the five C's of foreign language study:

 ❶ Communicate in languages other than English.

❷ Gain knowledge and understanding of other cultures.

❸ Connect with other disciplines and acquire information.

❹ Develop insight into the nature of language and culture.

Participate in multilingual communities at home and around the world. (p. 9)

Foreign language teachers are encouraged to provide direct instruction in learning strategies, such as *selective attention*, *activating prior knowledge, summarizing, questioning*, and *making inferences*. In this book, we describe these learning strategies and many others and we provide instructional guidelines and sample lessons for a variety of different learning strategies.

Learning strategies instruction and use is identified in the Foreign Language Standards as a means to help students become better language learners and to help them develop control over and responsibility for their own learning. In other words, learning strategies use helps students become self-regulated language learners. The importance accorded to learning strategies by the Foreign Language Standards is clearly stated: "Learning strategies are an integral part of language programs, providing students with the tools for a lifetime of learning." (National Standards in Foreign Language Education Project, 1996, p. 30).

Content-Based Language Instruction

Another trend of continuing interest in language education, also reflected in both the ESL and Foreign Language Standards, is the integration of content information into the language curriculum. When content is included in the language classroom, students learn to use the second language to acquire new information. Content has traditionally focused on cultural aspects of the target language, ranging from popular culture to art, literature, history, and the like. What is new in content-based language instruction is that the content is now often drawn from academic subjects such as science, social studies, and even mathematics. Instructional models for integrating content instruction with language learning have been developed both in ESL and foreign language education (see, for example, Cantoni-Harvey, 1987; Chamot & O'Malley, 1994; Mohan, 1986; Snow, Met, & Genesee, 1989).

Content-based language instruction has many advantages for students. In an ESL class, the introduction of subject matter content can help prepare students for the transition into the content classes taught in English. In a foreign language class, students can expand their language proficiency into content areas of personal interest or knowledge. Foreign language immersion classrooms provide a unique example of totally content-based language instruction.

Content-based language instruction is motivating for students when they have an intrinsic interest in the content topics studied. However, students also find that trying to learn content through a second language poses additional challenges because they must process both the new language and new information simultaneously. Learning strategies can help students meet these dual demands more successfully.

The accumulated evidence supporting the use of learning strategies with both first language content subject tasks and in second language learning point to the importance of combining strategies instruction with second language content.

Portfolio Assessment

Current trends in the assessment of student learning recommend that alternative forms of assessment, rather than standardized tests alone, be used to evaluate students' progress in school achievement. One increasingly favored approach to alternative assessment is the use of portfolios to gather chronological indices of student learning. Portfolio assessment can be defined as ". . . the evaluation of a collected, organized, annotated body of work, produced over time by a learner, which demonstrates progress toward specific objectives" (Barnhardt, Kevorkian, & Delett, 1997, p. 3). Students and teachers work together to select pieces of student work that demonstrate progress and achievement in meeting specified objectives. An advantage of portfolios over more traditional forms of assessment is that they can provide evidence of growth in many different dimensions of learning. In the language classroom, for example, the teacher might decide to collect examples of student writing, tapes of oral interviews, exercises for reading and listening comprehension, and learning logs in which students evaluate their own learning by indicating their strengths and areas of weakness.

Student self-evaluation can provide important information to add to assessment portfolios. An important dimension in language learning is students' development of appropriate learning strategies. However, standardized and other traditional tests do not capture these mental processes. Because learning strategies are most often not observable phenomena, teachers need to rely on students' own reports about the strategies they've used. For example, students might write learning logs about strategies used for a language task or complete an interview or questionnaire about learning strategies they find useful for different types of tasks. (Chapter 7 provides suggestions for student self-evaluation of learning strategies.)

The Cognitive Academic Language Learning Approach (CALLA)

The Cognitive Academic Language Learning Approach (CALLA) is an instructional model that integrates current educational trends in standards, content-based language instruction, learning strategies, and portfolio assessment. The CALLA model provides explicit instruction in learning strategies that will assist students in meeting national curriculum standards, learning both language and content, and becoming independent learners who can evaluate their own learning. CALLA is designed to accelerate academic achievement for English language learning (ELL) students and has been applied in ESL, EFL, and foreign language instruction. The theoretical framework of CALLA is a social-cognitive learning model that emphasizes the role of students' prior knowledge, the importance of collaborative learning, and the development of metacognitive awareness and self-reflection.

A CALLA curriculum has the following three components:

- High-priority curriculum content
- Academic language development with a focus on literacy
- Explicit learning strategies instruction

While this structure is straightforward, integrating the three components in actual instruction can be difficult without the guidelines of an instructional framework. The framework developed for CALLA is designed to assist teachers in incorporating the components and theoretical principles in planning instruction (Chamot & O'Malley, 1994).

The CALLA instructional design is task-based and has five phases in which teachers combine the three components of content, language, and learning strategies:

- Preparation
- Presentation
- Practice
- Evaluation
- Expansion

In the first phase, Preparation, teachers focus on finding out what prior knowledge students have about the content topic to be taught, their level of language proficiency, and their current learning strategies for this type of task. In the second phase, Presentation, teachers use a variety of techniques to make new information and skills accessible and comprehensible to students. These techniques include demonstrations, modeling, and visual support. This phase is followed by or integrated with the third phase, Practice, in which students use the new information and skills (including learning strategies) in activities that involve collaboration, problem solving, inquiry, and hands-on experiences. The fourth phase, Evaluation, has students self-evaluate their understanding and proficiency with the content, language, and learning strategies they have been practicing. Finally, in the fifth phase, Expansion, students engage in activities to apply what they have learned to their own lives, including other classes at school, their families and community, and their cultural and linguistic backgrounds. These five phases are recursive, thereby allowing for flexibility in lesson planning and implementation.

In this book, we use the CALLA instructional sequence as a framework for teaching learning strategies so teachers can more easily organize and plan their strategies instruction. (See Chapter 3 for a description of this instructional framework.)

How to Use This Book

This book is organized as a practical resource for language teachers interested in introducing learning strategies to their students. Chapter 1, the introductory chapter, first sets the stage by providing a rationale for teaching learning strategies as a means of fostering learner autonomy. It then relates learning strategies to several important trends in language education, including national standards, content-based language instruction, and authentic assessment. Finally, it describes the Cognitive Academic Language Learning Approach, the instructional model that we have used to guide our suggestions for teaching learning strategies.

Chapter 2 describes the model of learning underlying our approach to learning strategies instruction and provides definitions of twenty-seven learning strategies that language learners have found useful. An explanation of why it is useful, an example of its use, and suggestions for when to use it accompany each strategy definition.

Chapter 3 describes the application of the CALLA instructional sequence to the framework that we have used to develop our model for teaching learning strategies. Chapters 4 through 8 further develop each of the five recursive phases (Preparation, Presentation, Practice, Evaluation, and Expansion), with specific guidelines and sample activities for each.

Chapter 9 identifies learning theories that support learning strategies instruction, provides a review of learning strategies research in both native language and second language contexts, and discusses the link between motivation and learning strategies. Throughout the chapter, we draw on theory and research to provide a strong rationale for integrating learning strategies instruction into the language classroom.

Finally, Chapter 10 contains nineteen examples of learning strategy lessons for different ages, instructional contexts, and levels of language proficiency. These sample lessons were developed by language teachers and incorporate the learning strategies identified in Chapter 2. Each lesson identifies the target audience for which it is intended [English as a Second Language (ESL), English as a Foreign Language (EFL), content-based language instruction, or foreign language], the level of language proficiency, and the approximate grade level. However, most lessons are easily adaptable to different language contexts and proficiency levels, and many can also work well with various ages of students. We hope that these lessons will help you to begin learning strategies instruction in your classroom.

METACOGNITIVE MODEL OF STRATEGIC LEARNING

This chapter presents a metacognitive model of learning that learners use to work through a language task. The model organizes learning strategies according to the metacognitive processes of **planning, monitoring, problem solving,** and **evaluating.** Information on how, when, and why to use each strategy is given so that teachers can make instruction explicit, thus enabling students to reflect on and exercise control over their learning.

Instructional Objectives

This chapter will help you to:

- Provide a rationale for the strategies model.
- Show how each process works in coordination to assist learning.
- Define and give examples of individual language learning strategies.
- Present strategies that frequently work in combination.

The Metacognitive Model

Organizing Strategies into Four Processes

Learning strategies research has revealed a wealth of information on the types of strategies students use to learn. Over one hundred strategies have been identified by different language learning strategies researchers (Rubin, 1981; Stern, 1975; Wenden, 1987b; Oxford, 1986; O'Malley & Chamot, 1990; Chamot & Kupper, 1989; O'Malley, Chamot, Stewner-Manzanares, Küpper, & Russo, 1985a; Chamot, Barnhardt, El-Dinary, Carbonaro, & Robbins 1993; Chamot, Barnhardt, El-Dinary, & Robbins, 1996; Cohen, 1990; Rost & Ross, 1991). Chapter 9 provides an overview of the research on learning strategies. The practitioner is faced with the challenge of how to interpret and use this information in the classroom. The Metacognitive Model of Strategic Learning organizes learning strategies in such a way that they become manageable and helpful to students and teachers. It outlines the processes effective learners use to work through any challenging language learning task and describes ways to transfer strategy use to other subject areas, as well as to real-life situations. By using this model to guide instruction, the language teacher will provide students with a powerful approach that can help them throughout their lives.

The Metacognitive Model of Strategic Learning is based on extensive research on learning strategies in which data were collected on the strategy use of effective foreign and second language learners ranging from elementary through university level. (See Chamot & Kupper, 1989; Chamot et al., 1993; Chamot et al., 1996; O'Malley & Chamot, 1990; O'Malley et al., 1985a.) Learning strategies were chosen for inclusion in the model based on their usefulness and applicability to a broad range of learning tasks. Students can use these strategies for all of the modalities—reading, listening, writing, and speaking—as well as for the retention of vocabulary and content information. These are the strategies used by good learners; all have been successfully incorporated by teachers into second language instruction.

The Model consists of four metacognitive processes:

- Planning
- Monitoring
- Problem solving
- Evaluating

Students work through each of these processes for any challenging learning task. For example, in a typical classroom task, such as an interactive speaking interview of a classmate's leisure time activities, the good learner might begin **planning** by thinking about various activities in which people often engage in their free time. She continues **planning** by narrowing her focus to those activities for which she knows vocabulary in the target language. Depending on the extent of her knowledge, she may decide to gather additional vocabulary by asking her teacher, looking at her notes, or checking a dictionary. She thinks about how to formulate questions in the target language, and she anticipates the types of responses she may get to her questions. She then writes down her questions and/or some key vocabulary pertinent to her topics. She reminds herself of language features such as pronunciation and intonation. After she begins her interview, she **monitors** herself by listening to herself speak, watching the interviewee's face, and listening to the interviewee's answers to make sure her questions are clear and that the interviewee understands. She asks for clarification when she does not understand a response (**problem solving**). This good learner repeats the interviewee's main points to make sure she understands, and she gives feedback to show she is paying attention. After the interview is finished, she **evaluates** by reflecting on her use of language and any new words or phrases she acquired. She may think about whether she opened and closed the interview in appropriate ways. Finally, she makes written or mental notes of what she might do differently the next time to improve her performance. In this example, the student used all four processes to successfully complete the assignment. Her strategic behavior helped her prepare for the task, actually do the task, resolve difficulties and overcome her lack of information, and reflect on her performance.

As a teacher, are you aware of your own use of any or all of these metacognitive processes? Gather some examples to share with your students as you present the model to them.

Many of us use these processes every day. As teachers, we work through them for every lesson we plan, implement, and evaluate. However, many times we do not think consciously about why we use them. Without explicit implementation of the model, students will not be able to exercise control over their learning because they will not know how, why, or when to engage in specific strategic behaviors. Without this knowledge, they also will not be able to transfer strategies from one task to the next. By teaching the model explicitly, teachers can have an impact on students' learning beyond the language taught in their classrooms.

The Recursive Nature of the Model

The four strategic processes are not strictly sequential but may be used as necessary depending on the demands of the task and the interaction between the task and the learner. Figure 2.1 illustrates the

FIGURE 2.1

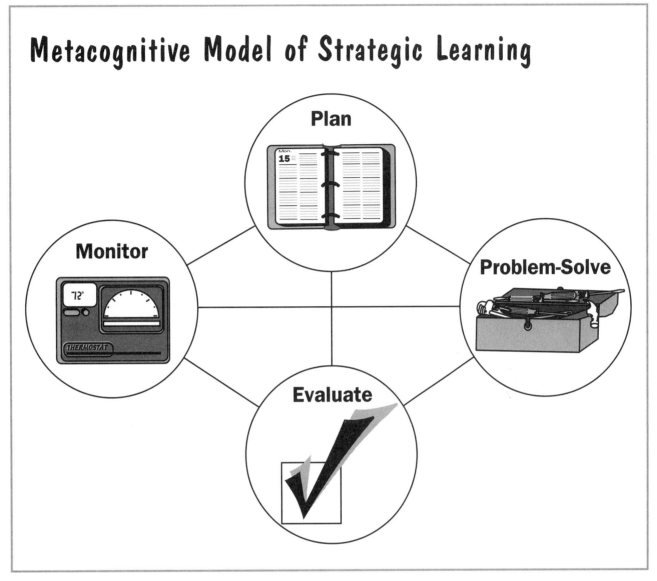

Metacognitive Model of Strategic Learning

Plan

Monitor

Problem-Solve

Evaluate

recursive nature of the model. For instance, when a student begins reading a story in the target language, he **plans** by setting his goals or thinking about what he wants to get out of the story and making predictions about the story based on the title and his prior knowledge of the topic. Then he moves on to the **monitoring** process and, as he reads, checks whether the story is making sense. However, as he reads he decides that, based on new information in the story, he needs to go back and revise some of his plans. He may decide to change his predictions, bring in new background knowledge, or even change goals. He continues reading and then decides to stop and **evaluate** himself after completing only the first part of the story. If he feels he did not understand an important phrase or idea, he may need to go to the **problem-solving** process. In other words, he is using each process as it is needed during the task, although not necessarily sequentially.

EXAMPLE

When explaining the recursive nature of the model to students, you may use the analogy of the writing process. You begin by brainstorming ideas and then writing the first draft. While writing, you may decide that you need to generate more ideas and examples, so you go back to the beginning process. You then revise what you have written based on feedback and your evaluation of your work. Finally, you work through the recursive process until you are satisfied that what you have written is good.

Individual Strategies in the Metacognitive Model of Strategic Learning

This section presents individual strategies according to each of the four processes, as well as strategies for remembering information. Each strategy description contains the metacognitive components necessary for explicit strategy instruction: a definition of the strategy, an example of how the strategy can be used, and an explanation of why and when the strategy is useful. Although a strategy is grouped according to the process in which it most often occurs, it may be used in more than one process depending on the task and how the strategy is applied. Figure 2.2 on pages 15–17 provides a summary of the strategies.

Planning Strategies

Can you think of an instance when you could have completed a task more successfully if you had planned more thoroughly for it?

Planning is a crucial first step toward becoming a self-regulated learner. The graphic of a calendar planner has been chosen to represent the planning process because planning for a learning task is similar to how people plan, organize, and schedule events daily, weekly, or monthly. Planning strategies help people develop and use forethought. They encourage thinking so that the learner reflects before beginning a task rather than diving into the activity unprepared and with little thought as to what will happen. During the planning process, good learners think about how they are going to approach and carry out the task. They set

FIGURE 2.2

Learning Strategies

STRATEGY	DEFINITION	OTHER POSSIBLE TERMS	METACOGNITIVE PROCESSES
Set Goals	Develop personal objectives; Identify the purpose of the task	Determine destination, Establish purpose, Plan objectives	Planning
Directed Attention	Decide in advance to focus on particular tasks and ignore distractions	Pay attention	Planning, Monitoring, Problem-Solving, Evaluating
Activate Background Knowledge	Think about and use what you already know to help you do the task	Use what you know, Elaborate on prior knowledge	Planning, Monitoring, Problem-Solving, Evaluating
Predict	Anticipate information to prepare and give direction for the task	Anticipate, Guess outcome	Planning
Organizational Planning	Plan the task and content sequence	Outline, Brainstorm, Priority list	Planning
Self-Management	Arrange for conditions that help you learn	Know yourself, Plan how to study	Planning
Ask If It Makes Sense	Check understanding and production to keep track of progress and identify problems	Monitor comprehension and production, Self-monitor	Monitoring
Selectively Attend	Focus on key words, phrases, and ideas	Scan, Find specific information	Planning, Monitoring
Deduction/ Induction	Consciously apply learned or self-developed rules	Use a rule, Make a rule	Monitoring

FIGURE 2.2 (*cont.*)

STRATEGY	DEFINITION	OTHER POSSIBLE TERMS	METACOGNITIVE PROCESSES
Personalize/ Contextualize	Relate information to personal experiences	Relate information to your experiences	Monitoring, Remembering information
Take Notes	Write down important words and concepts	T List, Semantic webs, Idea maps, Flow charts, Outlines	Planning, Monitoring, Problem-solving, Evaluating
Use Imagery	Create an image to represent information	Visualization, Mental picture, Draw a picture	Planning, Monitoring, Problem-solving, Evaluating, Remembering information
Manipulate/ Act Out	Handle tangible objects, role-play, and pantomime	Pantomime, Use objects, Role-play	Monitoring, Evaluating, Remembering information
Talk Yourself Through It (Self-Talk)	Reduce anxiety by reminding self of progress, resources available, goals	Positive thinking, Build confidence	Planning, Monitoring, Problem-solving, Evaluating
Cooperate	Work with others to complete tasks, build confidence, and give and receive feedback	Work together, Peer coaching	Planning, Monitoring, Problem-solving, Evaluating, Remembering information
Inference	Make guesses based on previous knowledge	Logical guessing, Use context clues	Problem-solving
Substitute	Use a synonym or descriptive phrase for unknown words	Paraphrase, Circumlocute	Problem-solving
Ask Questions to Clarify	Ask for explanation, verification, and examples; Pose questions to self	Questioning	Planning, Monitoring, Problem-solving, Evaluating

FIGURE 2.2 (*cont*)

STRATEGY	DEFINITION	OTHER POSSIBLE TERMS	METACOGNITIVE PROCESSES
Use Resources	Use reference materials about the language and subject matter	Look it up	Problem-solving
Verify Predictions and Guesses	Check whether your predictions/guesses are correct	Verification	Evaluating
Summarize	Create a mental, oral, or written summary of information	Make a summary	Evaluating
Check Goals	Decide whether goal was met	Keep a learning log, Reflect on progress	Evaluating
Evaluate Yourself	Judge how well you learned the material/did on the task	Self-evaluate, Self-assess, Check yourself	Evaluating, Remembering information
Evaluate Your Strategies	Judge how you applied strategies and the effectiveness of strategies	Learning reflections, Assessing techniques	Evaluating
Imagine with Keyword	Create a visual and personal association between meaning and sound	Keyword Imagery method	Remembering information
Group/Classify	Relate or classify words according to attributes	Ordering, Categorizing, Labeling material	Remembering information
Transfer/ Cognates	Use previously acquired linguistic knowledge; Recognize words that are similar in other known languages		Monitoring, Problem-solving, Remembering information

goals by thinking of their objectives for the task, and they come up with a plan of strategies to help them through the task so that they will meet those objectives. They decide to focus their attention on the task and to ignore distractions. Good learners think of what they already know about the task and the related topic and then predict what they might need to do based on this information.

Although planning always starts at the beginning, the process can be revisited throughout the task if one needs to rethink plans to get back on track. Following are descriptions of some of the most powerful planning strategies.

Planning Strategy 1

SET GOALS

(What is my goal for this task? What do I want to be able to do?)

DEFINITION: Goal setting involves understanding the task and deciding what you should get out of it.

EXAMPLE: If you are going to see a video of a reporter interviewing people about a social issue, your goal might be to understand each person's opinion.

WHY: Identifying your purpose gives you direction and allows you to plan appropriate and effective strategies.

WHEN: For all types of tasks

Planning Strategy 2

DIRECTED ATTENTION

(How can I focus my attention? How can I ignore distractions?)

DEFINITION: Directed attention involves making a conscious decision to focus all of your attention on the task at hand by ignoring mental, physical, and environmental distractions.

EXAMPLE: In your ESL class, you are reading a science text about magnetism. It is a beautiful day, and the birds are singing outside. You cannot wait until class is over so you can go outside and play soccer. You consciously tell yourself that you are going to focus on the science text for now and that you will think about soccer after class.

WHY: Focusing your attention is the first step in taking control of your learning. If you cannot control your focus of attention, little learning can take place. Directed attention helps you increase your level of concentration, a skill that can be transferred to other tasks.

WHEN: Whenever you are working on a challenging task; whenever you feel your attention wandering

Planning Strategy 3
• •

ACTIVATE BACKGROUND KNOWLEDGE
(What do I already know about this?)

DEFINITION: Activating background knowledge helps bring to mind information that you know about the topic, the world, and the language to help you do the task.

EXAMPLE: If you are asked to read a fairy tale in the target language, think about what you know about typical characters, settings, and plots used in fairy tales.

WHY: Thinking about what you already know helps you get ready for the task by familiarizing yourself with it. By having in mind what you already know, you'll find it easier to understand and learn new information by relating it to your background knowledge.

WHEN: Whenever you know what the topic is and you have adequate knowledge of the topic or of related information; whenever new information comes up in the task

Planning Strategy 4
• •

PREDICT
(What do I think will happen?)

DEFINITION: Predicting involves thinking of the kinds of words, phrases, and information that you can expect to encounter based on your background knowledge and/or on information you encounter during the task.

EXAMPLE: If you want to buy a concert ticket, think about what you will need to say to the cashier. For example, you will want to know how to ask about dates, times, and prices in the target language.

WHY: Anticipating information gives you direction for doing the task because you will be attuned to certain types of information.

WHEN: When you have knowledge of the topic; when new information is presented that allows you to refine or modify previous predictions or make new predictions

> **Tip**
> *Keep in mind that due to cultural differences, predictions based on knowledge of your own culture may not always be accurate or appropriate for the target culture.*

Planning Strategy 5

ORGANIZATIONAL PLANNING

(What might I need to do? How can I plan for the task?)

DEFINITION: Organizational planning involves planning how you can accomplish the learning task, generating content in sequence, and brainstorming words, phrases, and information to use in the task.

EXAMPLE: When you are writing a story, develop a plan for the organizational sequence of the content. For instance, what will be in the beginning, middle, and end of the story? Think about the words and phrases you will need in your story.

WHY: Developing a plan before beginning the task gives you direction for the task and helps make sure that you will complete the task. Planning can also help reduce your anxiety by building your confidence through knowing what it is you have to do. By organizing and thinking beforehand, you will already have certain ideas, words, and phrases that you can use in the task.

WHEN: For all types of tasks

Planning Strategy 6

SELF-MANAGEMENT

(How can I best accomplish this task? What do I know best?)

DEFINITION: Self-management involves seeking or arranging the conditions that help you learn and focusing on what you know, including language structures, topics, and personal experiences.

EXAMPLE: If you are going to talk about pastimes, you may choose not to mention rollerblading because you do not know how to say it. Instead, you might focus on soccer, for which you know the target vocabulary.

WHY: Focusing on what you know helps ensure that you will understand and be understood. Understanding the conditions in which you learn will help you perform to the best of your abilities.

WHEN: For any task

Monitoring Strategies

How conscientious are you about monitoring your progress as you work through a task? Do you consistently monitor the effectiveness of your teaching strategies and lessons?

After good learners have prepared an approach, they use monitoring strategies to measure their effectiveness while working on the task. A thermostat is used to represent the monitoring process because it symbolizes the two components of monitoring. First, people monitor how they are doing as they work, just as a thermostat monitors the temperature in a room at a given moment. Second, they monitor by making adjustments to how they are working as necessary, just as a thermostat can be adjusted to make a room cooler or warmer.

While monitoring, students should think about where their focus of concentration needs to be at any given time and then consciously focus their attention on a specific aspect of the task. Learners monitor their comprehension and production by thinking about whether they are understanding when reading or listening or if they are making sense when writing or speaking. Learners also think about how the information they are receiving or producing fits in with their knowledge of the world based on their own experiences. They rely on their knowledge of the rules of language to make decisions about the language they are processing. If the task has a visual component, they may imagine a picture or think of a relevant situation to help them understand and produce language. When good students feel frustrated or overwhelmed, they give themselves encouragement by thinking about their learning tools, that is, their strategies. They use social skills to work with and learn from others while completing the task. The following monitoring strategies help students regulate their learning.

Monitoring Strategy 1

ASK IF IT MAKES SENSE

(Do I understand this? Am I making sense?)

DEFINITION: This strategy involves checking your understanding by asking yourself, "Is this making sense to me?" or checking your clarity by asking yourself, "Am I making sense?"

EXAMPLE: As you are reading a story, periodically ask yourself if you understand what's happening. If you're telling a friend a humorous story and she doesn't laugh, she might have misunderstood you.

WHY: Asking yourself if everything makes sense helps you to keep track of how you're doing and to identify problems.

WHEN: For all types of tasks, especially more challenging ones

Monitoring Strategy 2

SELECTIVELY ATTEND

(What parts should I pay most attention to? Is this information important?)

DEFINITION: Selective attention involves choosing to focus on specific aspects of language or situational details that will help you perform the task.

EXAMPLE: If you have to read a train schedule to get to your destination, you might choose to focus on finding departure times and platform numbers.

WHY: Deciding to focus on specific information makes it easier to identify the critical information for your goal because you can give it full concentration and ignore distractions. You can also choose to focus on information you know to help you understand and communicate better. Focusing on information you don't know can help you pinpoint problems and expand your learning.

WHEN: Useful for a variety of tasks, especially if your goal requires you to understand or give specific information

Monitoring Strategy 3
● ●

DEDUCTION/INDUCTION
(Which rules can I apply to help me in this situation?)

DEFINITION: Deduction and induction involve your applying or figuring out rules about language, including grammar, phonology, and morphology.

EXAMPLE: When you are reading, you look at the ends of words to identify which ones are verbs in order to note the tense of speech.

WHY: Using your knowledge of language rules helps you comprehend and produce the language accurately. Deduction increases your self-reliance because you can monitor your performance based on information you have about the language. Feelings of self-reliance can lead to increased confidence in your learning abilities.

WHEN: Whenever you need to apply rules in order to understand and produce language and you have knowledge of the necessary rules

Monitoring Strategy 4
● ●

PERSONALIZE/CONTEXTUALIZE
(How does this fit with my experiences? How does this fit in with the real world?)

DEFINITION: Personalizing or contextualizing involves comparing the message to your background knowledge to see if it makes sense.

EXAMPLE: As you are reading a cooking recipe, think about your own culinary experiences to help you understand and figure out ingredients and the sequence of the steps.

WHY: Checking language input and output against what you know helps you ensure that it makes sense. Connecting information to your experiences makes it more meaningful to you and thus more memorable.

WHEN: For all tasks, however, be aware that cultural differences may exist; also useful for remembering

Monitoring Strategy 5

TAKE NOTES

(What important information can I write down?)

DEFINITION: Taking notes involves your writing down key words and concepts in abbreviated verbal, graphic, or numerical form.

EXAMPLE: You are reading a dense text about computers. You know you have to understand the text because you will have a quiz on the information. You take notes by making a T list, in which you jot down the main idea and supporting details of each paragraph.

WHY: You can refer back to notes at any time. Writing down important information in a format such as a T list, semantic web, or outline can help you remember and understand better because you are establishing additional mental links that organize the information.

WHEN: Whenever you need to remember or refer back to information; whenever information is complex; whenever written notes can help you perform the task

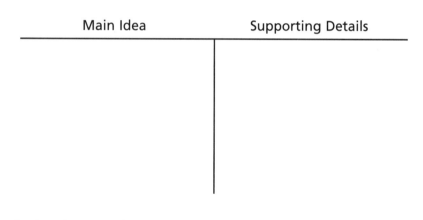

Main Idea | Supporting Details

Monitoring Strategy 6

USE IMAGERY

(Can I imagine a situation or draw a picture that will help me understand?)

DEFINITION: Using imagery involves creating an image that helps you represent information.

EXAMPLE: If you read a story that involves a change of seasons, your "mental movie" could depict changing scenery. When writing in the target language about your first trip to a city, play back images of the trip in your mind.

WHY: Forming pictures is a way to check if the information makes sense; you can watch for inconsistencies in your "mental movie." Mental links with images also help you remember the information.

WHEN: Whenever the content lends itself to vivid visual images; also useful for remembering

Monitoring Strategy 7

MANIPULATE/ACT OUT

(Can I use real objects or act out the situation to help me do this?)

DEFINITION: This strategy involves your manipulating tangible objects, role-playing, or pantomiming the situation to contextualize language.

EXAMPLE: If you are practicing phrases regarding health, you could role-play a visit to a doctor's office.

WHY: Objects and actions help you create mental links with information and these links help you learn and remember.

WHEN: Whenever available; easiest for concrete concepts and situations; can make abstract concepts more concrete; also useful for remembering

Monitoring Strategy 8

TALK YOURSELF THROUGH IT (SELF-TALK)

(I can do this! What strategies can I use to help me?)

DEFINITION: Self-talk involves making positive statements such as "I can do it" to help yourself get through challenging tasks.

EXAMPLE: If you're reading a scientific article in the target language, you could tell yourself, "Don't give up on this!" or "It's okay that I don't understand the whole thing."

WHY: Reassuring yourself while doing difficult tasks may enable you to do more than you thought you could because even if you can't do the task perfectly, you can probably do some of it.

WHEN: For all types of challenging tasks; helpful if you tend to get nervous when speaking in the target language or when taking a test

Tip

Be sure to choose a partner who keeps you on task and often gives you new ideas or helps you clarify your thinking. Remember that sometimes it helps to have somebody explain something to you. At other times, you need a chance to try to explain to somebody else so you can be sure you really understand it yourself.

Monitoring Strategy 9

COOPERATE

(How can I work with others to do this?)

DEFINITION: Cooperation involves your working with classmates to complete tasks and/or to give and receive feedback.

EXAMPLE: If you have to give a speech in class, practice with a peer, who will ask questions that he or she thinks the teacher or other students might ask.

WHY: Working with other people gives you a chance to share your strengths so that you all can do a better job.

WHEN: When classmates are available or the task requires group work; whenever you need feedback; also useful for remembering

Problem-Solving Strategies

When good students have difficulty at any time during a task, they choose a strategy from the problem-solving process. For instance, if they do not know the meaning of a word, they make an educated guess based on all available information. If they do not know how to say something, they think of another way to say it or they say something different. They use any resource available to them to solve the problem, whether it comes from within themselves, through reference materials, or from another person. The strategies included in the problem-solving process range from solving problems autonomously by making a guess based on the context to looking up information in a dictionary. Students who actively and appropriately engage in problem solving are more successful at learning tasks.

Evaluate your own problem-solving skills and strategies by reflecting on a recent task that you had some difficulty completing. Were you able to identify what your problems were? How did you resolve them?

Problem-Solving Strategy 1

INFERENCE

(Can I guess what this might mean?)

DEFINITION: Inferencing involves guessing the meaning of unfamiliar language based on what you know, the content, the language, and other contextual clues (for example, nonverbal cues and pictures).

EXAMPLE: You are reading a dialogue about school, and you repeatedly see the word meaning "to study," which is not familiar to you. Based on your knowledge of the language, you figure out that this word is probably a verb. Many of the words in close proximity to the unknown word are cognates such as mathematics, literature, biology, and music. Based on this information, you make a guess that the word must mean "to study."

WHY: Often, the information you need to solve problems is already available if you just look at other parts of the task and at your own resources. Drawing inferences can help you quickly solve problems yourself without having to go to another person or to reference materials.

WHEN: When something doesn't make sense to you; when necessary context is available

Problem-Solving Strategy 2

SUBSTITUTE

(How else can I say this? Is there another word that might fit?)

DEFINITION: This strategy involves substituting known words or phrases when you do not know or cannot remember a specific word or phrase.

EXAMPLE: You have lost your contact lens in the sink. You do not know how to say contact lens in the target language. You could describe it by saying that it is a small, round, plastic thing that you put in your eye to help you see.

WHY: Substituting allows you to quickly solve a problem so that you can keep communication going because it is difficult to know every word in the target language and constant use of a dictionary can impede and slow down communication. Substituting also helps you to communicate correctly because you are relying on language that you know.

WHEN: When you do not know how to say something; when you know another way to communicate what you want to say

Problem-Solving Strategy 3

ASK QUESTIONS TO CLARIFY

(What help do I need? Who can I ask? How should I ask?)

DEFINITION: Clarifying involves your asking for explanation, verification, rephrasing, or examples.

EXAMPLE: If your teacher says an unfamiliar word, such as *albañil*, when you're studying professions, you could figure out the meaning by asking questions such as "Does the person work in the city or country? Is it an indoor job or outdoor job?" Specific questions like this can give you the information needed to figure out the word's meaning without your just asking, "What does that mean?"

WHY: Pinpointing and communicating your problems by asking specific questions can help you solve comprehension and communication problems.

WHEN: Whenever something important doesn't make sense to you or you don't know how to say something and others who can help you are available

Problem-Solving Strategy 4

USE RESOURCES

(What information do I need? Where can I find more information about this?)

DEFINITION: This strategy involves your using reference materials such as dictionaries, textbooks, computer programs, CD-ROMs, and the Internet.

EXAMPLE: If you get confused when reading a novel and you notice an unfamiliar verb structure, you could look in your textbook index to locate information on the structure.

WHY: Looking up unfamiliar information in a reference source can help you solve complex problems, especially if no one is available to help you.

WHEN: When something crucial doesn't make sense to you or you don't know how to say something that is crucial to your message

Evaluating Strategies

After completing part or all of a task, good learners reflect on how well it went. This process allows them to see if they carried out their plans and to check how well strategies helped. Strategic students assess whether they met their goals for the task and if they did not, why they didn't meet those goals and what they can do differently next time. They evaluate the appropriateness of their predictions and guesses. If those were not correct, good learners think of how they can learn to make better ones next time. Regardless of whether the self-evaluation is positive or negative, it is important for students to learn from it so they can make improvements on the next task.

How do you assess whether a lesson you taught was successful? What methods do you use to evaluate your own performance as an instructor?

Evaluating Strategy 1

VERIFY PREDICTIONS AND GUESSES
(Were my predictions and guesses right? Why or why not?)

DEFINITION: This strategy involves checking whether your predictions and expectations were met while you carried out the task.

EXAMPLE: If you predicted that you might hear words for temperature, precipitation, sunny, or cold in a weather report, think about which of these words you actually heard.

WHY: Evaluating the appropriateness of your predictions and expectations helps you decide how well you've related your background knowledge to new information. It also reinforces your understanding of the information.

WHEN: After getting new information about a prediction or after completing the task

Evaluating Strategy 2

SUMMARIZE

(What is the gist of this? What is the main idea?)

DEFINITION: Summarizing involves your creating a mental, oral, or written summary of information.

EXAMPLE: If you watch a television program in the target language, you could periodically think about the gist or main points of the program to see if you really understand it.

WHY: Restating the gist of the message helps you decide how well you understood. It also reinforces your learning of that message.

WHEN: Whenever you want to check your understanding or communication

Evaluating Strategy 3

CHECK GOALS

(Did I meet my goal?)

DEFINITION: This strategy involves deciding whether you met your goal for the task.

EXAMPLE: If you are writing a letter to an e-mail pal, reread it to see if it communicates the information you wanted to share.

WHY: Asking yourself, "Did I accomplish what I set out to do?" should help you decide whether you need to go back and rephrase, add additional information, reread a text, or ask for more information.

WHEN: At the end of a task or whenever you aren't sure how well you're meeting your goal

Evaluating Strategy 4

EVALUATE YOURSELF

(How well did I do?)

DEFINITION: Evaluating yourself involves checking how well you understood or used the language in the task.

EXAMPLE: If you're reading a newspaper article for class, you could mentally give yourself a grade that represents how well you understood it.

WHY: Self-evaluating helps you identify your strengths and weaknesses so that you can do better next time.

WHEN: At the end of a task or whenever you aren't sure how well you're using or understanding the language; also useful for remembering

EVALUATE YOUR STRATEGIES

(Did I choose good strategies? What could I do differently next time?)

DEFINITION: Evaluating your strategies involves judging how well you applied the strategies to the task, judging how effective and appropriate your strategies were for that particular task, identifying why a strategy was helpful or not-so-helpful for the task, comparing the usefulness of various strategies on the same task, and thinking about better strategies you could have used.

EXAMPLE: If you made predictions based on your knowledge of Japanese foods, but you still didn't understand a restaurant video, think about why predicting didn't help. Maybe your knowledge of Japanese foods is more limited than you thought, and your predictions were incorrect. You could also think about other strategies that would be more helpful, such as paying attention to names that are given to specific dishes shown in the next restaurant video.

WHY: Assessing strategies use helps you decide when certain strategies work best so you can choose appropriate strategies in the future.

WHEN: For all types of tasks

Strategies for Remembering Vocabulary and Other Information

In addition to comprehending and producing information, students must learn to use grammar and the sound system and to remember information related to social and cultural behaviors, subject matter, and vocabulary. Students often mention the use of repetition to learn language, for example, "I keep going over the same word over and over again until it sticks." While repeated exposure to materials will increase students' chance of remembering information, the sheer volume of material in language acquisition indicates that more efficient strategies may be necessary. The strategies suggested here help students to learn and remember information for a long period of time by building bridges in the learner's mind. Information is retained and connected in the brain through mental links or pathways that are mapped onto an individual's existing schemata. If the links are numerous and personally meaningful, the information is easier to memorize and recall later. Making meaningful associations with new words and phrases can make vocabulary acquisition more effective and efficient.

What are your favorite strategies for remembering information? Share these with your students.

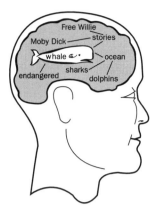

Remembering Strategy 1

IMAGINE WITH KEYWORD

(I use the keyword imagery method to remember vocabulary.)

DEFINITION:

Step 1: Think of a "keyword" that sounds like the new word, and imagine it as a picture.

Step 2: Think of a picture that describes the meaning of the new word or information.

Step 3: Link the pictures together mentally. Crazy-linking pictures are easy to remember.

Example: Spanish word: *pato*   Definition: duck   Keyword/image: a cooking pot

Interactive image: a duck wearing a cooking pot on its head

WHY: Using the keyword method creates a visual and personal association between meaning and sound. These mental links help you to remember the vocabulary item.

WHEN: Whenever you can think of an appropriate keyword that sounds like the target word and you can imagine pictures that represent the keyword and target word

Remembering Strategy 2

GROUP/CLASSIFY

(I create categories.)

DEFINITION: Grouping involves your creating categories by relating or classifying words according to attributes.

EXAMPLE: If the word means "sun," think of words that are associated with it, such as hot, suntan, and beach. When learning new vocabulary words, try grouping them into categories that are meaningful to you.

WHY: Grouping vocabulary creates mental links between words. These links help you recall related words.

WHEN: Whenever you are trying to remember a set of words that are somehow related or that can be categorized into meaningful groups

Remembering Strategy 3

· ·

TRANSFER/COGNATES

(I use my knowledge of this language or other languages. I use cognates from English or other languages.)

DEFINITION: This strategy involves using what you already know about language (prefixes, suffixes, and roots; verbs, nouns) to help you recognize and remember new words. It also involves recognizing words in the target language that are similar to words in English or other languages that you know and thinking about how the meanings are related (cognates).

EXAMPLE: The Spanish word *teléfono* is a cognate for telephone. The English word *basketball* is a cognate in many other languages. The words sound alike.

WHY: Focusing on word forms helps you deductively figure out and remember meaning. Learning cognates (words that sound similar in different languages) is an easy and quick way to increase your vocabulary.

WHEN: When you recognize the meaning of a word or know a rule that applies

Tip

Cognates are words that have obvious parallels to words in your native language, when the words have similar meanings. Beware of "false cognates." If the meanings aren't related, making a wrong connection could just confuse you.

Strategy Combinations

Learning strategies in action are complex behaviors that rarely occur as single instances. Normally we use strategies in combinations to complete a task. The following quotations were obtained from students through think-aloud interviews in which students verbalized their thoughts while working on a language task. They illustrate how many strategies can be used in a short amount of time. In the first example, a high school student studying Russian is reading in Russian the following sentence: "Larissa and Vadim study at the technical institute in the evenings."

> *"First I am going to look for words, root words, that I know of . . . right there is the root word of 'to study' and then 'institute.' I sounded it out in my head, and it sounds the same as in English and Spanish, so I put it together. That word kind of looks like 'in the evening' so I put it together, they probably study at the institute in*

the evening. That word right there also kind of looks like 'technical' in English, so I am guessing that that means the institute has something to do with technology."

The student begins by using *selective attention* to look for known root words. Then he uses *deduction* to construct the meaning of the word "study" by looking at its morphological root. The strategies *deduction* and *cognates* allow him to get the meaning of the word for institute. He *verifies* this guess through his knowledge of Spanish. He again uses *deduction* to identify the word for "evening" and *cognates* to identify technology. He puts the whole thing together by *summarizing* to see if the sentence makes sense to him. Thus, for trying to figure out one sentence, this highly effective student has used six different strategies for a total of eight strategy applications. He was able to successfully read the sentence by using a combination of strategies. He would not have been as successful had he relied on only one or two strategies.

Strategies are often more powerful when they are used in appropriate combinations. In the following example, a student is reading a dialogue. She uses her *background knowledge* to make an *inference*. However, she goes a step further by *verifying* her initial guess. Based on additional information in the text, she revises her *inference* and *verifies* her new guess. This time her *verification* reinforces her *inference*.

> *"It looks like a list of something because of the dashes—that's how I do lists, but now it looks like a dialogue because they ask a question and then they name a list of foods and it seems like a response to a question. So I decide that it's a dialogue."*

By using three strategies together—*background knowledge, inferencing,* and *verifying*—the student is able to accurately understand the text. None of these strategies in isolation would have been as effective as the three in combination. *Activating background knowledge, predicting,* and *verifying* are also usually used in combination. Teachers should be aware that although students will normally *make predictions* based on their *background knowledge*, they rarely *verify* predictions or inferences. Taking that final evaluative step of *verification* enables students to see whether their guesses were accurate. If they were accurate, then they can feel confident in their understanding. If guesses were not accurate, then students need to revise and to think about why their guesses were not correct so that they can make better guesses next time.

Goal setting and *goal checking* are two strategies that should always be used together. If learners set goals, they need to check whether they met their goals; otherwise, there is no point in setting goals. Evaluating progress towards their goals can give learners confidence if progress is being made. When students are not meeting their goals, then they may need to reflect on their plans and their actions for reaching their goals.

Assessing strategies use is one evaluation strategy that should be used with every strategy. Reflecting on how a strategy has worked can help students evaluate the usefulness of the strategy. Students need to think about whether the strategy was effective for the given task so that they will know how and when they can transfer the strategy to another task.

The problem-solving strategies are often used in combination as a series of steps that learners can work through when faced with a challenging task. When the learner encounters a problem, she first attempts to solve it herself by using *inferencing,* in which she relies on her knowledge and information provided in the task. If she is unable to solve the problem or she wants to *verify* her inference, she can ask a question of someone whom she feels would be a good, reliable source of knowledge about the problem area. If no one is available, she can then *access reference materials* and look up answers to her questions. Used in combination, these three strategies can help learners solve many problems.

This section presented some common strategies combinations. However, other combinations are possible. Task requirements and learner characteristics determine which strategies should be used and in which combination.

Conclusion

Many strategies are used in language learning. This chapter organized numerous strategies into a metacognitive model with four processes: **planning, monitoring, problem solving,** and **evaluating.** Teachers should teach the model to their students so that students understand the four processes. (See Chapter 5 for ideas on how to present the model to students.) However, teachers should be selective and thoughtful when choosing which strategies to teach their students. Teaching too many strategies at one time will overwhelm and confuse students. Conversely, teaching too few strategies may bore students by not challenging their intellects. Teachers should look at their instructional materials to determine which strategies to teach and when to introduce the strategies in the curriculum. More information on how to teach strategies through an instructional framework is presented in the next chapter.

Chapter **3**

INSTRUCTIONAL FRAMEWORK

Learning strategies instruction has helped students in many settings, from students with learning disabilities who are writing compositions (Harris & Graham, 1992), to first-language elementary students who are comprehending stories (Brown, Pressley, Van Meter, & Schuder, 1996), to ESL students who are presenting science projects (Varela, 1997). Across settings, successful strategies instruction includes several common elements (Chamot & O'Malley, 1994; Pressley, El-Dinary, Gaskins et al., 1992). This chapter explores the critical elements of effective strategies instruction and includes a discussion of factors that facilitate effective strategies instruction as well as a framework that describes how these elements work together.

Instructional Objectives

This chapter will help you to:

- Understand the roles of student and teacher beliefs in learning strategies instruction.
- Plan a classroom context that assists learning strategies development.
- Identify instructional techniques that foster learning strategies instruction for different levels of language proficiency.
- Select strategies and learning tasks that support strategic thinking.
- Apply the CALLA instructional framework.
- Scaffold learning strategies instruction.

Factors Facilitating Effective Strategies Instruction

· ·

Both individual and instructional factors can impact the effectiveness of learning strategies instruction. These factors include the beliefs of both students and teachers regarding learning, the social climate of the learning setting, and general approaches to instruction used in the classroom.

Student Beliefs

Learning strategies instruction is based on the idea that students are more effective when they take control of their own learning. Students' cultural or educational backgrounds may be at odds with this belief. For example, students whose prior schooling has been in highly structured, teacher-directed contexts may have had few opportunities for independent, self-regulated learning. However, for strategies instruction to have an impact, students must first believe they are capable of becoming more independent learners. They also must believe that what causes their success or failure is the use of effective or ineffective strategies, not luck or innate ability alone. Finally, students must be willing to take responsibility for their learning. Teachers need to nurture and encourage these beliefs and may need to provide extensive support so students can experience the success that comes by willingly using effective strategies.

Are your students prepared to take responsibility for their learning? If not, what beliefs stand in their way? How can you encourage them to look at learning differently?

Teacher Beliefs

The teacher, too, must believe that effective strategies use can determine student success. As one teacher stated, "I think strategies instruction helps the students if [teachers] really believe in it. If we don't believe in it or really use it ourselves, it's not really going to help them. But if we really believe in it, then maybe they'll use it as a part of their learning also."

If the teacher thinks successful learning is the result of ability alone, which is relatively fixed, it follows that low-achieving students are powerless to change. Strategies, on the other hand, are not innate and can be learned. If learning strategies instruction is to be successful, teachers must also believe that strategies can be taught. Teachers must have confidence that the individual strategies are effective, and they must communicate this confidence to students. A good way for teachers to do this is to offer personal examples of how they have used strategies for similar language tasks or in everyday life. One teacher, for instance, described *predicting* how much spaghetti would be needed at a dinner party and then *evaluating* the prediction by determining whether the guests had actually had enough.

Are you ready to give students more control over their learning? What fears do you have about students' becoming more independent? What would help you give up some of the control over learning?

Perhaps most importantly, teachers must believe that their students are capable of becoming more independent learners. This also requires that teachers be willing to give up some control over learning so that students can take more control. Teachers who adhere to the transmission model of learning or other teacher-directed approaches are likely to have difficulty making strategies instruction work for them.

Classroom Context

Giving students control over their learning does not mean giving up control of the classroom. Effective classroom management is critical, since a chaotic classroom impedes any form of learning, including strategies instruction.

Like learning a new language, learning to be an independent learner requires taking risks. The classroom environment must encourage students' risk-taking. Teachers who accept students' responses without judgment and who promote respect among classmates will have greater success with strategies instruction.

Language of Learning Strategies Instruction

What language of instruction will be most appropriate for introducing learning strategies in your classroom? Will you change the language of instruction as students become more proficient with strategies?

Since most learning strategies are mental operations and hence not directly observable, classroom discussions about learning strategies are important vehicles for identifying the strategies that students use and for modeling additional strategies. These discussions are relatively easy to initiate in students' native languages, but they are difficult to conduct in a second or foreign language when students are at beginning levels of language proficiency. Teachers of beginning-level students must decide whether to introduce learning strategies in the native language (assuming that all students speak the same first language and that the teacher is proficient in that language) or to teach students the vocabulary and expressions needed to talk about learning strategies in the target language.

Students will find it easier to talk about their own thinking and learning processes in their native language if this type of discussion is familiar to them. However, if their cultural and educational experiences have not emphasized the identification of individual approaches to learning, the discussion of learning strategies—even in the native language—could be bewildering. As one student explained, "In my country, we are not supposed to talk about ourselves in class, we are supposed to learn what the teacher says." In this situation, students may actually find it easier to talk about learning strategies in the second or foreign language if learning strategies are perceived as an important element of learning the new language.

Discussing learning strategies in the target language poses linguistic challenges for the teacher. How can students in the beginning-level class talk about their own thinking processes? We have observed both ESL and foreign language teachers introducing strategies in the target language successfully. They start slowly with a single strategy, often one that students are already using implicitly (for example, *cooperation*). The strategy is given a target language name, and the teacher demonstrates how to apply it, using simple language, gestures, and repetition as necessary. Teachers need patience and perseverance to teach learning strategies in the second or foreign language to beginning-level students, but the task is not impossible.

Instructional Approach

Effective strategies teachers focus on students' learning processes, as well as on products and outcomes. In addition to emphasizing curriculum content, they must strongly emphasize the thinking that students use to make sense of that content. Thus teachers focus not only on technically "correct" language use, but also on the message that students are trying to communicate and the reasoning behind their responses. This can be done by probing to find out how students arrive at their answers. During students' explanations, the teacher can point out when students use strategies, especially if they seem unaware that they are doing something strategic. Teachers can also help students avoid future mistakes by following up incorrect answers to find out where the student's logic went astray. Mistakes can thus serve as opportunities to remind students of effective strategies that might have helped them.

EXAMPLE

Use the following questions to elicit information about students' thought processes.

- What are you going to do?
- How did you come up with that?
- What makes you think so?
- What were you thinking about?
- How can you solve your problem?
- What led to that decision?

Encouraging students to talk about their thought processes helps make them more aware of the strategies they are already using. This metacognitive awareness is important because it enables students to call on those strategies whenever they face challenging tasks. In addition, the teacher can explicitly introduce other strategies that the students can try, since some students may never have thought of using a particular strategy. Others may have used the strategy without really thinking about it. Explicit instruction is a way to ensure that students are aware of the choices they have for learning, understanding, and solving problems. The framework presented later in this chapter will describe how to teach strategies explicitly.

Many teachers find it important to emphasize the value of strategies instruction as part of content as well as language instruction. Teachers need to make it clear that instruction in strategies can help students reach long-term goals in all types of learning, not just a specific, immediate goal in the language classroom. Learning strategies are not just a classroom activity for a particular vocabulary set or other language task. Developing learning strategies can help students become effective learners with a variety of tools to aid them in all types of learning and understanding. Teachers should point out that the strategies students are learning in the language classroom can help not only in language but also in other subject areas, as well as in any situation in which greater understanding is needed.

Teachers need to build students' metacognitive knowledge for each strategy that is introduced. This means naming and defining the strategy and explaining why the strategy works and when to use it. Teachers should explicitly discuss why and how each strategy can improve students' understanding, production, and learning. After explaining a strategy, the teacher can ask students why they think the strategy would help. Teachers can then supplement students' responses by explaining the theory behind the strategy (see sample explanations in the Metacognitive Model of Strategic Learning in Chapter 2). It is important to acknowledge that different strategies work better for different people and for different tasks. Teachers can encourage exploration of the kinds of tasks, situations, and purposes for which each strategy is more or less useful. This can be done in a formal explanation or discussion, but it also should occur informally when a student uses a strategy.

Finally, once a few strategies have been introduced, instruction should emphasize the coordination of strategies. The teacher can explain the importance of having a flexible repertoire or menu of strategies for language learning. The Metacognitive Model of Strategic Learning in Chapter 2 can serve to organize individual strategies. Thus the teacher

Tip

Coordinate with teachers of other content areas to plan to teach a core set of strategies across subjects. For instance, prediction in language learning and hypothesizing in science can correspond to estimation in mathematics and technical courses. Most strategies can be adapted for use across a wide range of content areas.

How will you encourage students to be flexible in their strategies use, rather than relying on just one or two comfortable strategies?

should remind students that good learners **plan, monitor, problem-solve,** and **evaluate** recursively during a given task; these are not just linear steps to follow. Students can also be reminded that different strategies can work for the same task. If one strategy does not work for a student, the teacher can encourage the use of another. Students need to understand that explicit instruction in strategies can help them become better language learners because it helps them add strategies to their repertoire of learning tools, makes them more aware of the strategies available to them, and encourages them to evaluate which strategies are most effective for them on different kinds of tasks.

EXAMPLE

Use the following questions for building students' metacognitive awareness.

• Did that strategy help you?

• Why was that strategy helpful for this task?

• Is there another strategy that might work better?

• In what situations does this strategy work well for you? When does it not work so well?

Course Level and Strategies Instruction

The strategies in the Metacognitive Model of Strategic Learning are designed to be taught to students at all levels of language proficiency. Although strategies are especially important for less proficient and beginning-level students, even the best students do not use strategies as thoughtfully and flexibly as they could. Less advanced students may need more modeling and coaching from the teacher. More advanced students need faster fading of scaffolding; teachers can release control to such students by providing less explicit cues to use strategies they have learned. Teachers may find different strategies more appropriate at different language levels, based on the specific tasks and goals they are working on in those classes. Some teachers find it helpful to start with a few basic strategies at lower levels and build up with more strategies at higher levels. It is also important to revisit previously taught strategies, exploring how they apply to more advanced tasks.

A Word about Scaffolding

A challenge teachers may face when teaching learning strategies is determining when and how to scaffold instruction to provide the appropriate amount of support. Evaluating students' strategies use is the critical first step in scaffolding. If it seems that students are not applying a certain strategy, then they may need stronger scaffolds. Teachers can provide extra support by giving more explicit reminders or revisiting practice opportunities. They may also need to give students more evidence that the strategy is useful to them. As students begin using a strategy more independently, the teacher needs to gradually reduce prompting and explicitness (see Figure 3.1). For example, coaching strategies can be done at first through verbal reminders and then later by

FIGURE 3.1

Scaffolding Strategies Instruction

Scaffolding: Ways to provide additional support when students need it

- If students understand a strategy but are hesitant to use it, try a mini-experiment (see Chapter 7) to prove the strategy's impact.

- If students have trouble remembering the full range of strategy choices, create a poster and refer them to it.

- If students have trouble choosing a strategy, offer one or two choices and have them try one of them.

- If students understand the strategy but have difficulty applying it themselves, provide some guided practice opportunities.

- If students are using a strategy inappropriately, model it for them again, describing how what you are doing differs from what you have seen them doing.

- If students seem to misunderstand the point of the strategy, explain it in a different way, perhaps using an analogy.

Scaffolding: Ways to reduce explicitness when students are ready

- Instead of telling students which strategy to use, have them choose strategies themselves.

- Instead of verbal reminders to choose a strategy, refer students to a poster of choices.

- When students practice strategies, give less teacher feedback and ask them to evaluate how well the strategies worked.

- If the strategies are getting repetitive for students, introduce some new strategies.

- Introduce a totally new context for using the strategy (such as for a speaking task rather than for reading) and have students discuss how to modify the strategy so it works for the new task.

referring students to a poster of questions that they can ask themselves to guide strategies use. As another example, early in instruction the teacher may suggest a specific strategy for students to try, but as instruction progresses students should choose strategies for themselves. The main point of scaffolding is that teachers should try to identify how much support students need and to provide just enough support while still working toward the eventual goal of student independence.

Cooperative Learning and Strategies Instruction

Cooperative learning is compatible with strategies instruction. A simplified form of *cooperation* (for example, practicing in pairs and brainstorming study approaches) is one of the strategies emphasized in the Metacognitive Model of Strategic Learning (see Chapter 2). More formal cooperative learning approaches, such as Jigsaw and Teams-Games-Tournaments (Slavin, Karweit, & Madden, 1989) also can be used to facilitate strategies instruction. Cooperative learning is an excellent way to scaffold instruction because it provides instructional support while increasing student responsibility for learning. Cooperative settings are also useful for identifying students' background knowledge of a strategy or a topic.

Which of the factors discussed here are most likely to affect strategies instruction in your classroom? Are there any other factors that may have an impact? How will you develop instruction to address these factors?

Selecting Initial Strategies to Teach

Each of the strategies presented in Chapter 2 is designed to be flexible for a variety of tasks and student levels. Teachers should feel free to be creative in how they apply the strategies in their classrooms.

EXAMPLE

The following guidelines can help teachers as they choose the first strategies to teach.

- Start with the simplest strategies (such as *imagery/visualizing*) and build to more complex ones (such as *summarizing* or *organizational planning*).

- Start with strategies that the students already use, and show them how the strategy can be expanded for more advanced uses or for different tasks.

- Start with strategies that have the widest applications in the class. Think of how to adapt the strategy for reading, listening, speaking, and writing and for learning content. Examine curricular goals and select strategies that will help students reach the most goals.

What strategies will you select to begin strategies instruction? Refer to Chapter 2 for strategies descriptions and think about which strategies meet these guidelines for your situation.

- Determine which strategies could help with specific current challenges that students are facing, and start with the strategies that students need most.

- Make sure that the strategies are well-matched to instructional objectives and to the tasks that students are expected to do. For example, *selective attention* may be more appropriate at lower levels where vocabulary and structural knowledge is more limited, while grammar-based *inferencing* might be better for students at higher levels. *Self-talk* is especially important for anxiety-producing activities, such as oral presentations and test-taking. *Questioning for clarification* may be more feasible when listening in a conversation than when reading a chapter in a novel.

- Start with strategies that the teacher understands well and finds effective. Teachers new to strategies instruction can build their own confidence and students' confidence by using strategies they believe in. Confused explanations of a strategy may only lead to unsuccessful attempts at using the strategy. The goal is for the whole class (teacher and students) to experience the effectiveness of strategies instruction.

- Try to determine the strategies that students use for similar tasks in their native language. Teach them the target language names for these strategies, and use those names as a basis for introducing learning strategies instruction.

Selecting Appropriate Tasks and Activities for Strategies Instruction

In effective strategies instruction, students learn how to apply strategies to legitimate learning tasks that could not otherwise be easily accomplished.

Integrate Strategies into Regular Course Work

Effective strategies instruction is not an extra activity or even a separate part of the regular language class. Rather, it is used to support language and content learning and to accomplish the goals of the curriculum. While initial explanations are needed, much of strategies instruction should occur while students are working on authentic, meaningful language tasks. Teachers should use the kinds of tasks and activities they would normally use for a lesson, integrating components of effective strategies instruction into the lesson, as described in this and the following chapters.

Use Appropriately Challenging Tasks

Lesson materials should present authentic language tasks and should be moderately challenging. If the task is too easy, students will not need strategies, but if it is too difficult, even appropriate strategies may not lead to success. The point of learning strategies instruction is for students to experience the benefits of using strategies. Students are not likely to apply strategies unless they can see how the strategies help them.

Are your current instructional tasks appropriately challenging for strategies instruction? What modifications, if any, would make your current lesson materials more appropriate?

An Instructional Framework

A framework to guide instructional planning can help teachers incorporate learning strategies into their lessons. In this section, we describe a framework that has been used successfully by second language teachers. This instructional framework provides guidelines for teaching the learning strategies identified in the Metacognitive Model of Strategic Learning (see Chapter 2).

Overview

The Metacognitive Model of Strategic Learning described in Chapter 2 provides an organized menu of effective learning strategies that students can use for a variety of language tasks. Research comparing more effective to less effective language learners shows that while all students use some strategies, good language learners use strategies more effectively. But even the best students are often unaware of the strategies that they are using. By becoming aware of their strategies use, students can make active decisions to help them face learning challenges. This chapter and the remaining chapters in this book are concerned with how the teacher can show students how to use learning strategies to become more independent learners. The CALLA instructional framework (Chamot & O'Malley, 1994) is an effective way to plan learning strategies instruction. This framework provides for explicit learning strategies instruction through a progression from teacher-guided activities to students' independent use of strategies, similar to the progression required to facilitate language learning. The five basic phases in the CALLA instructional framework are as follows.

Preparation
Students prepare for strategies instruction by identifying their prior knowledge about and the use of specific strategies (see Chapter 4 for techniques for eliciting prior strategies knowledge).

Presentation

The teacher demonstrates the new learning strategy and explains how and when to use it (see Chapters 2 and 5 for suggestions on presenting new strategies).

Practice

Students practice using the strategy with regular class activities of moderate difficulty (see Chapter 6 for a variety of Practice phase activities).

Evaluation

Students self-evaluate their use of the learning strategy and how well the strategy is working for them (see Chapter 7 for suggested evaluation activities).

Expansion

Students extend the usefulness of the learning strategy by applying it to new situations or learning tasks (see Chapter 8 for guidelines to help students transfer learning strategies to new contexts).

Can you think of a specific task that would lend itself well to presentation of the first three phases of learning strategies instruction?

The CALLA framework for learning strategies instruction emphasizes explicitness, metacognitive knowledge, and scaffolded support as the teacher and students work through these phases. The five phases are recursive, which means that teachers can move between phases as needed to help students develop skills for understanding and using learning strategies. For example, after eliciting students' prior knowledge about strategies to use for a specific task (such as learning new vocabulary) in the Preparation phase, the teacher might model another strategy for the same task in the Presentation phase. Then the teacher could briefly return to Preparation to ask students if the modeling has reminded them of any additional strategies they have used themselves. Similarly, after students have had an opportunity to apply a new strategy to a real task during the Practice phase, the teacher might want to return to the Presentation phase in order to describe another strategy that works well in tandem with the first. The recursive nature of the CALLA instructional framework provides flexibility in planning language lessons that integrate learning strategies instruction. Figure 3.2 illustrates the recursive quality of CALLA instruction.

Tip

Take one of your best lessons and work through the instructional framework to see how you can integrate elements of strategies instruction into your classroom activities, rather than teaching strategies separately.

In this framework, strategies instruction is not taught at a special time of its own. Nor is it separated from content in special strategies lessons or strategies activities. Instead, discussions about strategies and thought processes become a natural part of regular class activities. Strategies instruction that follows this framework is intended to be integrated into the authentic, meaningful language activities that the teacher uses already.

FIGURE 3.2

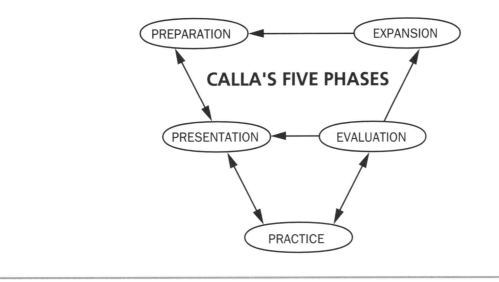

CALLA Instructional Sequence: Five Recursive Phases

CALLA'S FIVE PHASES

PREPARATION ← EXPANSION

PRESENTATION ← EVALUATION

PRACTICE

Figure 3.3 shows that strategies instruction starts out as more teacher-directed, with students taking more responsibility over time. An analogy for this framework is constructing a building from the ground up. First a foundation is poured (preparing students for strategies), then scaffolding is put in place to support the building in progress (presenting strategies and coaching students as they practice them). As the building is constructed, it begins to support itself, and the scaffolding is gradually removed (less explicit instruction and less coaching as students start using strategies independently and extending them to other areas). Yet, even once a building stands on its own, maintenance and repairs are occasionally needed (thus the need for strategies evaluation and evaluation of instruction, as well as the potential need to revisit earlier phases of instruction for additional support, as illustrated in Figure 3.2).

Figure 3.3 illustrates that even though there is a general progression from teacher direction to student independence, there are times when strategies instruction needs maintenance and repair, such as re-explaining a particular strategy or additional coaching to use a strategy that students seem to have forgotten. The instructional framework, like the strategies model, represents recursive phases. Even though all five phases might appear in an individual lesson, the overall progression from teacher direction to student independence will be more gradual over time.

FIGURE 3.3

Framework for Strategies Instruction

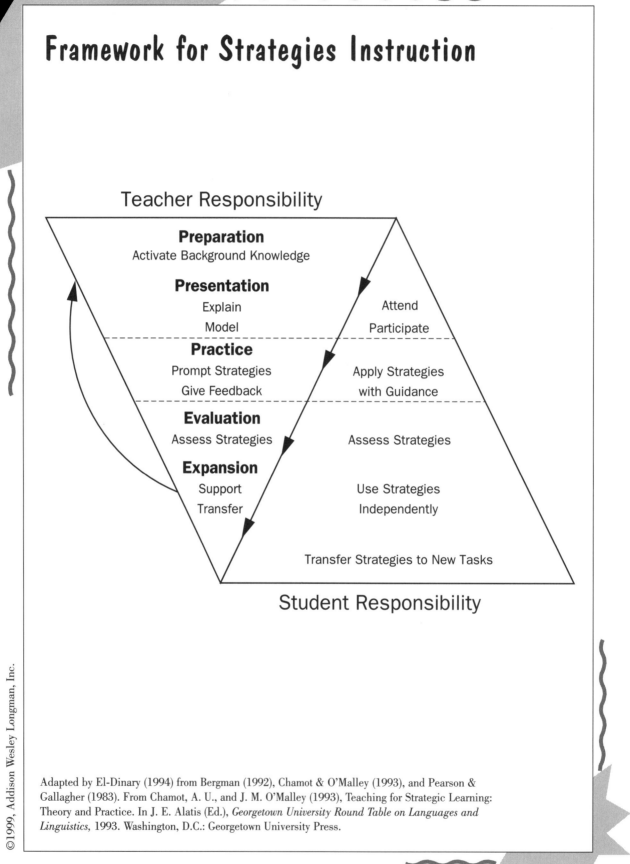

Teacher Responsibility

Preparation
Activate Background Knowledge

Presentation

Explain   Attend

Model   Participate

Practice

Prompt Strategies   Apply Strategies

Give Feedback   with Guidance

Evaluation

Assess Strategies   Assess Strategies

Expansion

Support   Use Strategies

Transfer   Independently

Transfer Strategies to New Tasks

Student Responsibility

Adapted by El-Dinary (1994) from Bergman (1992), Chamot & O'Malley (1993), and Pearson & Gallagher (1983). From Chamot, A. U., and J. M. O'Malley (1993), Teaching for Strategic Learning: Theory and Practice. In J. E. Alatis (Ed.), *Georgetown University Round Table on Languages and Linguistics*, 1993. Washington, D.C.: Georgetown University Press.

In learning strategies instruction, teachers pour a foundation for preparing students to learn about strategies by having them *activate background knowledge* of strategies they already use. This can be accomplished by conducting class discussions about what students do as they work on language tasks, having students keep learning strategies journals, and giving students questionnaires about strategies use.

After students' awareness of their own strategies gives them something to build on, the teacher can construct a scaffold for independent learning by explicitly presenting the Metacognitive Model of Strategic Learning. The teacher presents the idea that good learners **plan, monitor, problem-solve,** and **evaluate** during language tasks. The teacher also presents individual strategies to meet curricular goals and students' needs. Because good students may claim that they are already using strategies, it is important to acknowledge that good language learners use these processes naturally and automatically. It is also important to emphasize the value of explicit strategies instruction, as described in Chapter 5. Instruction that makes the strategies explicit helps students think about their strategies so they can develop conscious control of their learning and language use.

Although it is critical for teachers to present strategies in a way that students understand them, understanding a strategy is only the skeleton of the building. The real construction of independent learning happens when students practice strategies and try strategic thinking themselves. Again, it is important to practice strategies using moderately challenging tasks so students experience the benefits of the strategy. A moderate challenge that cannot be achieved without the strategy, but can be achieved with it, will show students the value of the strategy.

After initial practice, students need the support of reminders to use the strategies they have learned. Teachers can also support strategic thinking by asking students to explain how they figured out the responses they gave in class. For correct responses, this helps the student build awareness of effective thought processes; for incorrect responses, it helps students identify where their thinking went astray.

Another scaffold that students need as they practice new learning strategies is feedback about how they are applying strategies. Teachers can provide feedback by praising effective thinking and by pointing out the strategies that students are using. Early in strategies instruction, teachers should frequently prompt students to choose strategies for a task. If students have trouble choosing, the teacher can suggest specific strategies. Teachers also need to give students feedback when they use strategies, praising them for being strategic. As students become more

Tip ························

See Chapter 4 for ideas about preparing students for strategies instruction.

Tip ························

See Chapter 5 for ideas about how to present explicit strategies instruction.

What language learning task would be appropriate for your students to practice strategic thinking? Choose a task that could not be achieved without strategies, but that will allow your students to recognize the value of using strategies.

How will you emphasize strategies use while presenting your usual material?

Tip

Chapter 6 provides more detailed guidelines on the Practice phase of learning strategies instruction.

Tip

Chapter 7 explores different ways to encourage student self-evaluation of strategies, including the use of student learning journals, class experiments, and questionnaires.

When have you successfully transferred a strategy that you find effective in one area or task in your work or life to another area or task? Share these experiences with your students.

Tip

Chapter 8 provides suggestions and examples for the Expansion phase of strategy instruction.

independent in using strategies, the teacher can fade out prompting and coaching, making cues less frequent and less explicit.

All forms of practicing and coaching strategies use should be integrated into the curriculum, taking place in the context of regular language tasks. The instructional changes made by integrating strategies into the curriculum should not be reflected in the content but rather in the emphasis, that is, putting students' thinking in the spotlight and encouraging effective use of strategies.

Once students have had a chance to practice a strategy, the teacher should ask them to evaluate how well the strategy is working and which strategies might be best for a given task or problem. It is critical that students learn to identify whether a strategy is helping them and to learn to choose alternative strategies when one is not working. In our own research it became apparent that more effective language learners can apply alternative strategies when the first strategy is not successful in solving a problem, whereas less effective students tend to keep repeating the same strategy (or give up), even though it is not helping them (Chamot et al., 1996).

After students have internalized a strategy for one kind of task, the teacher can encourage them to expand its use by transferring it to other situations. If the strategy was introduced as a way to understand directions in the target language, the class can explore how it could help when giving someone else directions. Learning strategies introduced to assist in listening comprehension can be adapted for reading comprehension, and memory strategies can be applied to any type of information to be remembered, from vocabulary to subject matter content. Nonetheless, students rarely make such connections on their own, and sometimes the potential for transfer is not obvious.

There are several ways in which teachers can support the transfer of strategy use. One is to simply tell students about other situations in which they could use the strategy or to prompt them to try the strategy as they work on a new task. In many cases, however, the teacher will need to explain how to modify the strategy to fit the different task. It may also be useful to conduct class discussions in which students brainstorm other times that the strategy could help. Another way to support transfer is to provide a variety of contexts for practicing the strategy.

Sometimes students will make the connection on their own and transfer a strategy to a new situation. Whenever a student does this, teachers should seize the opportunity to point out and praise the expansion of the strategy. It may also be useful to talk about the challenge of recognizing new ways to apply strategies. Students may pay more attention to expanding familiar strategies when they realize that doing this is not always automatic.

Conclusion

● ●

This chapter described important factors that impact the planning of successful learning strategies instruction, including student beliefs, teacher beliefs, classroom context, and instructional approach. Guidelines for selecting initial strategies to teach and appropriate tasks and activities were outlined. The application of the CALLA instructional framework to language learning strategies instruction was described, and examples of recursive teaching and scaffolding were provided.

As with helping students to become proficient in a language, helping them to become independent strategic learners takes extensive explaining, modeling, and coaching. All of these strategies instruction activities take place while students are working on curricular goals. The reward for these efforts is a classroom of thinkers who can learn the language more efficiently and more thoughtfully.

PART TWO

CALLA Strategies Step by Step

Chapter 4

PHASE 1: PREPARATION

Implementing strategies instruction requires planning and preparation by teachers and students. The Preparation phase is the time to lay the foundation or groundwork for creating a learner-centered classroom that is then ready for strategies instruction. This phase needs to be embedded in the language instructional curriculum so that students see discussions about strategies and thought processes as a natural part of regular class activities. This chapter shares ideas and techniques that teachers can use in their classrooms to create a positive setting for strategies instruction.

Instructional Objectives

This chapter will help you to:

- Establish the roles of teacher and learner in the learning process.
- Build a foundation to focus on thought processes in the language classroom.
- Activate students' awareness of strategies they already use.
- Identify strategies your students already use to prepare yourself for instruction in learning strategies.
- Reinforce existing strategies and build on them.

Creating the Learner-Centered Classroom

A learner-centered classroom is an environment that creates and fosters independent students who are aware of their learning processes and who, through this awareness, are able to take control of their learning. A learner-centered classroom must initially be created by the teacher and then accepted by students. It does not occur automatically, but rather must be worked at so that all participants support the environment and are supported by the environment. Students whose learning abilities and strategies are acknowledged and encouraged will embrace strategies instruction as a way to further their own independence as active thinkers. However, the stage needs to be set in order for strategies instruction to occur successfully. Following are examples of activities shared by teachers who have successfully created learner-centered classrooms.

How aware are you of your own learning processes or strategies? Under what conditions do you "learn" most successfully?

Setting Learning Responsibilities

Traditionally, teachers shouldered much of the responsibility for learning in the classroom. However, in a learner-centered classroom teacher and students share responsibility. The teacher takes on the role of model and facilitator, and students increase their role as active participants who are ultimately responsible for their own learning. Students need a clear understanding of class expectations from the beginning in order for the learner-centered classroom to be successful. Classroom contracts (see Figure 4.1) and the use of learning analogies are two examples of how to start building a learner's expectations toward independence.

In the past, how have you made your students aware of the expectations of your course?

FIGURE 4.1

Sample Student-Teacher Classroom Contract

CHARACTERISTICS OF A GOOD TEACHER	CHARACTERISTICS OF A GOOD LEARNER
Interesting	Pays attention
Intelligent	Does homework
Understanding	Cooperates
Patient	Asks questions
Friendly	Independent
Organized	Listens to teacher and classmates
Good listener	Active in class

Classroom Contract

A classroom contract consists of an agreement between teacher and students or students and students regarding how each will contribute to and behave in the classroom. Contracts are most successful if students provide the input on the agreement with guidance from the teacher.

Can you remember your best or favorite teachers? What qualities made them good teachers? How would you characterize a good learner?

Students in different classes may come up with different characteristics, which is fine, because the point is that a sense of trust and shared responsibility has been established between teacher and student. Hang the posters in the classroom as reminders of the contract and for future reference. For example, if a characteristic of a good learner is to complete homework on time, then the teacher can refer to the contract if there is a problem with a student's attitude toward homework. The responsibility for the student's action has shifted completely to the student because she or he has agreed to behave in a certain manner.

Tip

Make copies of your classroom contract so students can have their own copies.

EXAMPLE

Following is an example of how to implement a teacher-student contract:

1. Ask students to think about some of the best teachers they have had and why they believe these teachers were so good. On poster board, write students' ideas of good teacher characteristics.

2. Then ask students to think of characteristics of a good learner and write these on a second piece of poster board.

3. When you have the two lists of characteristics, one for teacher's behavior and one for students' behaviors, tell students that you would like to make an agreement with them. That is, you promise to live up to the characteristics of a good teacher, if students make a similar promise to be good learners.

Tip

Write down several analogies for the student-teacher classroom relationship. Your analogies should reflect the teacher's role as facilitator and the students' role as active and responsible participants in the learning process.

Analogies

The teacher can also use analogies with students to explain the roles of teacher and students in the learning process. The teacher can guide, facilitate, present materials clearly, answer questions, model, and provide some practice opportunities, but the teacher cannot learn the language for students or even make students learn the language. Students must decide themselves that they want to learn, and they need to take initiative for seeking opportunities for learning.

Some well-known analogies that can be shared with students illustrate this point:

1 Learning a language is like playing on a soccer team. The teacher is the coach who presents different kinds of plays, gives advice and opportunities for practice, and provides feedback and support when it comes time to play a game. Students are the team players who actually play and must make decisions and evaluate themselves during the game.

2 Learning a language is like being in a theatrical play. The teacher is the director who provides direction, practice opportunities, and feedback. Students are the actors who must learn and bring alive the script in order to put on a good show.

Depending on the age and context of the class, choose an appropriate analogy that will demonstrate to students the foundation of the class. For instance, compare a teacher in a language classroom to a conductor with an orchestra. The Chinese proverb—"Give a man a fish and feed him for a day; teach a man to fish and feed him for a lifetime"—can also illustrate how the classroom will operate. The teacher gives students learning tools that they will always be able to use to learn a language.

Can you think of other appropriate proverbs to illustrate your role as a facilitator of learning?

Learning Reflections

The learner-centered classroom requires students' awareness of their learning processes. Ask students to reflect on the components involved in language acquisition so they realize what they need to do to learn the language.

Figure 4.2, "Self-Reflections on Language Learning," asks students to think about the different types of learning activities they find useful when studying a language. Students think about how they communicate through speaking, writing, listening, and reading and about what types of materials are used for language learning in each of the modalities.

Think of a time when you were learning a new language. Recall some of the learning activities that you found helpful. What did you find most difficult about learning a new language?

Students can also reflect on how learning a language is similar to and different from learning in other subjects (for example, math, science, and music). This generates an overall awareness of the learning process so students can then transfer to language strategies they may have acquired in other subjects. Conversely, students may realize that they need to be

FIGURE 4.2

Self-Reflections on Language Learning

HOW DO YOU LEARN A LANGUAGE?

1 How do you like to learn a language? What is successful for you?

____ Reading with a dictionary	____ Reading without a dictionary
____ Reading a textbook	____ Reading authentic materials (stories, ads, and so on)
____ Making vocabulary lists	
____ Watching TV	____ Learning songs
____ Listening to the radio	____ Speaking with classmates
____ Listening to tapes and repeating	____ Speaking with native speakers
____ Learning dialogues	____ Using a computer
____ Studying grammar	____ Translating
____ Writing letters	____ Videotaping yourself
____ Writing stories	____ Studying with friends
____ Studying by yourself	____ Focusing on pronunciation and intonation

OTHER WAYS:

2 What do you like best: reading, listening, writing, or speaking? Why?

3 What do you like least: reading, listening, writing, or speaking? Why?

4 Imagine your friend is planning to study [*target language*]. Write a letter giving advice about the best ways to learn. Include at least five specific things your friend should do.

Dear _____ ,

more active in a language class than in other classes. The worksheet shown in Figure 4.3, "Learning in Different Subjects," guides students through this reflection process. There are no right or wrong answers on a worksheet. The idea is for students to begin thinking about how they learn and the different approaches they use in particular settings. Students may find it interesting to share their ideas with classmates.

Tip ....

Have students share their answers with small groups before sharing them with the class.

Setting Personal Language Goals

A crucial step toward a learner-centered classroom is getting students involved in learning by having them set language goals for themselves. Having students set personal language goals increases their involvement by increasing the stake they have in the learning process. Giving students the opportunity to establish their own goals, in addition to or in collaboration with those set by the instructional program, allows students to reflect on their reasons for learning a second language, which may in turn lead to increased motivation.

Tip ....

Begin by simply asking students why they are studying the language, but try to get beyond the response, "It's required."

Have students write down their personal language goals on a piece of paper. Collect these and create lists of long- and short-term goals on the board to stimulate class discussion. Ask students to offer examples of short-term goals that would help a student reach the long-term goals you have listed.

Goal setting is a strategy that needs to be taught to students. Goals can be either long- or short-term. Long-term goals are usually a result of students' motivations for choosing the language of study. For example, long-term goals may originate in the following areas:

What were some of your personal goals when you studied a language in the past? How did you achieve those goals? How have you applied that language since you first studied it?

- Professional (I need to know the language for a career.)

- Educational (I want to be able to use the language on a college level.)

- Social (I want to be able to participate in conversations with friends who speak this language; I want to be able to function in the society.)

- Personal (My family heritage is related to this language, and I want to be able to travel to the target country.)

Short-term goals, which are set more often, are used as enabling steps toward long-term goals. For example, if a student's long-term goal is to be able to read detective novels in the target language, then he or she may focus on short-term goals such as reading short detective stories and focusing on vocabulary related to law enforcement and crime. Short-term goals are generally more immediately reachable than long-term goals.

FIGURE 4.3

Learning in Different Subjects

Think about how you learn in your various classes. Consider this statement:

Learning a language is different from learning other subjects.

Do you think this statement is true? Why or why not? Before you answer, read and answer the following questions.

1 Think about a class such as science or mathematics. List at least five things you are expected to learn in this class. Then do the same for your ESL class.

A CLASS IN SCIENCE OR MATHEMATICS	AN ESL CLASS

2 Think about what you do in these classes. Check the following statements that are usually true about these classes.

	SCIENCE OR MATHEMATICS	ESL CLASS
The teacher talks most of the time.	_____	_____
Oral participation of every student is very important.	_____	_____
Students have hands-on activities to do (for example, experiments, group work, drawings)	_____	_____
You have to memorize a lot of material.	_____	_____
You have a lot of reading to do for homework.	_____	_____
You have a lot of writing to do for homework.	_____	_____

FIGURE 4.3 *(Cont.)*

	SCIENCE OR MATHEMATICS	ESL CLASS
You have to practice speaking and rehearsing for homework.	_____	_____
You have listening to do for homework.	_____	_____
You take lots of notes in class.	_____	_____
You have to really pay attention to what's being said in class.	_____	_____

3 How are classes in ESL different from and similar to your classes in science or mathematics?

	SIMILARITIES	DIFFERENCES
TYPES OF INFORMATION LEARNED		
TYPES OF ACTIVITIES IN THE CLASS		
WHAT I DO TO STUDY		

Contributed by Lisa Küpper

The teacher needs to discuss with and model for students the difference between reachable and unreachable goals. For example, an unreachable goal could be, "I want to be fluent by the end of the year." This unclear goal needs to be narrowed and defined. Ask the student what it means to be fluent. If goals are not realistic, then students are likely to become discouraged and lose motivation when assessing progress toward the goals. However, setting reachable goals can build students' confidence and feelings of success.

Self-Assessment of Language Abilities

Closely related to setting personal language goals is self-assessing abilities and evaluating progress in the language. Generally, students expect teachers and administrators to evaluate whether learning has taken place. However, acquiring the ability to evaluate one's own strengths and weaknesses is a critical step toward learning how to regulate learning. As with setting personal goals, self-assessment can increase students' motivation by increasing involvement in language learning.

Self-assessment entails reflecting on one's prior experiences and knowledge, as well as the process that enabled them to get to their current status. Students think about what worked and did not work and why one learning approach was more or less successful than another.

In preparing students for strategies instruction, have them assess their language learning abilities at the start of the school year. Students who have had previous exposure to the language can rate their abilities in each of the modalities. Rubrics, which are rating systems for language assessment, can have number scales (e.g., 1–5, 0–100) or descriptive words (poor, fair, good, excellent). The type of scale itself is not as important as the fact that students have a clear understanding of how to use the scale. Students who are at the very beginning level can report on what areas they think will be difficult or easy for them in learning the language based on other learning experiences. Figure 4.4 shows an example of a worksheet for self-assessment combined with personal goal setting. However, teachers may need to make adaptations based on student population and curriculum objectives.

Self-Efficacy for Language Learning and Strategies

Motivation plays an important role in all types of learning, including language learning. Highly motivated students work hard, persevere in

FIGURE 4.4

Personal Language Goals and Self-Assessment

SHORT-TERM GOALS

Please rate your current ability in English (0 = no ability, 5 = excellent ability)

Reading:	0	1	2	3	4	5
Listening:	0	1	2	3	4	5
Speaking:	0	1	2	3	4	5
Writing:	0	1	2	3	4	5

Realistically, what are your goals for this term?

Reading:	0	1	2	3	4	5
Listening:	0	1	2	3	4	5
Speaking:	0	1	2	3	4	5
Writing:	0	1	2	3	4	5

What aspect of the language do you think you need to focus on this semester/year?

LONG-TERM GOALS

How do you want to be able to use English in your life?

What ability level do you need for your goal?

Reading:	0	1	2	3	4	5
Listening:	0	1	2	3	4	5
Speaking:	0	1	2	3	4	5
Writing:	0	1	2	3	4	5

Can you identify the students in your class that exhibit task-based confidence? Can you identify those who do not have confidence in their learning ability? How will you tailor strategies to each of these learners?

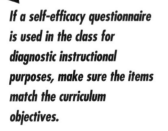

Tip

Students can complete a confidence questionnaire that reflects the task objectives in the curriculum at various intervals, starting at the beginning of the program of study, to see if there is any change in their self-perceptions.

Tip

If a self-efficacy questionnaire is used in the class for diagnostic instructional purposes, make sure the items match the curriculum objectives.

the face of difficulties, and find satisfaction in the successful accomplishment of a learning task. Self-efficacy or task-based confidence, which forms the basis for self-esteem and learning motivation, refers to learners' beliefs about their abilities to accomplish a task. Self-efficacious learners feel confident about solving a problem because they have developed an approach to problem solving that has worked in the past. They attribute their success mainly to their own efforts and strategies, believe that their own abilities will improve as they learn more, and recognize that errors are part of learning. Students with low self-efficacy, believing themselves to have poor abilities, choose less demanding tasks and do not try hard because they believe that any effort will reveal their own lack of ability (Bandura, 1992).

Strategies have been linked to motivation and particularly to a sense of self-efficacy leading to expectations of successful learning (Zimmerman & Pons, 1986; Chamot et al., 1993; Chamot et al., 1996). The development of an individual's self-efficacy is closely associated with effective use of learning strategies (Zimmerman, 1990). An individual's level of confidence is also correlated with frequency of strategy use. Elementary through college-level language students who reported a greater frequency of strategies use perceived themselves as more confident in their language learning abilities. (Chamot et al., 1993; Chamot et al., 1996).

Having access to appropriate learning strategies should lead students to higher expectations of learning success, since an important aspect in viewing oneself as a successful learner is self-control over strategies use. This type of self-control can be enhanced if strategies instruction is combined with metacognitive awareness of the relationship between strategies use and learning outcomes. Students with greater metacognitive awareness understand the similarity between a new learning task and previous tasks, know the strategies required for successful problem solving or learning, and anticipate that employing these strategies will lead to success (Paris & Winograd, 1990).

Self-efficacy can be used in language instruction to measure students' confidence levels in completing specific language tasks such as figuring out the main idea in a reading exercise. Figure 4.5 provides sample questions for measuring the self-efficacy of both older and younger students.

Students' self-perceptions are important to the teacher, parents, and the students themselves. If a student starts off with a low perception of his or her ability, then the teacher, parents, and student can work together to

FIGURE 4.5

Sample Self-Efficacy Items

FOR OLDER STUDENTS

Circle the number on the line that shows how sure you are that you could read a text in English and . . .

❶ . . . figure out the main topic or gist.

0——10——20——30——40——50——60——70——80——90——100

| Not sure | Somewhat unsure | Kind of sure | Very sure | Completely sure |

❷ . . . answer questions about very specific information.

0——10——20——30——40——50——60——70——80——90——100

| Not sure | Somewhat unsure | Kind of sure | Very sure | Completely sure |

❸ . . . use the text to accomplish a task in real life (for example, read a menu to order a meal).

0——10——20——30——40——50——60——70——80——90——100

| Not sure | Somewhat unsure | Kind of sure | Very sure | Completely sure |

FOR YOUNGER STUDENTS

Circle the answer that tells how sure you are that you can do these things while reading in your first language.

❶ When you read in your first language, can you figure out the most important information?

No way   Probably not   Maybe   Probably   Definitely

❷ If you read something in your first language in class today, can you answer questions about it?

No way   Probably not   Maybe   Probably   Definitely

❸ Can you understand written directions in your first language?

No way   Probably not   Maybe   Probably   Definitely

How can you be sensitive to students' own changing perceptions of their abilities throughout the year?

learn techniques and skills to help boost the student's confidence level. Used regularly, this reflection can also help identify problems a student is having during the school year (e.g., self-efficacy unexpectedly lowers) because self-efficacy is not static; it can change over time depending on a person's reaction to the task and perception of self. Knowledge of students' self-efficacy levels can also help identify which strategies are most needed by individuals.

Identifying Students' Existing Learning Strategies

Ask students what kinds of "tricks" they use to help them learn in other subjects. This should stimulate a lively class discussion.

After students have become familiar with their roles in the learner-centered classroom and have begun reflecting on themselves as learners, they are ready to begin learning strategies instruction. The next step is finding out what strategies students already use. This discovery helps students become aware of their existing strategies use and that of their classmates. By drawing on students' background knowledge of learning strategies, the teacher is acknowledging their abilities to actively contribute to the instructional process. All students come into strategies instruction with preferred techniques for learning, whether for languages or other subjects, and appreciate acknowledgment of their prior experiences.

Based on the strategies your students have named, how will you decide which strategies to present?

Identifying students' current strategies use also helps the teacher decide which strategies to focus on in the instruction. The teacher should build on strategies students already use. For example, if students already use the strategy of *inferencing* the meaning of unknown words based on the context, then start strategies instruction with this strategy. The teacher can identify students' existing strategies use to begin focusing on their learning processes by probing to find out how they arrive at answers. Students can become familiar with talking about their thought processes with strategies that are most familiar to them before moving on to new techniques.

The following sections present a variety of Preparation activities that teachers can use to activate students' awareness of learning strategies.

Class Discussions about Learning Strategies

Whole class discussions are useful for introducing the idea of learning strategies. Before beginning a class discussion, give students a few minutes to reflect individually on the strategies that they use (see Figure 4.6). In this way, students are not put on the spot to immediately come up with strategies but may participate as they become comfortable with the concept. Begin by discussing what students do to help them

FIGURE 4.6

Strategies Brainstorming

Directions Think about the strategies you use for each of the skill areas and jot down your ideas. Prepare to participate in a class discussion about useful strategies.

Reading: What do you do to help yourself read in English?

Strategy Description	Why Is This Strategy Useful?	When Is This Strategy Useful?

Listening: What do you do to help yourself listen in English?

Strategy Description	Why Is This Strategy Useful?	When Is This Strategy Useful?

Writing: What do you do to help yourself write in English?

Strategy Description	Why Is This Strategy Useful?	When Is This Strategy Useful?

Speaking: What do you do to help yourself speak in English?

Strategy Description	Why Is This Strategy Useful?	When Is This Strategy Useful?

understand and produce language. Ask students to brainstorm strategies they use for various language tasks, and have them discuss why different strategies have been helpful to them. The discussion can include talking about how strategies work differently or similarly for the four modalities: reading, listening, writing, and speaking.

A take-off on this activity is to have students share their favorite strategies for the tasks discussed. Write the strategies on the board. Then take a tally, by show of hands, of which students find this strategy helpful. The result is a list of favorite strategies in the class. Put these strategies on a poster and hang it in the class. As new strategies are introduced throughout the year, the list may grow and change.

Think of strategies that you've used to help you learn in various subjects. Can you apply any of them to language learning?

If students do not have previous foreign language experience, ask them what they do to help themselves learn in other content areas. Then see which of those strategies they think might apply to learning a new language. Let students know that as part of learning the target language, they will also be introduced to some strategies to help them learn more effectively. Tell students that everyone learns in different ways, and they need to be active in finding what works best for them.

The Preparation phase extends beyond the beginning of strategies instruction. The teacher may need to revisit it during the instructional process to elicit from students those strategies that they find useful. Class discussion about strategies that students find useful for specific tasks is an easy, quick way of preparing students for the presentation of new strategies.

Tip ....

Record which of the Preparation phase activities were most useful and successful for activating students' background knowledge. You may wish to draw on these again as you introduce new strategies.

Group Discussions and Structured Interviews

Once students are familiar with talking about strategies, they can form small group discussions (3–5 students). Working in small groups increases students' involvement in the discussion. Students are also likely to be more open with classmates in small groups than in a large discussion led by the teacher. Students of all ages are willing to talk to their peers about strategies and often are willing to try a strategy suggested by a peer (Chamot et al., 1996).

Begin small group discussions by focusing students' attention on specific language tasks that are represented in the curriculum. Give students structured interview guides that describe learning scenarios and ask students questions about what they do to complete the task (see Figure 4.7). Students can then share responses in their groups and discuss why they believe certain techniques are more helpful. Within a group,

FIGURE 4.7

Group Interview Guide

SAMPLE LEARNING SCENARIOS

(*Adapt content of scenarios to your curriculum*)

Directions Sit in groups of 3–4. Assign one student as coordinator/interviewer; this student will ask the questions on the interview guide. Assign a second student as recorder; this student will write down the strategies discussed during the interview. Both the coordinator and recorder will also answer the questions. (*Variation for a shorter amount of time: Give students only one scenario.*)

SCENARIO 1

You are studying a unit on weather. You need to learn weather-related vocabulary.
- What do you do to remember what the words mean?
- How do you remember how to spell the words?
- How do you learn how to pronounce the words?

SCENARIO 2

Your teacher gives you a folk tale. You must read it, answer written questions, and be prepared to retell the story.
- What do you do to get ready for reading?
- How do you know if you are understanding what you read?
- What do you do if you do not understand the story?
- What do you do if you do not understand a word or phrase?
- What do you do when you finish reading?
- When do you answer the questions?
- How do you find the answers?
- What do you do to prepare to retell the story?

SCENARIO 3

Your homework assignment is to write a letter to an electronic key pal who speaks the language you are studying.
- What do you do to get ready to write?
- How do you decide what to write?
- What do you do to make sure you are writing correctly?
- What do you do if you do not know how to write something?
- What do you do after you finish writing?

students may disagree on the usefulness of strategies. Let them discuss their differences and explore why they may use different techniques. Students can encourage each other to try new strategies.

This activity can also be done as a warm-up. At the beginning of class, present students with a single learning scenario that they will have in class and ask them to share and discuss their strategies for coping with the situation.

Think-Alouds

Can you think of a recent instance when verbalizing your thought process helped you complete a task?

A think-aloud is a technique in which a person verbalizes his or her thought processes while working on a task. As the name implies, it literally means thinking aloud, something people do in their everyday lives. In a language learning setting, a think-aloud reveals how a person processes language. Generally, these processes are the person's strategies for completing the specific language task. Because a think-aloud is in real time, students are not likely to forget their thoughts or make up false ones; thus the technique has a high degree of validity in connection with the task.

Collaborative Activity

The think-aloud can be done in a variety of ways. Students can work in pairs. One student is the interviewee and thinks aloud while working on an assigned language task; the other student is the interviewer and records the thought processes of the interviewee on a think-aloud record sheet, such as that shown in Figure 4.8. Upon finishing the task, students switch roles so each has a turn to think aloud. The think-aloud can be done with any language task: reading, listening, writing, speaking, vocabulary learning, grammar, or pronunciation. Pairs of students can work on the same types of tasks so they can compare and discuss strategies. Start students with a task for which it is easier to think aloud, such as reading, vocabulary, or grammar, and then move them on to other modalities. For listening, students can listen to part of a tape or video and then stop and say what they were thinking while listening. The same is true for speaking and writing. That is, students can produce some of the language and then report on their thoughts. They can also give their thoughts before starting and after finishing the task.

Tip ....

Students may enjoy recording your thoughts as you model a think-aloud. This is also good practice before they begin working in pairs.

Students will probably need training and practice thinking aloud, but once they are used to the technique, most enjoy having someone pay close attention to their thoughts. The teacher can model for students how to think aloud by working on a language task and telling his or her thoughts. He or she can either role play a student of the same age and ability as those in the class, or work with a language task that he or she actually finds challenging (maybe even in a different language from the one studied). Students can practice recording by taking notes on the

FIGURE 4.8

Learning Strategies Think-Aloud Record

Name _____

Partner's Name _____

Date _____

Language Activity _____

Directions Work with a partner. As you work through the task, tell your partner your thoughts about how you are doing the activity. What are you trying to understand or figure out? Your partner will write your strategies on the following chart.

Strategies	Is the Strategy Successful/Helpful? Why or Why Not?	
	Yes	No
Plan		
Monitor		
Problem-Solve		
Evaluate		

teacher's think-aloud and then discussing as a class some of the techniques observed. It is important that students do not view think-aloud thoughts as analogous to right or wrong answers. Each thought has its own value, and the process itself helps students become more aware of how they are learning.

Can you think of other ways to get students used to asking and answering these sorts of questions about their thinking processes?

Students can also learn prompts for encouraging classmates to tell their thoughts. The teacher can model these prompts by making the focus on thought processes a part of the classroom. Thus students will hear the teacher repeatedly use the questions. The prompts can be given in the target language or in English, depending on the students' language level.

In addition to pair work, the think-aloud can be used as a diagnostic tool for individual students. A teacher who knows a student is having difficulties can conduct an individual think-aloud interview with that student to identify problems and help provide additional solutions.

EXAMPLE

Following are some sample think-aloud prompts (prompts are in a hierarchy from general to more specific).

General prompts

- What are you thinking? What's going through your mind?
- How are you doing this? How are you figuring this out?
- What are you looking at? Why?
- How did you know that?

Prompts to get more information

- Is there anything else you are thinking?
- Can you tell me more?
- What were you thinking when you were silent a moment ago?

Prompts responding to what a student has said or done

- How did you figure that out?
- Why do you say that? How do you know? How does that help?
- Why did you change your mind?
- Why did you decide to speak/write about this?
- How did you come up with that? Why did you say that?
- Is that working for you?

Prompts for when a student faces problems

- What are you going to do about that?

- How will you figure it out?

Prompts at the end of the task

- Were you able to tell me out loud what was going through your mind?

- Is there anything you would like to add about what was going through your mind as you worked?

Individual think-alouds can be conducted after class or while the rest of the class is engaged in another activity. It may also be interesting to conduct individual think-alouds with some of the best students to see what makes them so successful. This gives ideas for strategies that can work for other students. The teacher can take notes during the interviews to record students' strategies, or audio or video tape the interview for a more in-depth analysis later. The advantage of taping the interview is that attention can be focused completely on giving appropriate prompts as opposed to trying to write down everything the student is saying.

Tip

Conduct a think-aloud with students who are struggling so that you can identify problems. Conduct a think-aloud with one of your stronger students to identify what makes them successful.

Questionnaires

Questionnaires provide a systematic way of collecting information on the strategies students use. The information is retrospective in that students have time to reflect on what they usually do in a situation. Questionnaires can be open-ended or closed. Open-ended questionnaires allow students a broader response range. However, since this is self-report data, keep in mind that students may not remember everything or may think information is irrelevant and not put it down.

EXAMPLE

An open-ended questionaire could include questions such as the following:

1. What do good learners of English do?
2. What are some things you do to help you learn English?
3. What are some things you do to learn new English words?
4. What is your definition of a learning strategy?

FIGURE 4.9

Sample Learning Strategies Questionnaire— High School and Adult

READING ENGLISH

Reading is a frequent activity you use for learning and using English. You may often read texts such as dialogues, stories, advertisements, and articles in English as part of classwork or on your own.

How often do you do each of the following to help you understand English reading material that is challenging?

1 I decide in advance what my reading purpose is, and I read with that goal in mind.
   Never   *Rarely*   *Sometimes*   *Often*

2 I decide in advance specific aspects of information to look for, and I focus on that information when I read.
   Never   *Rarely*   *Sometimes*   *Often*

3 Before I read, I think of what I already know about the topic.
   Never   *Rarely*   *Sometimes*   *Often*

4 I try to predict what the text will be about.
   Never   *Rarely*   *Sometimes*   *Often*

5 While reading, I periodically check whether the material is making sense to me.
   Never   *Rarely*   *Sometimes*   *Often*

6 I imagine scenes or draw pictures of what I am reading.
   Never   *Rarely*   *Sometimes*   *Often*

7 I encourage myself as I read by saying positive statements such as, "You can do it."
   Never   *Rarely*   *Sometimes*   *Often*

8 I work with classmates to complete assignments or solve comprehension problems.
   Never   *Rarely*   *Sometimes*   *Often*

FIGURE 4.9 (*Cont.*)

9 I use the context, like familiar words, pictures, and the content, to help me guess the meanings of unfamiliar words I read.

Never   *Rarely*   *Sometimes*   *Often*

10 I identify what I don't understand in the reading, and I ask a precise question to solve the problem.

Never   *Rarely*   *Sometimes*   *Often*

11 I use reference materials (dictionary, textbook, computer program, and so on) to help solve comprehension problems.

Never   *Rarely*   *Sometimes*   *Often*

12 After reading, I check to see if my predictions were correct.

Never   *Rarely*   *Sometimes*   *Often*

13 I summarize (in my head or in writing) important information that I read.

Never   *Rarely*   *Sometimes*   *Often*

14 I rate my comprehension by reflecting on how much I understood what I read.

Never   *Rarely*   *Sometimes*   *Often*

15 After reading, I decide whether the strategies I used helped me understand, and I think of other strategies that could have helped.

Never   *Rarely*   *Sometimes*   *Often*

16 I check whether I accomplished my goal for reading.

Never   *Rarely*   *Sometimes*   *Often*

Other Approaches I Use

_____

_____

_____

_____

_____

FIGURE 4.10

Sample Learning Strategies Questionnaire— Elementary School

SPEAKING ENGLISH

Following are some things that you might or might not do to help yourself speak in English, such as when you present a report, answer questions in class, or have a conversation. For each question, circle whether you do it *Almost Never, Sometimes,* or *Almost Every Time.* Tell what you really do, not what you think you should do.

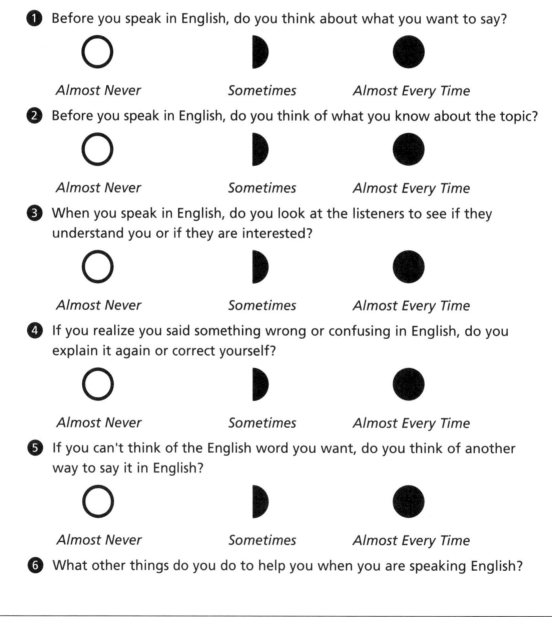

1 Before you speak in English, do you think about what you want to say?

       Almost Never   *Sometimes*   *Almost Every Time*

2 Before you speak in English, do you think of what you know about the topic?

       Almost Never   *Sometimes*   *Almost Every Time*

3 When you speak in English, do you look at the listeners to see if they understand you or if they are interested?

       Almost Never   *Sometimes*   *Almost Every Time*

4 If you realize you said something wrong or confusing in English, do you explain it again or correct yourself?

       Almost Never   *Sometimes*   *Almost Every Time*

5 If you can't think of the English word you want, do you think of another way to say it in English?

       Almost Never   *Sometimes*   *Almost Every Time*

6 What other things do you do to help you when you are speaking English?

Closed questionnaires, on the other hand, give students a response range in the form of a scale (e.g., always, sometimes, never; 1, 2, 3; useful, not useful). These types of questionnaires are used if specific information is to be collected. For instance, the teacher, armed with a set of strategies to teach, wants to find out how many students are already using these strategies. The learning strategies questionnaire can correspond to the Metacognitive Model of Strategic Learning as in Figures 4.9 and 4.10. This type of questionnaire is easily scored and quantified and can be used for pretest and posttest information if someone wants to see whether students' use of strategies increases over time or to compare strategies use across students.

Tip

Create a learning strategies questionnaire for your class that you will administer once at the beginning of the course and once at the end. This will help you see how your students' ideas about learning strategies have changed.

Diaries/Dialogue Journals

Tip

Consider having students write in their learning strategies journals at the end of every class. This supports the reflective/metacognitive nature of learning strategies and reinforces the seriousness of keeping the journal or diary.

Having students report on their strategies use through diaries and dialogue journals enables the teacher and the students themselves to discover their existing strategies use and also to track strategies use over time. Students can be given set times in class or at home to record their use of strategies in their journals. If possible, have students record their strategies use in relation to specific language activities that were done as part of the class or outside of class.

For instance, if students have an opportunity to speak with native speakers, either because they are living in the target country or have access to such speakers in the community, they can regularly write about how they cope with such situations. Diaries and journals establish a strong bond of trust between learner and teacher. They also make excellent additions to learning portfolios, especially if there is a section devoted to learning strategies.

Conclusion

Preparing students for strategies instruction requires planning and an initial investment of time for both teacher and student. However, once the foundation is laid instruction will proceed smoothly, since students become accustomed to reflecting on their learning processes and are willing to take responsibility for their learning. Teachers will have in-depth knowledge of their students' learning abilities and will be able to choose appropriate strategies for instruction. Teachers and students will be ready for the next phase of learning strategies instruction—the Presentation of new strategies.

Consider how well you have prepared your students for learning strategies instruction. What would you do differently when you next present a strategy? Which techniques or activities worked well?

PHASE 2: PRESENTATION

After the Preparation phase in which students' prior knowledge about and use of learning strategies have been discovered and discussed, the teacher is ready to move into the Presentation phase. In this phase, language learning strategies are explicitly modeled, named, and explained. This chapter provides concrete suggestions for presenting learning strategies explicitly. The first part of the chapter gives an overview of general guidelines to follow when introducing new language learning strategies. The second part suggests types of activities that teachers can use to help students understand what strategies are and how to use them.

Instructional Objectives

This chapter will help you to:

- Model strategic thinking through a think-aloud or story that demonstrates learning strategies.
- Name and explain the value of the learning strategy or strategies.
- Explain when to use the target strategy and give examples of appropriate tasks that the strategy will help to accomplish.
- Elicit student's experience with the target strategy or strategies.
- Discuss learning strategies with parents.
- Communicate with other teachers about learning strategies.

General Guidelines for Presenting Learning Strategies

Presentation of learning strategies, whether for language or other types of learning, is most effective when it is explicit, that is, when strategies taught are given names and students are told the reasons for using the strategies. Explicit instruction should also include suggestions about the tasks that a strategy helps to accomplish and the mental processes associated with use of the strategy. The guidelines that follow can help teachers ensure that their learning strategies instruction is explicit.

How explicit is your teaching in general? Do you explain to students exactly what you expect them to learn and perform, or do you find that they can usually figure it out on their own?

Teacher Modeling

Before asking students to practice a strategy, the teacher should demonstrate how the strategy is used by modeling it on a similar task. For example, students might be required to use the strategy of *inferencing* as they view a videotape of person-on-the-street interviews. To model this type of strategy use, the teacher could play a video of similar material, such as a news program with a live interview. While watching the video, the teacher can stop at one or two points where something said in the video is unclear and think aloud while trying to figure out words or phrases from the context, intonation, and other cues. Teachers should make their thought processes as clear as possible by writing them or illustrating them on the board or on an overhead.

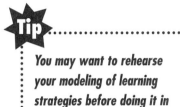

You may want to rehearse your modeling of learning strategies before doing it in front of your students.

Naming the Strategy

As teachers demonstrate their own thought processes in the modeling phase, they should name the strategy explicitly: "I am using *inferencing* when I figure out the words I don't know from the context." The strategy name (in the L2 or L1) should be written out for students on a board, a poster, or a strip of cardboard that the teacher can raise every time the strategy name is mentioned. Knowing the strategy names is necessary for the times when students are asked to evaluate their strategies use and to discuss which strategy is appropriate for a task. This explicit training leads to a more conscious understanding of strategies that, in turn, contributes to the learner's metacognitive knowledge and control over strategies use.

In what other areas of life is it important to give a specific name to an internal condition? Why?

Have students make learning strategy posters or strategy walls. A strategy wall is like a word wall. New words (or strategies) are written on poster board strips that represent bricks and they are displayed to look like a brick wall.

Explaining the Importance of the Strategy

As teachers think aloud while modeling application of strategies to a task, they can point out the usefulness of the strategy with specific examples: "As I am listening to this video and I hear words that I don't know, I have several choices. I can ignore them and just keep listening, or I can stop listening and get frustrated. I might give up at that point. But if I use the strategy *inferencing* and try to figure out the words, I can keep on listening and maybe I will learn some new words. I will feel happy that I have been able to continue listening to the video. The strategy helps me to understand even when I don't know all of the words I hear. *Inferencing* is important for me because I can use it to finish the task, instead of giving up." Students need to hear this type of explanation because they may not realize the value of strategic learning for themselves until they have practiced it over time.

Telling When to Use the Strategy

*Can you give an example from your own life of when you used **inferencing**? Can you give examples of your own use of other learning strategies?*

During the Presentation phase of the lesson, the teacher can describe typical situations in which the focus strategy may be helpful. The closer these are to the students' daily lives, the more memorable they will be. For example, the teacher might say, "Imagine your friend is talking to you on the phone, and a noisy truck drives by your window. You might miss a few words he said, but you can probably get what he's saying by 'filling in the gaps' with what you know he's been talking about. That's one way of using *inferencing*. Whenever you don't understand every word of what you hear or read, you can use the things you do understand to help you figure out the rest." Students should be encouraged to tell about some other times when they might be able to use the strategy. "Was there a time when you could not hear or understand every word and you used *inferencing*? For example, in my school days we were given photocopies that were of such poor quality, we needed to use *inferencing* to figure out some of the partially printed words."

Asking Students to Describe Their Use of the Strategy

After presenting a learning strategy by modeling it, naming it, and describing how and when to use it, teachers should give students an opportunity to share ways in which they have already used the strategy. This can be accomplished in many cases with a class discussion in which individual students describe how they have used the learning strategy. However, some students may be unwilling to speak up in class. When Robbins taught EFL at Doshisha Women's College in Kyoto, Japan, she found that her students could reflect on their experiences with using a particular strategy by writing in a learner diary. This has been a productive method for students to express their reactions to strategies instruction. Many students who are reticent about speaking

English in class with a native English-speaking teacher are extremely capable of responding to strategies instruction by writing about their own experiences and problems in language learning.

Suggested Activities for Presenting Learning Strategies

Learning strategies can be presented as part of the introduction of a new lesson topic or on their own when the teacher perceives that students are experiencing difficulties with a certain type of task. This section describes several activities that can be used as vehicles for presenting new strategies to students.

Sample Lesson for Introducing a Strategy

The lesson plan in Figure 5.1 provides an explicit presentation of a new learning strategy, *prediction*, to be used with a video. This lesson plan is scripted to give a concrete example of what a teacher might say while introducing a new strategy and discussing it with students. To show how the Presentation phase fits into an instructional sequence, this lesson plan includes all five phases of the Instructional Framework described in Chapter 3.

How much time (excluding watching the video) do you think it would take to teach the sample lesson in Figure 5.1? Would you teach the whole lesson in one day? Why or why not?

Teacher Think-Alouds to Present Strategies

The presentation of language learning strategies can be made more tangible through a teacher think-aloud while working on a typical language task. A think-aloud serves the dual purposes of modeling strategies use and of making instruction in strategies explicit. The teacher's first step in doing a think-aloud is to choose a task that will parallel those the students are required to do, while retaining some validity in terms of the level of difficulty for the teacher. For example, a teacher of English might use a text in Old English to demonstrate his or her own reading strategies for a think-aloud. The material used by the teacher should be challenging enough to require the use of some strategies and yet still be comprehensible to the students.

If all of the students share the same native language and the teacher has at least some proficiency in that language, the think-aloud can be done in the students' native language. A language learning task in their own native language will not only be interesting to students, but will also show the teacher as a good role model and a strategic language learner.

FIGURE 5.1

Script for a Lesson Presenting the Strategy *Prediction*

Preparation

❶ Discussing the students' use of the strategy

The teacher begins, "We often predict without thinking deeply about it in our daily lives. When you ask your parents for permission to do something, do you ever predict what they will say? For example, you want to borrow money to buy a new computer game, and you plan to ask your mother this evening. On the way home from school, would you imagine how she's going to answer you? Maybe she'll remind you of how many games you already have or how much money you've spent on other things. By thinking of what she might say, you can prepare your own responses, such as, "I know I have a lot of other games, but this one will help me learn about history." You might play the conversation through in your mind until you have the confidence to ask your mother for the money. Let's take a few minutes for you to think of other times when you try to guess what will happen next."

Students can form small groups to brainstorm ways they have used *prediction*. Then a representative from each group can write all of their ideas on the board for the class to read or say them aloud when the teacher asks for them.

Presentation

❷ Naming and explaining the strategy

"Today, we are going to watch a video about dinosaurs. Before we begin, I'd like you to guess what some of the words used in the video will be. When you guess what's coming up, it's called *prediction*. We use *prediction* to help us remember what we know and to get our minds ready for learning the new material.

Remember, we can learn best when new things are related to what we already know. If you're going to do a task on material you have some information on, use *prediction* based on that information to help you prepare for doing the task."

Practice

❸ Using the strategy

"What words do you know related to dinosaurs? Please predict some you think you'll hear in the video. [Teacher writes the words students suggest on the board, labeling

FIGURE 5.1 (*Cont.*)

them 'Predictions': 'large,' 'powerful,' 'eggs,' 'bones'.] Write the words you think will be in the video in your learner diary. You don't need to write all of the ones we've predicted, only the ones you think you will hear. Now, I'll play the video. You listen well for these words we've predicted. When you hear a word we've predicted, check it off on your paper."

❹ Checking the strategy

"Did you hear the words we predicted?" [Teacher marks the words on the board that were in the video.] "Was it easier to hear them because you were thinking about them before we played the video? Maybe it was because when you have a word on your mind, it's easier to notice it when you hear it. What else did you hear, besides the words that we predicted? What did the narrator say about the eggs, for example?"

Evaluation

❺ Evaluating the strategy's effectiveness

"Did *prediction* help you understand this video better? The next time you watch a video in this language, do you think you'll try to predict something about it first? In your learner diaries for this lesson, write about your own experiences using this strategy. Has it helped you in the past?"

Expansion

❻ Expanding the strategy to help accomplish other tasks

"What other times can we use this strategy?" [Teacher may review the situations that students suggested when asked to tell how they had used *prediction* in the Preparation phase.] "Before asking your teacher a question, perhaps you could predict, what the answer will be. When you're reading, you might use *prediction* when you think of how the story will end. Before a test, you should *predict* what type of questions the teacher will ask and what material will be on the test. This helps you prepare for the test more efficiently. For the next day or two, try to be aware of when you are using *prediction*. Write in your learner diary about the times you use it."

*Do you have students who rarely ask questions in class? How might you encourage them to **ask questions for clarification** whenever they need to?*

An example of a teacher's think-aloud in an EFL classroom in Japan is provided in Figure 5.2. The native English-speaking teacher did his or her think-aloud on a speaking task in Japanese as a way of modeling strategic processes and specific strategies described in Chapter 2. (Words in parentheses indicate the processes and strategies in the Metacognitive Model of Strategic Learning described in Chapter 2.)

Follow-up Strategy Instruction Based on the Think-Aloud

As a follow-up to the think-aloud, it is important that the teacher explain how his or her thought processes showed strategic thinking. Using an overhead or a chart on the board, the teacher can review the think-aloud to make students aware of the strategic processes he or she was modeling. Figure 5.3 provides an example of how the teacher reviewed the think-aloud that was modeled in Figure 5.2.

Teaching to Different Learning Styles: Charts, Visuals, and Movement

In addition to aural input from teacher modeling and think-alouds, many students may also benefit from visual and kinesthetic cues to use learning strategies. Learning strategies posters in the classroom can serve as visual reminders of the strategies that are being introduced and practiced. The teacher may also wish to display a poster of the strategies that are being taught with different thematic units, as in Figure 5.4.

Special graphics can be developed to illustrate specific learning strategies and can be used as simple aids for presenting strategies to students. Teachers can use these graphics as posters, transparencies, or handouts (which younger children can color). Figure 5.5 illustrates three such graphics.

The first graphic shows the first tool for learning: "Ask questions." This refers to the social-affective strategy, *questioning for clarification.* One of the most valuable skills that learners can develop is the ability to ask questions in the target language. This strategy should be presented along with some simple forms of questions being modeled by the teacher and then practiced by the students. Teachers should emphasize that questions are welcome throughout the class and should teach the desired behavior to indicate the need to ask a question (for example, by raising a hand or by using another culturally appropriate signal). While Western teachers expect students to raise their hands freely in a classroom situation, many students from other educational backgrounds may be extremely hesitant

FIGURE 5.2

Teacher's Use of Students' Native Language to Think Aloud

(Set a goal)

"The task I'm going to do is to make up a 30-second radio ad for my home state, Indiana. I want to encourage Japanese people who are traveling to the United States to include Indiana on their itinerary along with those other must-sees such as the Grand Canyon and Disney World."

(Plan)

"First, I'm thinking about what I know about Indiana. Most people think it's just flat and boring, but those aren't things that would attract a Japanese tourist. If I think about what I enjoy doing in Indiana, besides being with my family, the thing that springs to mind is SHOPPING! I know Japanese people like that! And it's so convenient to get to the shopping malls there. There's plenty of free parking, there are all kinds of nice stores, and the stuff is very cheap, even compared to other places in the United States."

(Think of what I know; problem-solve)

"Ok, now I'm going to start writing down what I want to say. The words I know I can use in Japanese are: [writes on sheet] *kaimono, mise, shoppingu sentaa,* or *mōru*—which is right, I wonder? [teacher asks a student for advice]— *yasui, benri.*"

(Monitor)

"Ok, I'm ready to begin. *Amerika ryoko no toki wa, Indiana shu e kite kudasai. Indiana shu wa ii kaimono ga dekiru tokoro desu. Nande?*" (When you go to America, please come to Indiana to go shopping.)

(Revise the plan)

"Now, I want to say that there are lots of malls, but I just realized that I'm not sure how to say 'many' with a thing like malls. *Ooi* comes to mind, but I think that's just for people. I'll just have to use the expression for 'various' and hope that conveys the idea."

(continued on next page)

FIGURE 5.2 (*Cont.*)

(Return to monitoring)

"Iroiro ooki mōru ga atte, benri desu." (There are various big malls where the shops are convenient.) "Next, I want to say that the things in the stores are cheaper than in other places. How should I do that? *Hoka no tokoro yori . . . Indiana no mise no hō ga yasui desu!"* (By comparison to other places, the things in Indiana's stores are cheap.) "I'm not sure that's clear. If this is wrong, I know it's going to sound bad, and my listeners might not even understand. I've heard *meibutsu* but I think that refers to local products. Well, I'll have to ask someone about that when I get a chance. I could beat up on myself at this point, but I'd better keep working so I can get this done quickly." *(self-talk)*

(Problem-solve)

"Maybe I'd better just say, *Mise no naka no, zenbu ga yasui desu yo! Desu kara, Indiana shu e, kaimono ni kite kudasai!"* (In the stores, everything is cheap! So, please come to shop in Indiana!)

(Evaluate)

"Well, how did I do? I think it gets across the ideas I wanted to present, so I met my goal. It may sound a little childish or foreign, but that's to be expected. I didn't mention anything about Indiana's being a safe place, but I'm not sure I can say anything about it in Japanese. In the future, I think I'll try to vary the sentence structure a little and find out for sure how to use the adjectives I want to use. I'm glad I was able to figure out most of what I wanted to say without having to look things up. Even though I did have to ask for some advice, I did it in Japanese. Thank you for helping me with my Japanese vocabulary."

---

to raise their hands when they want to ask a question. At certain ages, this is the result of not wanting to call attention to one's lack of understanding. Depending on the class size and level of formality, the teacher can devise alternative ways for students to indicate their questions. For example, older students may prefer writing their questions in a learner diary, as described earlier. Younger learners may enjoy displaying a "I have a question!" card on their desk or placing a special toy or other object on the teacher's desk to indicate that they would like to ask a question.

The second tool for learning is "Think about what you know." This refers to the cognitive strategy of *activating background knowledge* or *using prior knowledge*. Students are encouraged through the use of this tool to

FIGURE 5.3

Follow-Up to Teacher's Think-Aloud

Now, let's look at how this think-aloud showed what processes might be going through your mind while working on a language task.

Plan "What did I do to plan?" (I set a goal for myself, and I wrote down the words I thought I might use.) "Did I have to change my plan or plan more later on?" (I added to the things I wanted to say by discussing malls.)

Monitor "How did I monitor my work on this task?" (I looked at students to see if they seemed to be understanding me, and I listened to myself speaking.)

Problem-solve "Do you remember what one of my problems was?" (How to say "many shopping malls" or how to say "products.") "How did I solve it? Did I have to revise my plans at all?" (I asked students for help and changed the phrase to use something I was more certain about.)

Evaluate "After I finished, how did I evaluate my performance? Did I evaluate my strategy use?" (I thought I did a fairly good job, and I found asking for help was an effective strategy.)

---

use knowledge they already have to help understand what they are learning in English or another target language. As discussed in Chapter 4, teachers elicit their students' prior knowledge about learning strategies in the Preparation phase of the Instructional Framework. This strategy is taught explicitly during the Presentation phase. For example, even the youngest students of English have had some exposure to phrases in advertising and on children's TV programs and videos. When teaching the names of colors in English, a teacher could ask students to tell the colors they have already learned by referring to the characters on Sesame Street. For example, the teacher could show a picture or poster of those characters and have the students complete the teacher's phrases: "Big Bird is *(yellow),*" "Cookie Monster is *(blue),*" and "Elmo is *(red).*"

What kind of prior knowledge about colors might you elicit from older learners? What prior knowledge might you elicit about numbers, days of the week, months, and other vocabulary sets?

The third tool for learning is "Move to learn." This refers to the cognitive strategy of *contextualization.* Children and even older students enjoy moving around the classroom, and teachers should provide frequent opportunities for them to practice their new language in association with mime, gestures, rhythmic dance movements, and dramatic role-plays. Teachers should explain to students how these kinesthetic activities assist them in learning by using a strategy name to identify the activity, as in Figure 5.5. However, teachers should be aware that kinesthetics is

FIGURE 5.4

Learning Strategies for Different Thematic Units

THEME	STRATEGIES
School	☞ Ask questions
	☞ Activate background knowledge
	☞ Act it out
Friends	☞ Personalize
	☞ Use what I know
	☞ Encourage myself
	☞ Cooperate with classmates
Holidays	☞ Cooperate with classmates
	☞ Act it out (celebrations)
	☞ Draw pictures
	☞ Use real objects
Growing	☞ Use inferencing
	☞ Rate performance
Weather/	☞ Predict
Environment	☞ Selectively attend

FIGURE 5.5

Tools for Learning

Tool #1: Ask questions

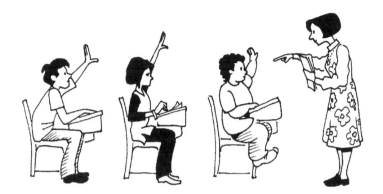

Tool #2: Think about what you know

Tool #3: Move to learn

Tip ....

Total Physical Response is a familiar language teaching technique. It can also be used as a learning strategy by explaining to students how physical actions that illustrate language meaning can help them remember words and sentences in the target language.

another area in which cultural sensitivity is essential. Movements that are permitted in Western cultures may be taboo in some African, Asian, or Middle-Eastern countries. An example is touching a classmate of the opposite sex, touching someone's head, or allowing too much or too little distance between two people. Teachers who are new to a culture should consult with colleagues before incorporating actions into lesson plans.

Games and lessons using gestures can be an enjoyable way to initiate discussions about cultural differences and similarities. Communicative gestures or movements can be effective mnemonic devices for remembering vocabulary and grammatical patterns. The teacher should always make explicit reference to these as learning strategies and explain that by associating the target language word or phrase with a gesture, a learner has a second way to remember and recall it. A video or photos of students performing gestures can be used for discussion and review as well as to decorate the class or accompany a list of the gestures learned on a poster.

Tip ....

Brainstorm with students about other possible icons to represent the four processes. Ask the artists in your class to draw the new icons on a poster to display in the classroom.

Visuals representing learning strategies help students associate names of strategies with the mental processes to which they refer. We have used charts with the icons described in Chapter 2 (see Figure 2.1, page 13) to present learning strategies to high school and college students to explain how learning strategies can be used before, during, and after a learning task.

Once students understand the general model, specific learning strategies can be presented for each stage of a learning task, as illustrated in Figure 2.2. This figure can be made into a poster that teachers can refer to whenever a new learning strategy is presented.

Telling a Story

Tip ....

Make a large picture or overhead transparency of each of the four processes. Show one picture at a time as you tell "The Mountain Climber Story." You might want to tell one part of the story only on a particular day and thereby build suspense about the rest of the story.

Like visuals, narratives are powerful vehicles for understanding and remembering conceptual information. In our research with presenting learning strategies to younger students, we have used a story that illustrates how learning strategies are applied by a fictional character to complete a task successfully. "The Mountain Climber Story" has been successful in helping younger students better understand what strategies are and how to use them. This story is about a girl who climbs a mountain successfully, using numerous strategies to achieve her objective. Figure 5.6 (pages 89–92) shows the visuals we used to illustrate the story to elementary school students. As with the icons used to illustrate the metacognitive model for older students, the names of strategies are added to the visuals of the mountain climber as they are introduced (not all at once, as in Figure 5.6).

FIGURE 5.6

The Mountain Climber Story

PLAN

- ☐ Set goals
- ☐ Preview
- ☐ Activate background knowledge
- ☐ Predict/Brainstorm

MONITOR

- ☐ Monitor sense
- ☐ Selectively attend to specific elements
- ☐ Use imagery
- ☐ Apply rules
- ☐ Relate information to background knowledge
- ☐ Self-talk to build confidence
- ☐ Cooperate with peers

PROBLEM-SOLVE

- ☐ Question for clarification
- ☐ Draw inferences
- ☐ Substitute/Paraphrase
- ☐ Use resources

EVALUATE

- ☐ Check goals
- ☐ Verify
- ☐ Summarize
- ☐ Self-evaluate
- ☐ Assess strategy use

From *Strategic Interaction and Language Acquisition* by A. U. Chamot and J. M. O'Malley, 1993. Washington D.C.: Georgetown University Press.

FIGURE 5.6 *(Cont.)*

THE MOUNTAIN CLIMBER STORY
(TO BE READ ALOUD)

Meet Sachiko. Sachiko is a very good thinker. She uses her mind to help her do all the things she wants to do.

Sachiko wants to climb Mt. Kumo. Mt. Kumo is very big. It will be a very long trip. Sachiko will have to think hard to climb the mountain. But Sachiko is a very good thinker. She knows that before she can start to climb Mt. Kumo, she has to **PLAN** for the trip.

Before her trip, Sachiko has to decide how high she wants to climb.
She sets a goal: "I want to climb all the way to the top of Mt. Kumo!"

Sachiko knows a lot about Mt. Kumo. Before her trip, she asks herself, "What do I remember about Mt. Kumo?" She studies her map of trails to help her remember all the things she knows about Mt. Kumo.

Before her trip, Sachiko has to think about what she needs to pack in her backpack. She predicts what will happen on her long trip so she knows what to pack. She asks, "What might happen? I might get hungry; I'll pack some rice crackers. I might get thirsty; I'll pack some water. I might get cold; I'll pack a coat. I might get tired; I'll pack a blanket."

FIGURE 5.6 *(Cont.)*

Sachiko decides to pay attention to hard parts of the climb. She asks, "What do I need to watch out for? I know there are some streams that I have to cross. I will watch out for them. I'll pack a rope to be ready for them."

Now Sachiko is ready to start climbing. Sachiko is a very good thinker. As she climbs, she needs to check how well she is doing. She needs to help herself so she can keep climbing.

Sachiko looks at the signs to see how far she has climbed. She looks at her map to make sure she is on the right trail.

Sachiko asks herself questions to see if everything is OK. She asks, "How am I doing?" "Am I tired?" "Am I thirsty?"

When she is climbing, Sachiko remembers what she knows about this mountain. She thinks about what she does to help her climb other mountains.

Sachiko sees a picture of Mt. Kumo in her mind and thinks about what she has to do. She looks up to see how far she has to climb. "Am I almost there?"

When she gets scared, Sachiko tells herself, "I can do it."
Sometimes Sachiko meets other climbers. They share climbing stories. They help each other.

FIGURE 5.6 *(Cont.)*

Sometimes climbing gets difficult. There are streams to cross. There are big cliffs. There are strong winds. But Sachiko is a very good thinker. She can solve her problems.

When Sachiko comes to the stream, she needs to choose how to solve her problem. What could Sachiko do?

She could use the map to find another trail. She could ask another climber to help her walk across. She could think about how she crosses other streams. Sachiko will use her rope to get across the big stream.

Because Sachiko is a very good thinker, she thinks about how well she did. After she crosses the stream, Sachiko asks herself, "Was my rope a good tool to cross the stream? Should I use a rope next time I cross the stream?"

Sachiko thinks and climbs, thinks and climbs. Finally, she reaches the top of Mt. Kumo! Sachiko is very happy.

She looks around and thinks about her climb. She thinks about everything she did to help her climb Mt. Kumo.

She asks herself, "How well did I do?"
"I packed enough water, but I would have liked more rice crackers. I will remember next time. I used good tools to cross the stream. I learned about how to climb a new mountain. And most important, I met my goal."

Sachiko is a very good thinker. She climbed all the way to the top of Mt. Kumo.

Teachers can read the story to students, indicating the appropriate illustration and metacognitive process—**plan, monitor, problem-solve, or evaluate**—for different parts of the narrative. Cultural elements can be added to the story by changing the heroine's name (we have used Sophie for French, Sachiko for Japanese, and Sarita for Spanish) and by having her select snacks for her climb that are favorite foods in the culture selected (for example, a baguette, rice balls, or tortillas). Later, when teachers introduce new learning strategies, they can remind students of different parts of the story that illustrate that strategy.

Any story that illustrates a strategic character who solves a problem can serve as a model for introducing the metacognitive processes of **planning, monitoring, problem-solving,** and **evaluating**. Many folk tales are excellent vehicles for introducing learning strategies. Figure 5.7 presents the folktale "The Man Who Stole Fire," which we have divided into sections to illustrate the four metacognitive processes.

Have students listen to or read a folktale such as "The Man Who Stole Fire." Then have them work in cooperative groups to identify parts of the story where Nanabozho **planned**, parts where he was **monitoring**, parts where he engaged in **problem-solving,** and parts where he **evaluated** his solution of the problem.

Communicating with Parents

When learning strategies instruction is part of the language curriculum in elementary or secondary schools, parents can provide support and encouragement to their children. Teachers can share information about learning strategies instruction with parents through newsletters, describing the types of learning strategies activities that are being taught. Newsletters should include a brief explanation of the value of learning strategies and concrete suggestions for ways in which parents can support strategies instruction. In bilingual and ESL/EFL programs, the newsletter should be in the parents' native language. Figure 5.8 provides an example of a newsletter that was sent to the parents of preschool and elementary age children who were studying English at the Kiwi International Service English school in Nara, Japan. The newsletter (in Japanese) described the approach being used by the school, that is, the incorporation of learning strategies and thematic content-based language learning.

Communicating with Other Teachers

Second-language and foreign-language teachers should inform their colleagues about the learning strategies instruction they are

When someone presents a new concept to you, would you prefer a visual image related to something familiar (as in the icons in Figure 2.1), a story as in Figure 5.6, or a different way altogether?

Collaborative Activity

Tip

Include information and discussion about learning strategies that you are teaching when you meet with parents for conferences or other parent-teacher activities.

FIGURE 5.7

A Folktale Illustrating the Metacognitive Model

THE MAN WHO STOLE FIRE

This is the story of how the Ojibwa people got fire.

Many, many years ago, when the Ojibwa first lived in Canada, they had no fire. They could not cook their food or get warm in the cold winters. Life was very difficult without fire. At that time the Ojibwa heard about an old man and his daughter who lived very far away. It was said that the old man and his daughter were warm in winter and could cook delicious food. They had fire, but they would not give any of their fire to the Ojibwa.

A young Ojibwa boy named Nanabozho lived with his grandmother because his parents were dead. Nanabozho loved his grandmother dearly, and she loved him. But his grandmother was old, and she began to lose her teeth. It was very hard for her to eat raw meat because she could not chew it. And in the winter she was so cold that she shivered, even though Nanabozho put warm blankets around her shoulders. Nanabozho looked at his cold and hungry grandmother. He knew he had to help her. Then he remembered that the old man and his daughter had fire. He decided to steal some fire from them. He thought about how he could get fire from the old man and his daughter, and he **made a plan.**

Nanabozho walked many days and finally he got to the house of the old man and the daughter. When Nanabozho saw the young girl, he changed himself into a little rabbit. The young girl saw the rabbit and picked it up. She petted the rabbit, then took it into the house. She stirred the fire and began to make soup for dinner. Nanabozho thought to himself, "My plan is working. Everything is going well!"

But when the old man came home and saw the rabbit sitting under the table, he thought the rabbit would make the soup even more delicious. He told his daughter to get a knife to kill the rabbit. Now Nanabozho (who was changed into the rabbit) did not expect this problem. He knew he had to do something to **solve his problem.** He thought of a way to get the fire and save himself from the knife.

FIGURE 5.7 *(Cont.)*

When the young girl took a sharp knife and tried to catch the rabbit, the rabbit jumped towards the fire. As he jumped, Nanabozho quickly changed himself back into a boy. He grabbed a burning stick from the fire and ran as fast as he could. The old man chased him, but Nanabozho had an idea how to escape. He set fire to the grass behind him, and soon there was burning grass between Nanabozho and the old man. The old man could not follow him because of the fire, so Nanabozho got home safely. That is how he **solved his problem.**

When Nanabozho got to his grandmother's house, he built a fire to keep her warm. Then he cooked meat and made soup for her to eat. Nanabozho took good care of his grandmother and he gave fire to all the other Ojibwa. He was happy. He thought, "My plan worked. Now all the Ojibwa homes are warm in winter and glowing with fire."

And that is how the Ojibwa got fire.

Adapted from "The Fire Stealer," retold by Pat Rigg in *Voices in Literature.* Copyright © 1996 by Heinle and Heinle.

implementing and find out whether teachers of other subjects are also teaching learning strategies. Teachers of mathematics, for example, may be teaching their students how to *estimate*, while science teachers are probably asking students to *make hypotheses* before conducting experiments. Both of these strategies have much in common with the language learning strategy of *inferencing* during listening or reading. Metacognitive strategies of **planning, monitoring**, and **evaluating** are useful for all school subjects and even for learning and problem-solving situations outside of school.

> **Tip**
>
> *Ask your colleagues what strategies they teach their students. Have them identify the specific names they give to strategies, and decide if these strategies have counterparts in language learning.*

Learning strategies instruction from more than one teacher can help students understand contextual demands and different applications of the same basic learning strategies. In one elementary school immersion program, for example, first- through sixth-grade teachers met to plan a learning strategies scope and sequence to integrate into both the target language and content curriculum, with appropriate learning strategies to be introduced and reviewed at each grade level.

FIGURE 5.8

Learning Strategies Newsletter to Parents

TOOLS FOR LEARNING

The teachers at KIS (Kiwi International Service) school have been studying this summer and have some new tools they want to share with their students. They are language learning strategies. Research has shown that these techniques are used by effective (successful) language learners and that any student can learn to use them to improve his or her language learning ability. KIS teachers will explain how to use these techniques and give students practice activities for each one. In the "School" theme, the strategies will be as follows:

1. **Ask questions**   When you don't understand clearly, ask a question (in English or in Japanese) to find out exactly what you need to know. For example, your teacher says, "I have two (mumbles) in my pencil box." If you ask, "Please say it again" and the teacher says, "I have two (mumbles) in my pencil box," you still don't know what the word (mumble) means. So it's better to ask, "You have two WHATS in your pencil box?" to show your teacher the part you did not understand. Now he or she can explain, "I have two erasers" and point to them so you can understand.

2. **Activate background knowledge**   Use the knowledge you already have to help you understand what you are learning in English. For example, you know many things about school already: There are teachers, students, classes, and so on. When you are learning about them in English, if you think of what you know you will be familiar with many of the things that your teacher is talking about. Your mind will be ready to associate the new words in English with the words you already know in Japanese.

3. **Act it out (Move to learn)**   At KIS this summer, we have learned many gestures, or movements, to go with English words and phrases. If you use a motion while saying a word or phrase in English, your brain will have two things to associate with the meaning. It will be easier to remember the word later. It's like having a person's home and work phone numbers; if you can't locate them at one place, you will probably find them at the other.

Special Request to Parents

You can help us by explaining these techniques in simple language to your children. After your child has studied them, ask him or her to demonstrate how he or she used the techniques in class. You can also practice them at home when you are teaching your child other material.

Conclusion

Language teachers can present learning strategies explicitly to students in a variety of ways. However, teachers should always model strategies, refer to them by name, explain why they are important, suggest when to use a specific strategy, and elicit from students how they are already using a strategy. As a result of this explicit presentation of learning strategies, students will acquire the metacognitive knowledge they need to use strategies independently and begin to have more control over their own learning processes.

In this chapter, we suggested a number of activities that teachers can use during the Presentation phase of learning strategies instruction. We also encouraged teachers to use their imaginations to design activities that help their students understand how to use learning strategies. Creative ways in which teachers are already presenting new information and skills to their students can be adapted to include the presentation of learning strategies.

Did any of your teachers ever present learning strategies? Were they explicit? What insights have you gained from their instruction?

PHASE 3: PRACTICE

In Chapters 4 and 5, we suggested ways in which teachers can identify the learning strategies students are already using (the Preparation phase) and explain new strategies by using explicit modeling (the Presentation phase). Presenting strategies in a way that students understand is the foundation for building independent learning, but the real construction of independent learning happens when students practice strategies and develop strategic thinking themselves. This chapter explores ways to provide successful practice opportunities for strategic learning. The first part of the chapter suggests general guidelines for practicing learning strategies, and the second part suggests types of activities that can promote the use of strategic processes by students.

Instructional Objectives

This chapter will help you to:

- Integrate strategies practice into your regular course work.
- Select appropriate levels of learning tasks for practicing strategies.
- Employ various techniques to encourage students to use strategies.
- Provide students with supporting information about strategies.
- Give students guidance for applying strategies.
- Scaffold strategies instruction so that students will be able to apply strategies with increasing independence.

General Guidelines for Practicing Learning Strategies

Strategies instruction places students' thinking in the spotlight and encourages effective strategies use while students work on classroom tasks. The examples in this chapter show simple but powerful ways teachers can encourage strategic practice as part of language practice.

Integrate Strategies Practice into Regular Course Work

Throughout this book, we have emphasized that effective strategies instruction is not an add-on, but rather a way to support language learning in an existing curriculum. Students should practice strategies while working on authentic, meaningful language tasks that are part of the language class. When teachers include learning strategies in their teaching, the instructional shift is not a matter of content but one of emphasis.

In planning lessons, identify language practice activities. Then add learning strategies practice to these activities.

Select Appropriately Challenging Tasks

For a language task to be an effective choice for learning a new strategy, it should be authentic and moderately challenging. In strategic learning it is critical that these criteria be met. If students respond negatively to strategies instruction, the first thing the teacher should do is examine the task to see if it meets these criteria.

An authentic language task, for example, is one that is based on real communicative or informational needs. It is designed to provide students with an opportunity to use the target language for a meaningful purpose. It is nearly always better to select a strategy to fit the task at hand, rather than to contrive a task to teach a particular strategy. For example, if an ESL class opens with a discussion of the weather, *prediction* could be taught in the context of predicting weather and then checking predictions. Even very young students with limited vocabulary can predict weather by drawing pictures. Once students are used to making weather predictions, the discussion could turn to predicting words that students can expect to hear when they listen to a weather report.

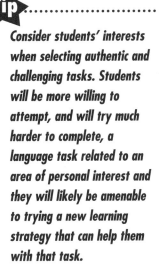

Consider students' interests when selecting authentic and challenging tasks. Students will be more willing to attempt, and will try much harder to complete, a language task related to an area of personal interest and they will likely be amenable to trying a new learning strategy that can help them with that task.

The difficulty of the task should represent a slight stretch for students. Students are not likely to apply strategies unless they personally experience success with and perceive the benefit of strategies for making a task easier and learning more efficient. If the task is too easy, students will not need strategies to succeed; they may therefore see strategies as a waste of time. However, if the task is too difficult students may not be able to succeed even when they do use appropriate strategies.

Tasks representing a slight stretch are those within Vygotsky's Zone of Proximal Development (ZPD) (see Chapter 9). Think of a language task in your own ZPD. What learning strategies might help?

For example, students who are just beginning to decode words—very young children or older students learning a new writing system—could initially learn reading comprehension strategies while they listen to stories or articles at their comprehension level that the teacher reads aloud. The teacher should select a text that is rich enough to inspire *predictions, visualizations,* and *relations to background knowledge,* which are strategies appropriate for even the youngest students. Students can then practice word decoding on simple texts, using decoding strategies that include *using context clues, applying phonics rules, substituting a word that makes sense, looking back for information,* and *skipping unknown words* when getting too bogged down. This approach allows students to experience rich, meaningful literature at their comprehension level while their decoding level is catching up.

Encourage Students to Practice the Strategies Introduced

The sample worksheet in Figure 6.1 is in English, the native language of the students in a beginning-level Spanish class. How could you adapt this worksheet for ESL or EFL students?

When students learn a new strategy, teachers will need to explicitly guide them to practice it during language learning tasks. One way to provide guidance is to add instructions to the task that remind students to use the strategy. Figure 6.1 provides an example of a worksheet developed to guide beginning-level high school Spanish students in practicing several strategies for reading a short story.

The teacher can model how to use the worksheet by giving examples. Since the lesson presented in Figure 6.1 focuses on *prediction,* the teacher can ask students why they would want to use this strategy for reading. The teacher also can model predictions and other strategies by thinking aloud while reading a story. Then students can think aloud in pairs while reading a different story and, finally, discuss the strategies they used.

Tip ....

Thinking aloud may not be easy for some students, but you should reassure them that they will improve with practice. For many students, it is easier to get started thinking aloud on a math problem.

Strategies practice with young students will probably be most successful if it begins with teacher modeling of the target strategies on part of the actual task (or a similar task) that students are asked to complete. This serves as a reminder of the strategies and how they work, and it helps students understand the level of work expected of them. However, to discourage parroting of the teacher's example, the teacher should remind young students that their use of strategies will be unique. Students should also be invited to try thinking aloud. Young students in ESL, bilingual, or immersion classes can try thinking aloud while they listen to the teacher read a story, while they work on a math problem, or while they read aloud from a class text.

FIGURE 6.1

Guided Learning Strategy Practice

BEFORE READING

1 Use the strategy *grouping* to give a category name to the following words that occur in the story you are going to read:

[list of 10-12 words that can be grouped in semantic categories]

2 Now look at the word list above and circle at least three words in Spanish that are *cognates* with English.

3 Look at the title, pictures, format, and questions at the end of the story. What do they tell you about the story? Write four *predictions* about the story based on these clues.

4 Before reading this story, what strategies do you think will be most helpful to you? Write them down and briefly tell why you think each strategy will help you understand the story.

WHILE READING

1 Work with a partner to read the story.

2 Take turns thinking aloud as you read. Do this by stopping after one or two paragraphs and telling your partner what you were thinking about as you were reading. Then your partner can tell you what he or she was thinking about.

3 Take notes on your partner's *think-aloud*, and have your partner take notes when it is your turn to think aloud.

AFTER READING

Be prepared to discuss the following questions with the class.

1 What did you learn from your partner's think-aloud?

2 What did you learn from your own think-aloud?

3 Which strategy (or strategies) proved most helpful in understanding the story?

Adapted from a lesson developed by Christine McCloy, Fairfax County (Virginia) Public Schools.

Coach Students to Use Strategies When Given Frequent Cues and Feedback

Tip

Just as your students are at different levels of language proficiency, they are also at different levels of proficiency in using learning strategies. Some students will need repeated reminders to use a strategy, whereas others will need only occasional reminders.

How could you convey the feedback examples in Figure 6.2 to beginning-level language learners?

Which strategy or strategies do you use most often while reading for comprehension? Could you teach one of your reading strategies to your students? If so, how? If not, why not?

Students need to be coached in their use of strategies during practice activities. In Figure 6.1, coaching was provided by teacher reminders and through the structure of the tasks. After initial practice, students need the support of reminders to continue using the strategies they are learning.

Students need feedback about how well they are applying the strategies. For example, teachers should praise particularly relevant and insightful *inferences*, creative and detailed *imagery*, and concise *summaries*. Another simple but effective way to provide feedback is to simply restate what the student said. This echoes the strategy back to that student and others so everyone has a chance to think about what the student did. In addition, a simple restatement reinforces strategy use by showing that the teacher thinks it is important. Restating how a student uses a strategy can be an effective way to accept all students' responses while encouraging strategic thinking. Young students can be especially sensitive when their response is called "good" or "okay," while another response is "great." Restating the response removes such judgments and shows students that all appropriate responses will be accepted. Figure 6.2 suggests a variety of ways to provide feedback when students talk about their thinking.

Teachers can also use a guided activity to coach students in the appropriate application of strategies taught in class. Individual students or pairs can be asked to record their strategies on the chalkboard or an overhead transparency. For example, after reading a short story for which students were asked to *create summaries, use inferences,* and *visualize* the setting, the teacher can call on several students in the class to share their results. As students describe their strategies use, the teacher provides feedback, such as: "Carmen, please read us your summary. [Carmen reads.] How did you decide what ideas to include in your summary?" "Jairo, were there any words in the story you weren't sure of? What inferences did you make? How did you make them?" "Alicia, what did you visualize while you were reading the story? Why is it a good idea to visualize when you read?"

Parents can be included in feedback about strategies use, especially with younger students. Parent-teacher conferences can include discussions about strategies the individual student is using. Report cards and graded homework can also include comments about the student's strategies. Teachers might even consider giving a grade for learning strategies use. These actions are all ways that teachers can show parents that learning processes are valued in the classroom, in addition to content outcomes.

FIGURE 6.2

Teacher Feedback to Students

- Ask the student for elaboration about the task he or she has just completed.
- Ask the student to identify the strategy (or strategies) he or she used.
- Rephrase what the student did to complete the task.
- Name the strategy that the student used for the task.
- Ask why the student chose that approach or solution.
- Ask whether the strategy worked.
- Explain why the strategy was effective.
- Ask what else the student could have done for that task.

Encourage Students to Choose Their Own Strategies and to Develop a Repertoire of Strategies

Once several strategies have been introduced, students need opportunities to practice choosing strategies for themselves. Teachers can ask students to reflect on their thought processes while they work on language tasks, either orally or in writing. When students are first coordinating their repertoire of strategies, they may need frequent prompts to choose strategies for a task and even suggestions of specific strategies to try. As students become more independent in using strategies, cues should be less frequent and less explicit. Even very young students can learn to choose strategies from a poster and eventually will remember the strategies options they have chosen and learned.

Teachers should continue to give students feedback whenever they use strategies, praising them for being strategic and pointing out when a particular strategy is successful. If one strategy is not working for a student, the teacher can encourage the student to select a different strategy. If students rely on only one or two strategies most of the time, teachers should encourage them to try others.

Tip

Make individual copies of classroom learning strategies posters and distribute them to your students. These can be laminated for durability and kept inside students' notebooks.

How could you encourage a student to practice a learning strategy when he or she professes a lack of interest?

Focus on Students' Learning Processes, Not Just Products

One of the easiest and best ways to encourage strategic thinking is to put less emphasis on "correct" content or language production and to put more emphasis on the thinking that leads to students' responses.

The core of strategies instruction should be based on a habit of focusing on students' thought processes. Thinking aloud does not have to be a formal, structured activity. During daily classroom tasks, teachers can frequently ask students about the reasoning behind their responses. Following are some sample questions for focusing on thinking.

- What are you going to do?
- How did you come up with that?
- What makes you think so?
- What were you thinking about?
- How can you solve your problem?
- How did you decide that?

What aspects of your students' behavior and performance do you tend to praise most often? How might you modify your pattern of praise to include a greater focus on learning strategies?

Students should be encouraged to talk about their thinking regardless of whether their answers are right or wrong. Students should not interpret "What makes you think so?" as "wrong answer" or even "good answer." When students seem to be lagging behind in comprehension or production, or when they give incorrect responses in class, focusing on thinking can reveal flaws in logic or inappropriate choices or application of strategies. Teachers can then use these opportunities to remind students of effective strategies they could have applied. Conversely, examining thinking behind insightful responses can give all students a model of effective thinking and can help good students be more aware of what helps them learn. Teachers should get in the habit of praising good thinking more than good outcomes.

As students describe their thinking, teachers should be sure to point out any strategies that they are using—especially when the students seem unaware that they did something strategic. For example, "So it seems like you have a picture in your mind of what this would be like. You're using *imagery*."

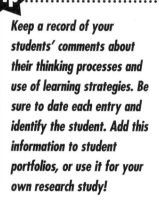

Keep a record of your students' comments about their thinking processes and use of learning strategies. Be sure to date each entry and identify the student. Add this information to student portfolios, or use it for your own research study!

When students correct themselves, teachers can help them focus on their own thinking processes by asking them questions such as "Why do you say that? Why did you change your mind? What were you thinking when you corrected yourself?"

When prompted, even very young students can describe their use of learning strategies. In our work with elementary school students, we found numerous instances of children's descriptions of their strategies and thinking processes (Chamot, Keatley, Barnhardt, El-Dinary, Nagano, & Newman, 1996). Some examples are provided in Figure 6.3.

FIGURE 6.3

Elementary School Students' Insights into Their Learning Processes

I try to look at the title to see what it is like. . . . I think that it is recycling. . . . "From Iron to Silverware" because it is from one thing to another, that it says that it converts to something else. . . .

Sometimes, I picture what they said, a picture like the character's actually saying it, or like a narrator telling . . . what's going on and everything.

[When I don't know a word] I read the first data. I think about what the first data says. In this case, "age" is the same as the first part of *agemasu*.

I think that this will be the easiest [picture] to make a story about . . . there was another picture I liked a lot . . . but I could not think of a story I could use.

[I'm thinking about] what I can use to organize my ideas.

When I have to spell them but I don't know . . . sometimes I just, like, pretend those letters are in front of my face . . . in the words. . . . It helps me.

I think about the stories I have heard and then those that happen in my life and then those that happen in the papers and then I use my imagination to think of different or creative things . . . because I don't always like stories that are true to life.

Interviewer: What are you thinking about at this moment, before starting to read? [Examines picture] That this story could be a fantasy. . . . Because I think that the story is going to be very funny and things are going to happen that can't happen.

[The man is] a little strange . . . because he always carries the umbrella. . . . He must really like the umbrella. . . . When it rains, he runs without using the umbrella even though he gets wet. . . . The umbrella must be really precious.

Source: Chamot, A.U., Keatley, C., Barnhardt, S., El-Dinary, P., Nagano, K., and Newman, C. (1996). "Learning Strategies in Elementary Immersion Classrooms." Final report submitted to International Research and Studies Program, U. S. Department of Education, Washington, D. C. Available from ERIC. Document No. ED 404 878.

Suggested Activities for Practicing Learning Strategies

In this section, we suggest specific activities that provide practice in using learning strategies. The suggestions include both interactive and individual activities, as well as activities that can be conducted in class or assigned for homework. Most of these activities will be familiar to many teachers and may already be a part of their instruction. In using these and other activities to practice learning strategies, teachers must be sure to make explicit the strategies to be practiced, their purpose, and how to use them.

Cooperative Learning and Group or Pair Work

*Is **cooperation** a strategy that you use frequently in your own life? What are some ways that you have worked cooperatively with others recently?*

Any type of cooperative learning or group activity can become a vehicle for practicing learning strategies. *Cooperation* should be identified as a strategy, and students can be asked to explain the various benefits that this strategy provides.

Assigning roles to different members of a cooperative group helps ensure that all members participate and make contributions to the group assignment. Typical roles include Coordinator/Task Master, Recorder/Note-taker, Cheerleader/Encourager, and Materials Organizer.

Tip

Make a poster describing the different roles for cooperative learning activities, and use it to remind students of the responsibilities of each group member.

As part of the cooperative learning task, teachers should remind students which strategies to practice. They also should provide a way for students to record the strategies they used during the cooperative learning or group activity. For example, students can be provided with a sample worksheet to complete as they work on a jigsaw cooperative learning activity.

Reciprocal Teaching

Reciprocal Teaching is a cooperative reading technique developed by Palincsar and Brown (1984, 1986) for low-achieving readers in native language contexts. This technique asks students working in groups to use several learning strategies designed to improve reading comprehension. Students sit in groups of four and quietly read through a section of the text. One student then acts as the discussion leader and, after *summarizing* the main points of the text, *questions* the others in the group about the text, indicates any areas of difficulty, and makes a *prediction* about what might occur in the next section of the text. Then the group members continue reading the second section of the text, and a second student acts as the discussion leader. Students continue in this fashion until they have read the entire text. The intent is that through overt and guided practice of these reading strategies, students will internalize them and begin using them independently for other reading assignments. Figure 6.4 presents an adapted version of Reciprocal Teaching that includes *using prior knowledge* as an additional reading strategy.

Tip ....

You may find that Reciprocal Teaching requires practice before students can use all of the strategies independently. Start with one or two strategies, and gradually add the others.

Role-Playing Activities

A number of learning strategies can help language students engage successfully in role-playing activities such as dialogues, improvisations, and skits. All of these activities involve oral interaction in the target language, usually for an audience. Dialogue practice may require memorizing or paraphrasing a role in a prepared conversational exchange, which might be provided by the teacher or the textbook or created by students. Learning strategies that students have reported helpful in memorizing dialogues of this sort include *visualization/ imagery* and *contextualization*.

Can you remember any special techniques you used to memorize dialogue when performing in a school play or similar activity?

Students can use *visualization* to create powerful mental images of themselves in their roles, the personalities of the characters played by other participants in the dialogue, and the physical setting in which it is taking place. By using *contextualization*, students can use physical actions, props, facial expressions, and even a particular tone of voice to trigger the next part of the dialogue being memorized. These two strategies are also helpful in unrehearsed improvisations and in longer skits or plays that require memorization and rehearsal.

Problem-Solving Activities

Problem-solving activities can also be combined with learning strategies practice. Examples are jigsaw and information gap activities, in which individual students have different pieces of information that they need to share to complete a task. These types of activities require students to use language to acquire and communicate new information in order to solve a problem or engage in a simulation.

Learning Stations

Activities organized around learning stations in content-based classrooms can exploit a wide variety of learning strategies to integrate into learning activities. In one CALLA classroom, for example, the teacher set up five different learning stations in an ESL-Social Studies

FIGURE 6.4

Reciprocal Teaching Strategies for Reading

ENGLISH: READING STRATEGIES

STRATEGY NAME	PROMPTS TO ELICIT THE STRATEGY
Use what you know	I remember. . . .
Summarize	This is about. . . .
Ask and clarify	Where . . . ?
	Who . . . ?
	When . . . ?
	What happened . . . ?
	Why . . . ?
	How do you know . . . ?
	What's the reason . . . ?
	What does it mean . . . ?
	What would have happened if. . . ?
Predict	I think what's going to happen is. . . ?

Adapted from Palincsar and Brown (1984). "Reciprocal Teaching of Comprehension-fostering and Comprehension-monitoring Activities." *Cognition and Instruction, 1,* 117–175.

middle school classroom. These low-intermediate students were studying the characteristics of life in desert regions. The teacher reminded them of the learning strategies they would be practicing: *cooperation, resourcing, predicting, using prior knowledge, imagery*, and *note-taking*. Then the teacher divided students into groups and assigned the initial learning stations (each group would eventually rotate to each of the five stations). The teacher explained that while all learning stations would require them to use the strategy of *cooperation* since they would be completing group assignments, some learning stations would require them to use only some of the other strategies.

The teacher called students' attention to the names of strategies posted on the bulletin board and asked students to give brief examples of how they had used each strategy. Then she gave a brief overview of the tasks at each of the learning stations and explained that students would find detailed directions for their task at the learning station. She next divided the class into groups of four and assigned them to each of the five stations. Each learning station consisted of four desks pushed together, a sign with the title of the learning station, one group worksheet for students to complete, and the materials needed to complete the activity.

Students worked for about 15 minutes at their initial learning stations, and then the teacher asked them to move counterclockwise to the next station. Students worked at three different learning stations the first day. Over the second and third days, they continued through the last two stations and then returned to the original stations to complete their group tasks. At the conclusion of each class, the teacher dismissed students one group at a time by asking a representative from each group to describe one of the learning strategies their group had used. If the student called on was able to describe a learning strategy, the group could leave, but if the student had difficulty in describing one of the group's learning strategies, other group members were asked to help. In this way, the teacher ensured that students were aware of the learning strategies involved in their group tasks.

Reader Response Groups and Writers' Workshops

Interactive reading and a process approach to writing are highly strategic approaches to reading and writing in a second or foreign language. Students may need to be reminded of the strategies they are using during these types of activities. In Reader Response activities, students sit in small groups to discuss a book or story they have read. Initially, the teacher leads the discussion, but eventually students should be able to conduct their own Reader Response groups. The teacher, often with

What kinds of classroom management techniques have you used successfully for cooperative or independent learning activities similar to learning stations?

Tip..........................

Set up a permanent learning station in a corner of your classroom for learning strategies. Provide names of strategies, icons, samples of student work with learning strategies comments, and other learning strategies artifacts.

Collaborative Activity

input from students, provides open-ended questions to guide the discussion. Questions about strategies used to comprehend the reading text can be used to elicit individual reflections on learning strategies used before, during, and after reading. Figure 6.5 provides examples of the types of questions language learners can discuss in a Reader Response group.

In a writers' workshop, students alternate between individual and collaborative work as they plan their stories, reports, or essays, develop drafts, revise those drafts, and eventually share their final drafts in published form. Each of these recursive stages of the writing process provides many opportunities for practicing learning strategies. During initial brainstorming, for example, students can identify the strategies they use to generate ideas. When they share their initial drafts, they can discuss the thinking processes and strategies they used as they developed their ideas, the problems they encountered, and how these problems were solved. Problems that were not successfully solved can be shared with group members, whose suggestions for strategies can be sought. During the revision process, teachers might ask students to keep notes on decisions made or to think aloud to a tape recorder as they work on revising their compositions. These notes or tapes can be used as a basis for a writer's conference in which the teacher helps individual students work through revisions to their writing.

Using Technology to Practice Learning Strategies

Language activities involving word processing, computer games and exercises, video, CD-ROM, e-mail, and the Internet can all provide opportunities for practicing learning strategies. Writing strategies such as *using prior knowledge, organizational planning, note-taking, outlining,* and *questioning for clarification* are helpful for students who compose at the computer keyboard. Similarly, when students read a text on the computer screen that is part of a CD-ROM or has been downloaded from the Internet, helpful reading strategies include *using prior knowledge, predicting, making inferences, using imagery* or *visualization, using cognates,* and *note-taking.*

Language games and exercises on the computer are motivating and can provide additional practice and feedback. We suggest having students work at a computer in pairs so they can discuss and share useful learning strategies for solving the problems presented on the monitor.

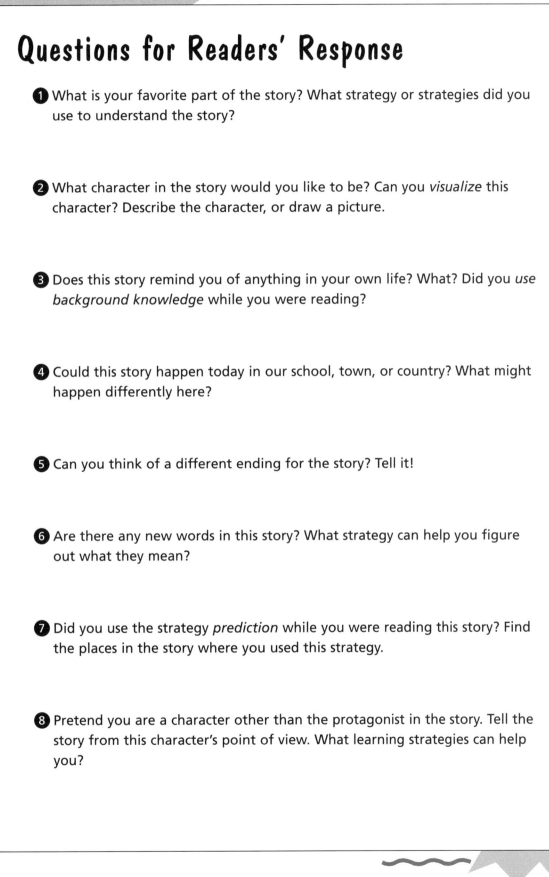

FIGURE 6.5

Questions for Readers' Response

1 What is your favorite part of the story? What strategy or strategies did you use to understand the story?

2 What character in the story would you like to be? Can you *visualize* this character? Describe the character, or draw a picture.

3 Does this story remind you of anything in your own life? What? Did you *use background knowledge* while you were reading?

4 Could this story happen today in our school, town, or country? What might happen differently here?

5 Can you think of a different ending for the story? Tell it!

6 Are there any new words in this story? What strategy can help you figure out what they mean?

7 Did you use the strategy *prediction* while you were reading this story? Find the places in the story where you used this strategy.

8 Pretend you are a character other than the protagonist in the story. Tell the story from this character's point of view. What learning strategies can help you?

In your personal use of e-mail, how concerned are you about spelling and other mechanical aspects of writing? What level of accuracy should you require of your students?

Projects involving e-mail and research on the Internet are gaining widespread use as more computers become available in classrooms. Language students can benefit from exchanging e-mail messages with key pals who are native speakers of the target language. Using learning strategies such as *planning* and *cooperation* to draft e-mail messages can help students overcome concern about making mistakes in their e-mails. Some students may want to *use resources* to check points of grammar or vocabulary before sending their messages. In reading e-mail answers and in conducting research on the Internet, students can use a variety of reading strategies, such as *selective attention, inferencing, summarizing* and *note-taking* (for research), and *questioning for clarification.* Teachers can suggest strategies that students can practice while engaged in on-line activities, or they may ask students to explain which strategies they plan to use (or did use) and why. (See Warschauer, 1995, for suggestions and applications of technology to language learning.)

Practicing Learning Strategies for Homework and Tests

Learning strategies can also be practiced as part of homework assignments. For example, teachers may assign specific strategies such as *grouping* and *visualization* as students read a narrative or expository text and identify important words or concepts to remember. When students prepare oral reports, teachers can suggest a number of rehearsal strategies, such as using note cards, practicing in front of a mirror, practicing with friends or family members, and recording and then evaluating their own performance.

Tip

Before teaching new test-taking strategies, ask students what strategies they already use to study for tests (Preparation phase). Pay special attention to the strategies used by students who are good test-takers.

Students can also use learning strategies when studying for and taking tests. Test preparation strategies include *selective attention* to important information, memory strategies such as *grouping, imagery, note-taking,* and *making graphic organizers,* and *self-assessment.* Useful test-taking strategies are *self-talk* to overcome anxiety, *selective attention to directions and questions, planning* and *time-management, questioning for clarification* as appropriate, and *checking back.*

Conclusion

This chapter suggested a variety of ways that teachers can provide students with practice opportunities for learning strategies, as well as ways to give students feedback about their use of strategies. The practice opportunities described were all in the context of lessons in the regular curriculum. Teachers need to be explicit in their expectations that students practice learning strategies within the context of classroom activities. This is accomplished by shifting the focus of instruction away from an emphasis on content outcomes and instead placing greater emphasis on thought processes. Instead of just emphasizing vocabulary memorization, lessons should focus on what students can do to remember the words and their meanings. Instead of only discussing what details students can recall about a story, a learning strategies lesson should focus on how students are developing an understanding of the story while they read it. Students at all levels are capable of talking about their thinking. With teacher support, they can apply strategies that they have been taught and describe how they are doing so. Through activities such as those described in this chapter, students learn to apply the strategies that teachers present to them, building up their capability for independent learning.

What test-taking strategies have worked for you in your own academic career? Can you teach any of these strategies to your students?

Chapter **7**

PHASE 4: EVALUATION

The fourth phase of learning strategies instruction, Evaluation, focuses on evaluating the new learning strategies that students practiced in the third phase, Practice. This evaluation is done in large part by the students themselves as a way of developing their metacognitive ability; that is, their ability to reflect on their own approaches to learning. Self-evaluation provides students with an opportunity to take control of their own learning by selecting or rejecting particular learning strategies. Thus the Evaluation phase is crucial to self-regulated learning. This chapter begins with general guidelines for the Evaluation phase and then suggests various types of evaluation activities.

Instructional Objectives

This chapter will help you to:

- Show students how to identify the learning strategies they used for a recently completed learning task.
- Encourage students to reflect on their own learning processes.
- Plan activities in which students evaluate the effectiveness of the learning strategies they have used for a specific task.
- Assess how effectively students are applying the strategies taught.
- Include learning strategies evaluations in assessment portfolios.
- Evaluate your own learning strategies instruction.

General Guidelines for Evaluating Learning Strategies

Although the focus in the Evaluation phase is on student self-evaluation, teachers are also engaged in evaluation activities. First, teachers need to evaluate how their students are applying the learning strategies that have been taught so that they can adapt their instruction to students' needs. Second, teachers need to evaluate their own learning strategies instruction. By reflecting on their degree of success in integrating learning strategies instruction into their classrooms, teachers can build on their strengths and find ways to improve any area of their instruction that is not meeting their students' needs.

Teachers should be aware that asking students about their thinking processes after they have completed a specific task may not yield complete or fully accurate information. Retrospective methods of collecting information about students' use of learning strategies (for example, questionnaires, discussions, and interviews) are always subject to the possibility that students may not report accurately on the strategies they actually used for the task. This can occur when students report what they perceive to be information desired by the teacher. Or it can occur simply because students may not be able to remember all of the strategies they used during the task. In spite of these potential limitations, we have found that students can report on at least the major strategies they used during a task and that such reports provide both students and teachers with useful insights into the language learning process.

Many of the approaches used in the Preparation phase to identify the strategies that students already use prior to learning strategies instruction can also be used to help students evaluate their use of the new strategies they've learned. For example, brainstorming discussions about strategies, group work and interviews, checklists, questionnaires, and diaries or dialogue journals can be used in both the Preparation and the Evaluation phases.

The concept of evaluating one's own approach to learning may be quite new to some students. For example, students who are accustomed to teacher-directed classes may expect the teacher to conduct all types of evaluation. Because they believe that evaluation is exclusively the teacher's role, they may react negatively to the idea of evaluating themselves in any way. Cultural factors may also inhibit some students from self-evaluation. For students whose cultures discourage what could be perceived as boasting, it can be difficult to claim that they have been successful in a task, even if that success can be attributed to the learning

How do you currently evaluate your own teaching? Do you concentrate on specific aspects of your teaching? Why or why not?

Tip ....

Student self-reports on their strategies use will be more reliable if you use more than one way to collect information (for example, combine questionnaires with interviews) and collect this information on an ongoing basis. The strategies that students report consistently are more likely to be accurate reflections of actual mental processes than those reported for only one type of measure or on only one occasion.

To what extent can—or should—the learning strategies teacher try to either circumvent or ignore cultural values related to self-evaluation?

strategies employed. Conversely, students whose cultures encourage individuals to promote themselves as a means of asserting their own value may experience great reluctance to admit to less than total success on a learning task.

Tip ....

Students need to be reminded not to label particular strategies as "good" or "bad," but rather as more effective or less effective for a specific task.

We believe that teachers need to acknowledge their students' beliefs and values while encouraging them to reflect deeply on their own learning. Self-evaluation does not necessarily have to be made public (although in many classes, free discussion of successful and unsuccessful strategies can become a springboard for both conversations in the target language and reflection on similarities and differences between class members). This chapter provides a number of options for students to evaluate their own use of learning strategies so that teachers can select self-evaluation activities that are appropriate for their students.

Whether self-evaluation activities are conducted as a group or individually, teachers need to make sure that students understand the purpose of self-evaluation. By making students aware of their responsibility for selecting appropriate strategies for future tasks, teachers provide students with an important tool for autonomous learning.

Tip ....

Add questions about learning strategies use to work samples that are to be included in student portfolios. For example, if students write a book report or complete a quiz, have them identify and evaluate the learning strategies used for this task at the end of the report or quiz.

Teachers should not only plan self-evaluation activities, but also be constantly on the lookout for students' spontaneous use of strategies. They also should ask students to comment on the level of success of a strategy used independently. Thus, when a student responds correctly, the teacher might ask, "How did you figure that out? How did you do that?" When the student explains, the teacher can follow up by identifying the learning strategy the student used and then asking, "Do you think that's a good strategy for this type of task? Why or why not?" In this way, self-evaluation of learning strategies can become an ongoing part of classroom activities.

In classrooms in which teachers maintain portfolios of students' work, examples of learning strategies evaluations should be included in the students' portfolios. This provides documentation of students' growth in understanding why and when to use learning strategies and in choosing and adapting the strategies that work best for them.

Suggested Activities for Evaluating Learning Strategies

In this section of the Evaluation phase chapter, we describe a number of self-evaluation activities that teachers can use to promote their students' independent use of learning strategies. Suggestions for explaining the purpose of self-evaluation are included with each self-evaluation activity.

In your own educational experiences, did a teacher ever ask you to evaluate your work? If so, what was your reaction? If not, why do you suppose your teachers did not include self-evaluation in their classes?

Class Discussions

A simple way for students to evaluate the success of their learning strategies use is for the teacher to lead a class discussion immediately after students have practiced one or more learning strategies with a language task. For example, after a cooperative group activity in which students prepared and practiced a role play, the teacher might follow up with a general self-evaluation discussion in which students are invited to comment on how they used the assigned strategies, whether they used additional strategies, and which strategy or strategy combinations worked best for them. One way to conclude such a discussion is to ask students to reflect on why the teacher asked them to evaluate their own use of strategies. This type of reflection will help them understand the purpose of the Evaluation phase of learning strategies instruction.

In classes in which students' limited target language proficiency or unwillingness to speak out hinders class discussions, a more structured way of eliciting their strategies self-evaluations can be used. Figure 7.1 describes an example of a structured class discussion for the Evaluation phase.

Teachers may wish to provide written directions for students to refer to during the structured class discussion. Written directions can be especially helpful for students who are hesitant about speaking in the target language. Another option to consider is allowing students to initially discuss their use of learning strategies in their native language, prior to reporting on it in the target language. This option may be necessary for beginning-level students. What is most important is that students understand the importance of reflecting on their own use of learning strategies.

Written directions should be very simple so students can understand them. Go over the directions with students before asking them to discuss their evaluations.

Learning Strategy Checklists

Checklists can also be used for students' self-evaluation of their learning strategies applications. Checklists can be completed either as a whole class activity or individually. Individual checklists are particularly useful with students who find it difficult to participate in class discussions, because of either limited target language proficiency, inhibitions about describing their own successes, or failures in using learning strategies. Checklists consist of a series of statements about the use of learning strategies related to recent language tasks students have

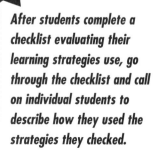

After students complete a checklist evaluating their learning strategies use, go through the checklist and call on individual students to describe how they used the strategies they checked.

FIGURE 7.1

Structured Self-Evaluation Discussion (Following a Role Play)

1 After students have completed their role plays, have them sit in groups different from the role play groups.

2 Explain that they are going to report on the learning strategies they used during the preceding activity. If you asked them to practice specific strategies, remind them of this (for example, two good strategies for preparing and practicing a role play might be *planning* and *substitution*). Indicate that they may have used a variety of other strategies as well.

3 Have students discuss with each other the strategies they used to prepare for a role play. One student should record the answers.

4 Call on each group to share the strategies used in their group, and list those strategies on the board or on an overhead.

5 For each strategy listed, ask for a show of hands from those students who used it and record the number of students reporting that they did. You may want to ask some students to describe how they used a strategy.

6 Remind students that a learning strategy might work well for one person or a particular task, but not work well for a different person or task. This is why it is important for them to personally evaluate the strategies they use. Go through each strategy on the list again, asking students to raise their hands if they think the strategy really helped them with the task. You can record negative answers in a separate column. Your list will now look similar to the following.

STRATEGY	HOW MANY USED IT?	STRATEGY HELPED	DID NOT HELP
Planning	15	13	2
Substitution	12	9	3

7 Follow up with a discussion of why the strategies did or did not help and what other strategies could have been helpful.

8 Conclude by asking students to tell why they think you asked them to evaluate their use of learning strategies. Accept all answers.

completed. Since the language of the checklist must be comprehensible to students, beginning-level language students may need checklists in their native language. Checklists may be used to ask students to indicate either whether they have used a learning strategy for a specific task or which strategies they have used during a particular time period. Figure 7.2 provides examples of both types of checklists.

Charts and Graphic Organizers

Visual representations of information are a useful way for language learners to express higher-level thinking in spite of limited language proficiency. For example, Venn diagrams can be used to compare and contrast information as varied as shades of meaning of a pair of cognates (for example, English *ball* and French *balle*) or similarities and differences between two cultures. Similarly, timelines can be used to display the events in a story as well historical events. The K-W-L chart is a graphic organizer that is especially useful in identifying prior knowledge, setting learning goals, and reflecting on what has been learned (Ogle, 1986). The teacher prepares a large chart with three columns, one marked K (for "What We Know"), the second marked W (for "What We Want to Find Out), and the third marked L (for "What We Learned"). Students brainstorm what they already know about a lesson's topic, identify some of the additional things they would like to learn, and then complete the first two columns of the K-W-L chart. After engaging in learning activities, students reflect on what they have learned and complete the third column. By adding a fourth column to the K-W-L chart, teachers can provide a learning strategies evaluation activity. The fourth column's heading is H, for "How We Learned." Figure 7.3 presents a completed K-W-L-H chart that illustrates an ESL lesson focusing on a science topic.

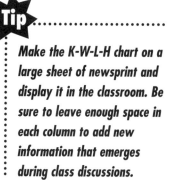

Make the K-W-L-H chart on a large sheet of newsprint and display it in the classroom. Be sure to leave enough space in each column to add new information that emerges during class discussions.

Another way to use graphic organizers during the Evaluation phase of learning strategies instruction is to have students construct flowcharts that describe how they used one or more strategies during an activity or lesson. Teachers can help students evaluate strategies used during the processes of **planning, monitoring, problem-solving,** and **evaluating** a learning experience by showing students how to construct a flowchart that describes their thinking during the process. Teachers can supply cutout shapes to represent different points in the entire process. For example, rectangles could be used to represent different points in the learning task, circles could represent points at which difficulties were encountered, and triangles could represent learning strategies that were used to solve problems.

Plan a flowchart for the activities and learning strategies you used on a recent task. Is your flowchart linear or recursive? What differences might you expect between your flowchart and your students' flowcharts?

FIGURE 7.2

Learning Strategies Checklists

TASK CHECKLIST

Think about our unit on *The First Americans.* What learning strategies did you use? Check the learning strategies you used for each activity. Describe other learning strategies you used.

ACTIVITY	LEARNING STRATEGIES
1 We watched a video about the Inuit (Eskimos).	____ I made predictions before watching the video. ____ I thought about what I already knew about the Inuit. ____ I used the video pictures to understand new words. ____ I used these other strategies: _____ _____
2 We used the library to look up information on our topics about Inuit life.	____ I used selective attention to find information on my topic. ____ I took notes on important information. ____ I made inferences about the meanings of new words. ____ I used these other strategies: _____ _____
3 We presented oral reports on Inuit life.	____ I planned an introduction, a body, and a conclusion. ____ I cooperated with classmates to plan and practice. ____ I asked for feedback to evaluate my oral report. ____ I used these other strategies: _____ _____

FIGURE 7.2 *(Cont.)*

TIME CHECKLIST

Keep a record of your learning strategies for five days. Make a check each time you use one of the learning strategies.

LEARNING STRATEGY	DAY 1	DAY 2	DAY 3	DAY 4	DAY 5
❶ I planned what to do before working.					
❷ I made predictions during reading.					
❸ I used selective attention to focus on important information when listening.					
❹ I took notes during class.					
❺ I related my prior knowledge to new information.					
❻ I used imagery to understand and remember new words and ideas.					
❼ I cooperated with classmates to study and learn.					
❽ I asked questions for clarification.					
❾ I checked my work.					

FIGURE 7.3

K-W-L-H Chart

K	W	L	H
(Students' Prior Knowledge)	(What Students Want to Find Out)	(What Students Learned)	(How Students Learned)
Plants grow in soil.	Do plants need light?	Plants need light.	We put one plant in sunlight and the other plant in a dark closet. We watered both plants. The plant in the closet died.
Plants need water.	How do plants get food and water?	Plants get water through their roots. The water goes up the stems to the leaves.	We put a white carnation in water with red food coloring. The red went up the stem and the carnation became pink.
Plants have roots and leaves.	What do roots and leaves do?	Plant leaves make food, and the stems take food to the roots.	
Most plant leaves are green.	Why are plants green?	Plants make their own food by photosynthesis. This is an interaction of the green color in leaves (chlorophyll), water, carbon dioxide in the air, and sunshine.	We watched a video that showed how photosynthesis works. We used these strategies: • *Selective attention* as we observed the plants, carnation, and video • *Prior knowledge* as we compared new information with what we already knew • *Imagery* as we tried to imagine photosynthesis happening in our plant • *Note-taking* during the video and observations • *Cooperation* as we worked with classmates and talked about plants

Adapted from Ogle, D. (1986). "The K-W-L: A Teaching Model That Develops Active Reading of Expository Text." *The Reading Teacher, 39*, 564–70.

Learning Logs

A learning log is an individual student's summary of what has been learned over a given period of time. Keeping a learning log can serve as an ongoing reminder to students to use strategies, especially when the learning log is included in the student's assessment portfolio. Learning logs can take many forms, ranging from carefully controlled to completely unstructured. In beginning-level language classes, for example, teachers can dictate or write on the board for students to copy in their journals brief summaries of what has been accomplished in class. For example, "Today we learned how to talk about our favorite foods. We learned how to say which foods we like and which foods we do not like." At the other extreme is a completely open-ended learning log in which the teacher merely directs students to write in their notebooks what they learned that day.

Young students and beginning learners can indicate their evaluation of a strategy by circling appropriate drawings or adjectives in their learning logs. Figure 7.4 shows a sample learning log for young children just learning to read. Under "Lesson", students can be asked to draw or copy a simple picture that represents the lesson, story title, or content area. Students can then put a check mark next to the strategies they used, draw a picture in the next column to show how they used it, and circle the happy or sad face to show whether the strategy worked well for them. Students can later be asked to explain their logs during a sharing time.

A semistructured learning log format can also be used for students to evaluate their use of learning strategies. Figure 7.5 shows a learning log for a unit based on CALLA. This approach asks students to evaluate their learning of vocabulary, content, language, and learning strategies, as well as their attitudes towards the information presented in the unit.

Students first complete this type of learning log individually. Then the teacher can lead a class discussion in which students are called on to describe how they each used the learning strategies they did. For example, if a student has checked "Read and listen selectively for new information," the teacher can then ask, "When did you use the strategy of *selective attention*? What was the task you used it with? What did you do? Did *selective attention* help you do the task? Why or why not?" The main purpose of these questions is to encourage reflection on the part of the student about his or her application of strategies to language learning.

Tip

If you already use learning logs with your students, you can expand them to include students' comments about the learning strategies they are practicing.

FIGURE 7.4

Learning Log for Children

NAME			DATE
LESSON			

STRATEGY	✓	HOW	HELP?
VISUALIZE			☺ ☹
PREDICT			☺ ☹
USE WHAT I KNOW ME			☺ ☹
SKIP ✖			☺ ☹
LOOK BACK			☺ ☹
GUESS ?			☺ ☹

FIGURE 7.5

Learning Log for Science

NAME _____ DATE _____

Complete the Learning Log for the unit LIFE ON EARTH: STRUCTURES AND FUNCTIONS. Check the items that you know or can do, then answer the questions.

LEARNING LOG

VOCABULARY

I can explain the meanings or draw pictures of these words:

❑ structure	❑ cell	❑ kingdom
❑ function	❑ reproduce	❑ plants
❑ organism	❑ simple organism	❑ animals

SCIENCE KNOWLEDGE AND SKILLS

I can:

❑ Identify the characteristics of living things.
❑ Describe the differences between plants and animals.
❑ Describe the characteristics of simple organisms.
❑ Name and describe the five kingdoms of living things.

LANGUAGE

I can:

❑ Discuss what I know about plants, animals, and other living things.
❑ Read and understand science information about life on earth.
❑ Listen to and understand science information about life on earth.
❑ Write a lab report of an experiment with living things that grow in soil.

LEARNING STRATEGIES

I can:

❑ Use my prior knowledge about living things.
❑ Read and listen selectively for new information.
❑ Observe carefully and take notes on my observations.
❑ Cooperate with classmates to conduct a science experiment.

(continued on next page)

FIGURE 7.5 *(Cont.)*

THINKING ABOUT YOUR LEARNING

A. How successful do you feel about learning the different parts of this unit?

1 Vocabulary

❑ Not very   ❑ Somewhat   ❑ Very

2 Science knowledge and skills

❑ Not very   ❑ Somewhat   ❑ Very

3 Language

❑ Not very   ❑ Somewhat   ❑ Very

4 Learning Strategies

❑ Not very   ❑ Somewhat   ❑ Very

B. Think about your learning and complete the following sentences on a blank sheet of paper.

1 This is what I learned in this unit:

2 This is what was difficult or confusing:

3 This is how I am going to learn what was difficult:

4 The most interesting thing in this unit was:

Adapted from Chamot, A. U. and O'Malley, J. M. (1994). *The CALLA Handbook: Implementing the Cognitive Academic Language Learning Approach.* White Plains, NY: Addison Wesley Longman, Inc.

Journals and Diaries

Another form of student reflection is the journal or diary. These are more open-ended than learning logs, as students are asked to write about their experiences in using learning strategies with minimal direction from the teacher. Students often keep a special notebook exclusively for the purpose of their journal or diary. In it they jot down their own accounts of how they have used the learning strategies taught in class, their evaluations of how well the strategies worked, and any other comments they wish to make. Students' journals or diary notebooks can be completely private, or they can be used as dialogue journals with the teacher or with another student. In a dialogue journal, the student writes his or her personal comments, and the teacher, or another student, responds in writing in a similar personal vein. That is, the teacher comments on the ideas expressed by the student with a personal comment but refrains from any corrections of what the student has written. The teacher, or other student, might also include with the comment a question designed to elicit further reflection on the student's use of learning strategies. Figure 7.6 shows several students' dialogue journal entries and their teachers' responses.

Tip

It is just as important for students to record strategies that do not work as those that do. Be sure to have them describe the exact context in which a strategy was successful or unsuccessful.

Diaries are similar to journals but may focus more on how a student uses learning strategies over a particular time period. That is, instead of writing only about how one has used the strategies taught in the language class, students can use a diary as an opportunity to write about many different kinds of applications of learning strategies in their daily lives.

Keeping a diary about their use of learning strategies over a period of time can help students understand which strategies have general applications and which might be domain-specific. For example, a foreign language student may discover that the learning strategy *inferencing* works as well for reading Molière in French as for reading Shakespeare in English, but this strategy may not be appropriate when trying to understand new scientific terminology in a biology textbook.

Students should write daily in their learning strategies diaries, recording all learning tasks and their procedures for completing the tasks. For familiar and easy tasks, a student might indicate that no special learning strategies were needed, while when the student faces a challenging task a number of strategies might be described. The value of the learning strategies diary is in the personal reflections elicited and in the students' increasing metacognitive understanding of their own thinking processes. After students have kept their learning strategies diaries over a period of time, teachers can ask them to read through their diary entries and

FIGURE 7.6

Learner Diaries

SCHOOL-YEAR LEARNER DIARIES

In one class, the teacher asked students to write on this topic: "A problem I had with learning and how I solved it." Here are some of the answers given.

❶ Michiko: I have many problems about English. One of them is I can't communicate my thoughts in English. It is difficult for me. I want to speak English frequently, [sic: fluently] but I can't do. When I speak English, I feel fear. I want to improve my ability, but it is difficult. Next, I can't write a English sentence without a dictionary. It is very important for me. Someday I want to be a frequent speaker of English.

Teacher's response: Try writing a journal in English every day. Don't worry about grammar. It's only for you to read.

❷ Student: When I was a little child, I wondered why people could sing English songs without watching the words of the song. It was because they love Beatles or other singers and they listened songs again and again. Not only listening but also translating into Japanese. If I understand, I would image that song and made a video clip in my head. It was not painful work for me. I believe we must study English with enjoyment. I wish I'll be able to understand English songs without translation someday.

Teacher's response: I'm sure you will be able to understand them someday! Your idea is cool! By the way, making a video clip in your head is called *visualizing*. It helps you remember a lot better, doesn't it?

SUMMER LEARNER DIARIES

Many of the students from this particular class tried some of the things that were suggested in the break between the first and second semesters: keeping a journal, speaking English with classmates on the telephone, listening intensively to tapes or movies, and so on. Their learner diaries after the summer vacation reported on their activities:

❸ Mayuko: In this summer, I didn't go abroad. I want to speak English well. But there is no opportunity to speak out. I thought how could I speak out English. When I thought about it, my friend who is senior student came and asked me to practice together. We spoke English all the time, when we were together. When we were in video shop, we spoke English. 'Look! This is the movie, which our friend said the best.' 'Yes, yes.' She can speak English so fluently that I can study English from her. I can train my speaking out skill throughout summer vacation.

Teacher's response: Wonderful! You're taking advantage of any chance you get to speak English. You're a good "environmental engineer" (a term used in the class's supplementary reading materials; *Language Hungry*, by Tim Murphey).

identify the strategies that were most successful for completing learning tasks. A class discussion in which students share their experiences with learning strategies applications can provide an understanding of individual differences in the use of strategies. It also can promote the sharing of information about how to use learning strategies for particular tasks.

Students should be encouraged to write their journals and diaries in the target language because of the language practice involved. However, teachers should also accept entries in students' native languages, especially for beginning-level students. The goal is for students to reflect on their own learning strategies, and it can be difficult for them to write these reflections in another language. In general, students will incorporate more and more of the target language in their journal and diary entries as they become more proficient in the language.

Try keeping your own learning strategies diary for a week or more, preferably in your second language. Were any aspects difficult to complete? Why?

Learning Strategy Experiments

A learning strategy experiment provides an opportunity for students to compare the results of a learning task that was completed without learning strategies to the results of one completed with learning strategies. For example, the teacher might first ask students to listen to a weather forecast in the target language and answer questions about the information presented. Then, the teacher could ask students to *use prior knowledge* to identify the parts of a weather forecast (today's, tomorrow's, and the next few days' expected local and national or international weather) and *selective attention* to identify key words for items such as city, high temperature, low temperature, and the expectation of sunny, rainy, or stormy weather. Students can then recall and jot down all of the words they already know in the target language about weather forecasting (*use prior knowledge*) as well as key words to listen for (*selective attention*). Next, students listen to another weather forecast using the learning strategies and answer similar comprehension questions. The teacher follows up with a discussion or written evaluation comparing students' performance when they used the learning strategies with their performance without strategies.

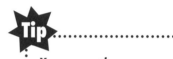

You can use the same approach for reading comprehension activities.

Have students work in pairs or small groups to compare their "before" and "after" comprehension worksheets.

Collaborative Activity

Another type of learning strategies experiment was observed in a third-year high school Spanish class. The teacher had been teaching a number of learning strategies since the beginning of the school year and in the spring decided to conduct a mini-experiment with her students. First, she described the Spanish task, which was to read a short story in cooperative learning groups and demonstrate comprehension by retelling the story in Spanish. She would call on one member from each of the six cooperative learning groups to retell the story and would grade the group according to that member's performance (this was to encourage cooperation as group members read and discussed the story). She then asked two of the groups to step out of the classroom for a few minutes, as she needed to have a "private talk" with the rest of the students. This "private talk" consisted of reminding the remaining students (these formed the "strategies groups") of two of the learning strategies they had been practicing in class with similar reading tasks: *selective attention* (*atención selectiva*) and *imagery* (*visualización*). She asked two of the strategies groups to use the first strategy as they read and provided them with a poster board and felt-tip markers to record the major words and ideas in the story. She also provided the other two strategies groups with poster board and felt-tip markers and asked them to draw pictures of the main events in the story on their poster boards. Next, the teacher asked the students waiting outside (the "nonstrategies" groups) to return to the classroom. She then proceeded to hand out the story and explain the task, without mentioning strategies.

Each group of students read the short story with the goal of comprehending it and being able to retell it as completely as possible. The nonstrategies groups went about the task in a very different way from the strategies groups. They quickly identified the most proficient Spanish speaker in the group and asked him or her to translate the story into English. The strategies groups, on the other hand, concentrated on applying their assigned learning strategies (either *atención selectiva* or *visualización*), leaving little time for translation.

When all students had completed the reading task, the teacher asked students from the nonstrategies groups to summarize the story in Spanish. The students' summaries consisted of a few general statements about some of the characters and one or two events from the story. The students were unable to identify the main ideas in the story or even to state its theme. In contrast, the strategies groups were able to retell the story in some detail, as they could rely on their poster boards on which they had either written the main ideas in the story (*atención selectiva*) or had illustrated the main events of the story (*visualización*). At one point, a student from the nonstrategies group exclaimed angrily, "It's not fair! Why didn't you let us use the strategies?" The teacher smiled and reminded him that his group could have used the learning strategies if they had wished—after all, the class had been practicing these learning strategies for the last six months! She then led a class discussion to evaluate the usefulness of the two learning strategies employed by the strategies groups. By using the mini-experiment approach to the Evaluation phase of learning strategies instruction, the teacher was able to have students experience successful uses of language learning strategies.

Tip

This type of mini-experiment is most successful when students are experienced in cooperative learning structures.

What kind of a mini-experiment would work best with your students—one in which the whole class is involved in comparing the results of using or not using learning strategies or one in which you divide the class into "strategies" and "nonstrategies" groups?

Questionnaires

Teachers can ask students to complete questionnaires to evaluate learning strategies used for a task. While the format of the questionnaire can be similar to the one used in the Preparation phase to identify strategies that students are already using, the questions should refer to a specific task that has just been completed. Figure 7.7 shows a self-evaluation questionnaire developed for an ESL language arts activity.

The open-ended questions at the end of the self-evaluation questionnaire provide students with an opportunity to reflect not only on what they have learned, but also on the strategies they used for learning purposes.

Even beginning-level language students can complete self-evaluation questionnaires in the target language if the questionnaire is short and the teacher explains each item. However, some teachers may prefer to develop questionnaires in the students' native languages in order to encourage students to engage in deeper reflection. In this case, the teacher may wish to assign the self-evaluation questionnaire as homework. After completing the questionnaire in the native language, students can be asked to follow up with a discussion of their questionnaires in the target language.

Tip

Be sure the questionnaire describes real tasks that students do in your classroom. You may also wish to include some items that reflect nonstrategic behaviors, such as abandoning the task. This helps guard against any tendency of students to give high ratings indiscriminately for every item!

When you complete a questionnaire, do you always give accurate answers? Why or why not?

Interviews

Interviews to evaluate learning strategies applications can be conducted by the teacher or by students, either individually or in small groups. As in the Preparation phase, both retrospective interviews and think-aloud sessions are useful approaches to identifying students' learning strategies. However, the purpose of such interviews in the Evaluation phase is for students and teachers to find out which of the instructed learning strategies were used for a recently completed task (*retrospective interview*) or are being used during an ongoing task (*think-aloud interview*).

A structured interview format is recommended when students are interviewing each other or when teachers are interviewing small groups of students. Asking the same questions of all participants in the interviews makes it possible to compare the results more easily. Structured interviews conducted in the Evaluation phase can be constructed in a similar way to the ones in the Preparation phase, but the questions should refer to a specific activity that students have recently completed. Figure 7.8 shows an adaptation of the group interview guide used in the Preparation phase (Figure 4.7, page 67) for

FIGURE 7.7

Learning Strategies Questionnaire

(The teacher may read the questionnaire to students and explain items as necessary. Part A should be completed immediately after reading the folktale. Part B should be completed after students have written their own folktales.)

Name _____ Date _____

READING STRATEGIES

Part A We have just read an African folktale about *Anansi the Spider*. Think about how you read the folktale. Answer the questions about the strategies you used. And remember — there are no right or wrong answers!

1 Before starting to read, I thought about what I already know about stories like *Anansi*.
No, I didn't do this.   I did this a little.   I did this a lot!

2 I looked at the title and illustrations and predicted what the story might be about.
No, I didn't do this.   I did this a little.   I did this a lot!

3 As I was reading, I pronounced each word in my head.
No, I didn't do this.   I did this a little.   I did this a lot!

4 I used the context (other parts of the story) to make a good guess about the meaning of new words. (Skip this question if there were no new words.)
No, I didn't do this.   I did this a little.   I did this a lot!

5 As I was reading, I tried to focus on what the characters did and said.
No, I didn't do this.   I did this a little.   I did this a lot!

6 I made predictions about how Anansi would solve the problem.
No, I didn't do this.   I did this a little.   I did this a lot!

7 When there were new words in the story, I asked a friend or the teacher what they meant. (Skip this question if there were no new words.)
No, I didn't do this.   I did this a little.   I did this a lot!

8 After reading the story, I thought about the most important points.
No, I didn't do this.   I did this a little.   I did this a lot!

9 What other strategies did you use while you were reading the folktale about *Anansi the Spider*?

FIGURE 7.7 (*Cont.*)

WRITING STRATEGIES

Part B After reading the story about *Anansi the Spider*, we wrote our own folktales. Think about how you wrote your folktale. Answer the questions about the strategies you used. And don't forget — there are no right or wrong answers!

10 Before starting to write I brainstormed ideas for my folktale.
No, I didn't do this.   *I did this a little.*   *I did this a lot!*

11 I planned my story by thinking about (or making notes about) the characters, plot, and where the story would happen.
No, I didn't do this.   *I did this a little.*   *I did this a lot!*

12 I didn't need to brainstorm or plan before writing; I just started writing.
No, I didn't do this.   *I did this a little.*   *I did this a lot!*

13 While I was writing, I thought about the people who would read my story.
No, I didn't do this.   *I did this a little.*   *I did this a lot!*

14 While I was writing, I tried to remember what I already know about the parts of a story.
No, I didn't do this.   *I did this a little.*   *I did this a lot!*

15 When I couldn't think of a word I wanted, I looked in the dictionary.
No, I didn't do this.   *I did this a little.*   *I did this a lot!*

16 When I couldn't remember a word I wanted, I just used a different word.
No, I didn't do this.   *I did this a little.*   *I did this a lot!*

17 When I finished my first draft, I asked a classmate to read it and make suggestions.
No, I didn't do this.   *I did this a little.*   *I did this a lot!*

18 I revised my story to make it better.
No, I didn't do this.   *I did this a little.*   *I did this a lot!*

19 I made the changes needed for my final draft.
No, I didn't do this.   *I did this a little.*   *I did this a lot!*

20 What other strategies did you use to write your own folktale?

Adapted from Chamot, A. U. and O'Malley, J. M. (1994). *The CALLA Handbook: Implementing the Cognitive Academic Language Learning Approach*. White Plains, NY: Addison Wesley Longman, Inc.

FIGURE 7.8

Group Interview Guide to Evaluate Learning Strategies

(The following activities are examples. Teachers should adapt them to reflect actual activities in their own classrooms.)

Directions Have students sit in small groups. One student in each group will be the interviewer and will ask questions for each activity. Another will be the recorder and will write down the answers to the questions. A tape recorder can be used as a backup for recording the interviews.

ACTIVITY 1: VOCABULARY

We have just finished a unit on food and nutrition. You have learned many new vocabulary words, such as health words, the names of foods, and the food groups.

What learning strategies did you use to:
• Learn the meanings of new words?
• Learn how to spell the new words?
• Learn how to pronounce the new words?
• Remember the new words?

Which learning strategies helped you? Which learning strategies were not helpful? Why?

ACTIVITY 2: READING COMPREHENSION

Today we read a story about Anansi the Spider. Then we answered questions about the story, and we had to retell the story in our own words.

What learning strategies did you use:
• Before you started to read?
• While you were reading?
• When you had a problem? (new words, new grammar, words in unfamiliar order, and so on)
• After you finished reading?
• To answer the questions?
• To retell the story?

Which learning strategies helped you? Which learning strategies were not helpful? Why?

Adapted from Sarah Barnhardt, 1996. National Capital Language Resource Center, Georgetown University/George Washington University/Center for Applied Linguistics, 2600 Virginia Ave., Suite 105, Washington, DC 20037.

purposes of self-evaluation. Note that each example refers to specific activities just completed in the class.

In a *think-aloud* interview during the Evaluation phase, students are asked to describe their thoughts as they work on a task or on part of a task. The same Learning Strategies Think-Aloud Record used in the Preparation phase (see Figure 4.8, page 69) can be used for students to record their use of learning strategies in real-time. The only difference now is that students have had instruction and practice in using some specific learning strategies. By thinking aloud, students will find out whether they are applying the instructed strategies. Follow-up class discussions can identify which instructed strategies were used by students, whether the students found them effective, which strategies were not used, and why one or more students chose not to use them.

Is it easy for you to think aloud? For example, do you talk to yourself silently as you plan a lesson or go over a list of things to do? The next time you are working on a task that is somewhat challenging, try turning on a tape recorder and thinking aloud!

Stimulated Recall

Teachers can use stimulated recall to help students remember what strategies they were actually using during a learning activity. In this technique, students are videotaped as they work on an individual task or cooperative learning activity. During the Evaluation phase, the teacher plays back the videotape, pausing the tape from time to time and asking students if they can remember what they were thinking at that particular moment captured on the tape. This technique has been effective in helping students recall their thinking processes, strategies, and affective responses during a conversational interchange (Robbins, 1996).

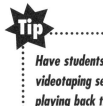

Have students take charge of videotaping sessions and playing back the videotape. You can also have students try to guess what other students were thinking as they watch the videotape.

Portfolio Assessment

When learning strategies instruction is integrated into a class, students' progress in using learning strategies needs to be assessed, just as their progress in developing proficiency in the target language is assessed. Portfolio assessment is gaining increasing acceptance as an alternative to traditional tests. A portfolio consists of samples of a student's work collected on a regular basis throughout the school year. Since the work samples are collected over a period of time, they demonstrate the progress the student is making in reaching the instructional goals of the class. Artifacts that can be included in an assessment portfolio in a content-based language class include the following:

- Teacher observation notes
- Records of books or stories read
- Science experiment notes
- Tests and quizzes
- Maps and timelines
- Math problem solving
- Printouts from computer-assisted exercises
- Copies of e-mail correspondence with key pals

- Writing samples
- Book reports
- Graphic organizers
- Art projects
- Social studies projects
- Video and audio tapes of oral language production and role plays

Tip

Plan which self-evaluation activities will be included in student portfolios as you prepare unit plans. This will help you avoid the problem of including all self-evaluation activities. Portfolios should represent typical examples of the individual student's work, rather than a file of all of his or her work!

The selection of artifacts to include in a portfolio is often made jointly by the teacher and the student.

Students' self-evaluations of their use of learning strategies are important additions to their individual assessment portfolios. Interviews, discussion notes, questionnaires, tape recordings of think-alouds, checklists, journal and diary entries, learning logs, and other self-evaluation activities can be included in students' portfolios.

Teacher Self-Evaluations

Tip

A reflective journal does not have to be lengthy. It is more important for it to be ongoing. Many teachers find that a good time to make their journal entries is on Friday afternoons immediately after the last class. A short paragraph—even two or three sentences—reflecting on that week's learning strategies instruction is all that is needed. Over time, this record will provide valuable personal insights into the progress of learning strategies instruction in your classroom.

Although the major purpose of the Evaluation phase is for students to develop their ability to evaluate their own use of learning strategies, teachers should also be continually evaluating the impact of learning strategies instruction on their students, their lesson planning, their use of materials, their teaching techniques, and their use of assessments. One way to carry out this process of reflection is by keeping a journal to record observations, insights, concerns, and decisions. A reflective journal can become a valuable tool as the teacher implements learning strategies instruction in the language classroom.

A more structured approach is to complete a self-evaluation checklist of learning strategies instruction on a regular basis. Figure 7.9 provides such a checklist for teachers. This checklist is organized according to the Instructional Framework presented in Chapter 3, thereby making it possible for teachers to evaluate their learning strategies instruction for each of the five phases: Preparation, Presentation, Practice, Evaluation, and Expansion.

FIGURE 7.9

Teacher's Checklist for Learning Strategies Instruction

	Often	Sometimes	Rarely
PREPARATION			
1 I ask students to describe the strategies they already use.	❏	❏	❏
2 I include activities such as think-alouds and discussions to help students become aware of their strategies.	❏	❏	❏
PRESENTATION			
3 I select strategies to teach that are appropriate for the task.	❏	❏	❏
4 I give the strategy a name and explain it.	❏	❏	❏
5 I tell students why and when to use the strategy.	❏	❏	❏
6 I model how to use the strategy with the same kind of task.	❏	❏	❏
PRACTICE			
7 I choose challenging tasks for students.	❏	❏	❏
8 I provide activities for students to practice the strategies.	❏	❏	❏
9 I remind students to use the strategy or strategies I've taught.	❏	❏	❏
10 I encourage students' thought processes by asking them how they figured something out.	❏	❏	❏
11 I point out any strategies I see students using.	❏	❏	❏
12 I praise good thinking more than right answers.	❏	❏	❏
EVALUATION			
13 I encourage students to evaluate their own use of strategies.	❏	❏	❏
14 I discuss with students which strategies they find most useful for the tasks they have just completed.	❏	❏	❏
15 I encourage students to choose the strategies they prefer.	❏	❏	❏
16 I promote student autonomy by fading cues to use strategies.	❏	❏	❏
17 I evaluate how I teach strategies and revise as necessary.	❏	❏	❏
EXPANSION			
18 I suggest to students how they can use the strategies in other subjects and in daily life.	❏	❏	❏

Adapted from Sarah Barnhardt, 1996. National Capital Language Resource Center, Georgetown University/George Washington University/Center for Applied Linguistics, 2600 Virginia Ave., Suite 105, Washington, DC 20037.

Conclusion

To what degree do you engage in self-evaluation in your daily life and in your professional life? How can you help your students to become self-reflective learners?

This chapter presented a variety of techniques that teachers can use during the Evaluation phase of learning strategies instruction. The focus of this phase is on student self-evaluation, which is essential for students to develop an understanding of their own learning processes. Students need to find out what learning strategies work best for them for specific tasks, why they work, what strategies are not effective, and when and why they are not effective. Through self-evaluation, students are able to develop and tailor their own individual repertoire of learning strategies. When students understand how they learn and which strategies are most useful to them individually, they are better equipped to regulate their own learning and to develop increased independence as language learners.

Teachers are also learners, and their reflections on their approach to teaching language learning strategies can provide an impetus to further development not only as a teacher, but also as a lifelong learner.

Chapter

PHASE 5: EXPANSION

A critical component of effective learning strategies use is the ability to transfer the application of a strategy from a familiar context to an unfamiliar context. This phase of learning strategies use is called Expansion. While it is relatively easy for students to practice and evaluate a strategy when instructed by the teacher to do so, real ownership comes from knowing how to choose an appropriate strategy when faced with a new task. Matching a familiar strategy to a new task completes the cycle of strategies instruction, as students must rely on their own background knowledge of both the strategy and the task. However, since few students complete this step on their own, most need guidance from the teacher. Expanding the use of the strategy to new contexts completes the instructional model. The Expansion phase should be included with instruction of all learning strategies.

Instructional Objectives

This chapter will help you to:

- Show students how to transfer learning strategies to new tasks.

- Provide explicit suggestions for applying learning strategies to different content subjects and to learning outside of school.

- Help students identify additional contexts in which a learning strategy can be useful or not useful.

- Show students how to keep learning logs or diaries that describe their new applications of learning strategies.

- Help students expand their use of learning strategies by teaching others how to use strategies.

PHASE 5: Expansion   **139**

General Guidelines for Expanding the Use of Learning Strategies

Can you remember an occasion when you discovered that you could transfer a learning strategy to a new task? What caused this insight?

Students may be able to evaluate the usefulness of a strategy for a particular task such as *inferencing* for reading but still not automatically transfer this strategy to another type of task, such as listening, even though *inferencing* works as well for listening as for reading. Language teachers should not be surprised that learning strategies are difficult to transfer because early research on learning strategies in first language contexts reported complete failure in strategies transfer (Gagné, Yekovich, & Yekovich, 1993). However, in studies in which students had to consciously evaluate a strategy's effectiveness, the strategy was successfully transferred to new tasks (see, for example, Palincsar & Brown, 1984; Ghatala, Levin, Pressley, & Lodico, 1985). Students' metacognitive awareness of the learning strategies they know and of when and how to use them is essential for the strategies transfer.

In addition to this metacognitive awareness of learning strategies, students also need an understanding of the requirements of the new task and its similarities, as well as differences, to the task with which they are currently using the strategy. Task knowledge together with strategy knowledge are key to the successful transfer of learning strategies.

Given the difficulty of transferring learning strategies, teachers need to explain to students why the transfer of strategies to new tasks is important and how a strategy can be used in a new context. Teachers can promote transfer by following the basic guidelines and suggested activities presented in this chapter. In this way, students learn that strategies can transfer to other language tasks, to other academic tasks, and to real-life situations.

As with all learning strategies instruction, teaching students to expand their use of learning strategies needs to be scaffolded. At first, the teacher gives strong support by explicitly asking students to transfer the strategy to a new task such as another class or homework assignment. Students then are asked to report back on the effectiveness of the strategy transfer. This encourages reflection and the development of automaticity of strategy transfer. Once students are comfortable with applying strategies to new contexts when instructed to do so, they can begin to identify the new contexts themselves. The final step is for students to choose an appropriate strategy for any given task. At this point, students can still be encouraged to reflect on and describe their choice of learning strategies. This will increase their metacognitive awareness of their own learning and thinking processes.

Tip

During the Planning stage, before students begin working on a new task, ask them to identify similarities and differences between the new task and previous tasks.

Tip

Have students construct a classroom chart that shows a grid with the types of language activities they practice and the learning strategies that are introduced (see Figure 8.1). Have them check off the learning strategies that can be used for a variety of language learning tasks as they begin to expand their use of learning strategies.

FIGURE 8.1

Learning Strategies for a Variety of Tasks

	READING A STORY	LISTENING TO DIRECTIONS	WRITING A REPORT	TALKING ABOUT HOBBIES
Attend selectively	✓	✓	✓	
Activate background knowledge	✓	✓	✓	✓
Make inferences	✓	✓		
Cooperate	✓	✓	✓	✓
Predict	✓	✓		✓
Visualize	✓	✓	✓	✓

Suggested Activities for Expanding the Application of Learning Strategies

The Expansion phase does not necessarily require extra teacher preparation or instructional time. Rather, expansion should be integrated into regular class activities. The types of expansion activities chosen will reflect the emphasis of the instructional curriculum of a given classroom. Variations are limited only by the imaginations of teachers and students.

Expanding through Discussions

Including the Expansion phase in learning strategies instruction can be as simple as combining discussions with the Evaluation phase. After students evaluate the effectiveness of the strategy for a specific learning task, the teacher can ask them in what other situations they think they would find the strategy useful. Students can brainstorm a list of additional language learning activities that have occurred recently in the language classroom. They then can discuss and decide how the learning strategy might be used in the new context. By discussing why and when the strategy might be useful, students reinforce their explicit knowledge of the strategy as introduced by the teacher in the Presentation phase. Students can also think about whether they have already used the strategy before without realizing that the technique was a strategy and had a name. In this way, students have an opportunity to demonstrate that they are "experts" on a particular strategy by sharing their experiences.

The Expansion phase often flows without interruption from the Evaluation phase, so there is often no apparent break between the two phases. Expansion activities are also frequently assigned as homework.

Have students keep personal records of their own "expert" strategies. They can refer to these records in future strategies discussions to see what new uses they have found for each strategy.

The teacher should mention times when the learning strategy may not have worked well and have students suggest possible reasons why. Students could even brainstorm new contexts in which they think the strategy would not transfer well, again giving their rationale. Understanding the limits of transfer is an important part of appropriate strategies use. As students reflect on why a strategy may not always be helpful, they are reinforcing the importance of choosing strategies appropriately. The use of *inferencing* is an example of how the context of a task affects the usefulness of a learning strategy. When reading a literature text, the reader may find that *inferencing* is extremely helpful when guessing at the meanings of unfamiliar words and in reading between the lines for ideas that are implied but not directly stated. However, when reading expository text, the reader may find that a new technical term needs to be understood precisely, and the context may provide only the most general of clues. Figures 8.2A and 8.2B describe cooperative group activities in which students can record their ideas on when to use a learning strategy on a different task—and when not to. The first activity (interviewing people in the community) is designed for advanced students, and the second activity (acting out a story) is for intermediate-level students.

If students have difficulty coming up with additional contexts for a particular learning strategy, the teacher can provide examples. However, ultimately the students need to be able to decide on other applications for the strategy in order for transfer to become automatic. It may be useful to talk directly about the process of transfer, including the challenge of recognizing times that students could benefit from applying a strategy they already know. Raising students' awareness of transfer can help them be on the lookout for transfer opportunities.

Expanding to Other Language Activities

Following discussions, students can be instructed to use a particular strategy in another language context. For example, if students *predicted* before reading a story, then ask them to *predict* before watching a movie. If students practiced using *substitution* when writing a letter, then ask them to *substitute* when engaging in a conversation. Expanding strategy use occurs in the classroom and at home with different types of tasks. Teachers can assign the use of a strategy with a new task for homework. The next day, students report on how they used the strategy and whether it worked. Figure 8.3 is a worksheet that students can use to describe how the strategy worked with a new task.

FIGURE 8.2A

Cooperative Group Activity (Advanced Students)

INTERVIEWING PEOPLE IN THE COMMUNITY

Directions Divide students into groups and have them interview community members about a topic, such as an aspect of local history, a current issue in the community, or the environment. Each group first chooses strategies from a chart of the Metacognitive Model of Stategic Learning. Then group members comment on how they used the strategies, as illustrated below.

STRATEGIES WE CHOSE TO USE	WHEN AND HOW WE USED THE STRATEGIES
Planning Strategies	
✓ Think of what I know about the subject	Before we planned our questions, we thought of what we knew.
__ Predict what people will say	We didn't use predicting because we didn't know enough to predict.
✓ Set a goal	We want to interview four people by next week.
Monitoring Strategies	
✓ Using what I know	We need to use what we know in order to understand the answers people give us.
✓ Cooperation	We have to cooperate to make sure our group is successful.
__ Self-talk	We didn't visualize or self-talk for this project.
__ Visualizing	
✓ Self-questioning (Am I understanding? Am I being understood?)	When we are talking to people, we need to see if they are understanding us; when we listen to them, we need to be sure we are understanding them.
Problem-Solving Strategies (complete this after you have found some problems)	
✓ Inferencing	We had to guess what some words meant.
__ Substitution	We didn't need to use substitution.
✓ Questioning for clarification	Sometimes the interviewer had to ask a question to make sure what a person said.
Evaluating Strategies	
✓ Goal-Checking	We checked that we met our goal.
__ Self-evaluation	
✓ Strategy evaluation	We talked about what strategies helped us to finish this project.

FIGURE 8.2B

Cooperative Group Activity (Intermediate Students)

ACTING OUT A STORY

Directions Assign students to groups, have them read a simple story, and then act it out with their group. Have each group decide which strategies they will use and then report on the strategies they actually used, as in the example in the following chart.

STRATEGIES WE CHOSE TO USE	WHEN AND HOW WE USED THE STRATEGIES
Planning Strategies	
__ Think of what I know about the subject	We didn't know the subject of the story, so we couldn't think about what we knew about the subject.
✓ Predict what people will say	We looked at the title and the pictures to predict what the story was about.
✓ Set a goal	Our group wants to make a funny skit about this story.
Monitoring Strategies	
✓ Using what I know	We need to use what we know to understand the story and to think how to act it out.
✓ Cooperation	We help each other to understand the story.
__ Self-talk	We didn't need to use self-talk.
✓ Visualizing	Some of the group members drew a picture of things in the story.
__ Self-questioning (Am I understanding? Am I being understood?)	We didn't use self-questioning.
Problem-Solving Strategies (complete this after you have found some problems)	
✓ Inferencing	We guessed at some of the words we didn't know in the story.
✓ Substitution	To make our play, we had to use different words that were easier for us to say.
✓ Questioning for clarification	We asked the teacher a question about some things we wanted to say.
Evaluating Strategies	
✓ Goal-Checking	When our classmates laughed, we knew we had met our goal.
✓ Self-evaluation	Everybody thought they had done a good job in our play.
✓ Strategy evaluation	We thought the strategies we checked were helpful.

Teachers should keep in mind that students may need help modifying a learning strategy to fit a new task. For instance, students may be adept at *visualizing* during a listening task as a way of mentally organizing incoming information and monitoring whether it makes sense. However, they may need assistance as they try to use *visualizing* for speaking in order to organize what they want to talk about and monitoring whether they have expressed it clearly. This could require brief additional explanations, modeling, or coaching by the teacher.

Expanding to Other Academic Subjects

Very often language teachers find that they teach more than just linguistic information. As they teach a language, they usually discover that they are also teaching history, social customs, literature, arts, music, culinary habits, and the like. In content-based ESL and foreign language programs, the Expansion phase of learning strategies instruction provides an opportunity for students to extend their use of strategies beyond the language to other subject areas, including science, mathematics, and social studies, and to learning tasks outside of school. To encourage the broad transfer of strategies applications, teachers should give students assignments to use strategies in many different contexts. For example, students can be assigned to use the strategy *imagery* in their history class by drawing a timeline or making mental pictures of key historical events to assist recall of these events.

Students can be asked to create their own learning strategies lessons for a content subject of their choice or for a learning situation outside of school. Learning strategies are routinely used in many programs designed to help individuals manage their lives more successfully. These include strategies for improving athletic performance, maintaining a diet or exercise program, and developing artistic or musical abilities. When students recognize that language learning strategies have a great deal in common with the strategies they use in other aspects of their lives, they will find it easier to transfer strategies between contexts.

Can you identify the learning strategies you use for any of your leisure activities? Do they relate to language learning strategies? How?

Students can also compare and contrast strategies used in different school subjects. For example, teachers can point out how *predicting* for reading in the literature class is similar to *hypothesizing* in the science class and to *estimating* in the math class. Students can make graphic organizers to illustrate how strategies are similar and different across subjects. Figure 8.4 shows how learning strategies can be compared across academic content areas.

FIGURE 8.3

Expanding Strategies Use

Part A Use one of the strategies you learned in class at home. Look at the example. Then complete this worksheet.

Example
I used _inferencing_ in class to help me with <u>reading in English</u>.
At home, I will try to use it for <u>listening to the radio in English</u>.

I used _____ in class to help me with _____

At home, I will try to use it for _____

Part B At home, after using the strategy to meet your goal, write about how you used it and whether it helped.

Tomorrow, I will be ready to tell
• how I used the strategy.
• whether it helped me.

_____

_____

_____

_____

_____

FIGURE 8.4

Comparison of Learning Strategies Used in Different Subjects

CLASS	STRATEGY NAME	WHEN I CAN USE IT OR WHEN I HAVE USED IT	HOW IT HELPED ME
Language/ Reading	Predict	When I have some information and am expecting more	It prepares me for listening or reading by making me aware of what may be coming up. It prepares me for speaking or writing by reminding me of my choices and helping me plan.
Science	Hypothesize	Before I begin an experiment or a lab	It helps me decide what is important about the data I will be gathering and lets me think carefully about how I will analyze it.
Math	Estimate	When I only need to have a rough idea of the answer	It allows me to choose between multiple choice answers, or lets me know how to proceed with a problem.
Art	Imagine	When I am beginning to work on a project, I imagine how it will look when it's finished	It helps me to set my goals for a project and encourages me as I work.
Social Studies	Forecast; Identify Cause and Effect	When I am studying a historical event, a trend, or a geographical feature and wonder about its effects	It helps me to understand the "big picture" by helping me to see how events come from historical, social, or geographical causes.

Expanding to Nonacademic Situations

Do you have a favorite story about how you learned a new strategy for dealing with a nonacademic problem? Share it with your students!

Strategies also are useful in nonacademic, everyday-life situations. Ask students how they can use strategies in their social lives. For instance, students might use *prediction* when deciding how much food to prepare for a party of ten hungry adolescents. The teacher can model how she uses strategies by sharing a personal strategy, such as: "I always lose my car in large parking lots at shopping malls or airports. My sister taught me a strategy to solve this problem that she says is an old hunter's trick. After walking away from the car, turn around and look at it, making a visual 'snapshot' image of the car in relation to permanent features of the scene, such as buildings, signs, and trees—not other cars because they might move! You may need to turn around more than once and take additional mental snapshots if it is a long way to the entrance of the mall or airport terminal. Later, when you return, all you have to do is *visualize* your snapshots—and there is your car." By giving her own examples, the teacher models for students how to transfer strategies. Transferring strategies to situations outside the class in which initial instruction occurred is the key to developing life-long learning skills. Figure 8.5 identifies areas of life experience in which learning strategies can play an important role.

Expansion through Positive Feedback

Tip

To increase your awareness of the positive feedback you give students, turn on a tape recorder for several classes. Then listen to your own reactions to students' use of learning strategies. How could you increase your encouragement?

Positive feedback for oneself begins with receiving positive feedback from someone else; this acts as a model and helps build self-confidence. Teachers can provide students with encouragement and praise when they describe how they have used a strategy in a new context. For example, when a class has learned to use *substitution* to assist writing, the teacher can praise the student who then expands use of the strategy when speaking in class. By highlighting these spontaneous teachable and learnable moments, teachers are truly integrating strategies instruction into their curriculum. Students are also likely to be receptive to these teachable moments because they illustrate authenticity and truthfulness in the learning strategies instruction. When students feel that their contributions to the expansion of learning strategies to new contexts are valued, they begin to understand that they, themselves, are an intrinsic part of the instruction and are true learning partners with the teacher.

Young students could also be motivated by ongoing games that encourage the expansion of strategies. For example, students can be encouraged to think of themselves as detectives looking for opportunities to use their strategies. Team or individual competitions can be structured, with a reward for the group that finds the most new strategies applications that week. Or rewards can be given to individuals or to the whole class after they discover a certain number of new strategies opportunities.

FIGURE 8.5

A Teacher's Examples of Learning Strategies in Daily Life

TIMES WHEN I USED STRATEGIES FOR LEARNING IN EVERYDAY LIFE

1. Learning to ride a bike

   PLANNING

   > I set the goal of learning to ride a bike,
   > I planned when and where I could practice.

   MONITORING

   > I got help and advice from other people about how I was doing.
   > When I fell, I told myself, "You can do it. Try again!"

   PROBLEM-SOLVING

   > If I needed a hand to steady me, I asked someone to run along with me as I rode.

   EVALUATING

   > When I finally could ride alone, I congratulated myself!

2. Learning to drive a car

   PLANNING

   > I set my goal for passing the driving test by a certain date.
   > I planned times to practice with other people.

   MONITORING

   > I checked to see if I was following all of the laws as I drove.

   PROBLEM-SOLVING

   > When I made mistakes, I tried to understand how I could avoid them in the future.
   > If I failed the written test, I found out what questions I missed and studied them again.

   EVALUATING

   > When I passed the driving test, I celebrated!

Expansion through Learning Logs

Students can begin to take responsibility for expanding their use of learning strategies by making a chart, or learning log, that shows when and where they use strategies. These learning logs can be done either individually or as a class project and could include a poster, such as the example in Figure 8.6, that can be displayed in the classroom.

Students' individual learning logs that describe how they have expanded their use of learning strategies to tasks outside of the language class can be included as part of their assessment portfolios. These Expansion phase learning logs can be compared to learning logs completed during the Evaluation phase of learning strategies instruction as a way of checking which of the strategies used for class assignments have been transferred to outside tasks.

Over a summer break, students can be asked to write a summer learner diary telling their language learning goals for the summer and the strategies they used to help them achieve those goals. Foreign language students who travel abroad often have wonderful opportunities to practice their target language in challenging, authentic situations that require the application of strategies. These learner diaries can be shared with other students to show the expansion of strategies use into circumstances outside the classroom.

When teaching listening comprehension, the teacher can require students to do a number of outside listening assignments with material that they choose. The worksheet shown in Figure 8.7 encourages learners to apply strategies outside of class and report back about how well the strategies worked. Our experience has been that students are motivated by having the freedom to choose material, as well as their preferred learning strategies, in this type of outside listening activity.

Expansion through Teaching Others

The expansion of strategies can take place through other venues aside from applying the strategy in a new context. Peer teaching allows students an opportunity to instruct others in the use of the strategy. In this case, both the student teaching and the student learning are expanding the strategy to a new use. Students can teach other students, their siblings, and even their parents how to use a strategy. Students can

Tip

For younger students, have a contest to see who can use a strategy in the widest range of situations, with students keeping written records in their logs.

Tip

As a class project, have students create a book that includes short essays and explanations of their favorite strategies and how to apply those strategies outside of school. They can share the book with another class or with next year's students.

FIGURE 8.6

Learning Log Poster

STRATEGY NAME	USED IN CLASS FOR	USED OUTSIDE OF CLASS FOR
Inferencing	Reading new words	Listening to songs
Using what I know	Understanding a story	Understanding a cartoon
Visualizing	Drawing a picture for new words	Solving a math problem
Questioning for clarification	Following instructions	Finding a new place
Self-evaluating	When I finish a project, telling how well I did	Telling my parents about how well I'm learning

FIGURE 8.7

Outside Listening Activity Report

WHAT I LISTENED TO

A video titled _____

A song by _____ called _____

A movie titled _____

A TV program about_____

A conversation between _____ and _____

Other _____

MY GOALS FOR LISTENING

___ To get the general idea

___ To tell a friend about it

___ To write a short summary

___ To learn new vocabulary

___ To learn the song lyrics

I MET MY GOALS USING THESE STRATEGIES

_____

_____

ON THE BACK OF THIS SHEET, I WILL WRITE THE FOLLOWING:

___ The general idea of the material I heard

___ What I told my friend

___ A short summary

___ The new vocabulary I learned and examples of how to use the word

___ The song lyrics and my comments about them

IF I DIDN'T MEET MY GOAL

___ I had trouble meeting my goal because _____.

___ I think I know what to do now. Next time I will try the following technique to

solve my problem: _____.

___ I want the teacher to solve my problem.

expand their knowledge of strategies by interviewing their parents about the strategies they used in school or use now at work and in everyday life. The use of learning strategies expands to contexts outside of school and becomes part of students' lives in discussions with family members and peers. Parents who are aware of their child's strategies instruction can help with the expansion process by reminding students to use strategies when they are faced with a challenging homework assignment. Figure 8.8 illustrates ways in which students can teach learning strategies to others.

Tip ·····················

Brainstorm with students some effective ways to teach learning strategies to others. Some students will probably imitate your teaching techniques, while others may have ideas of their own!

FIGURE 8.8

Learning by Teaching

Think of times when you had a chance to teach people outside of this class. Write down where or whom you taught, what you taught them, and the strategies you suggested.

WHERE I TAUGHT OTHERS	WHO AND WHAT I TAUGHT	STRATEGIES I SUGGESTED
At my club	When new members join, I tell them how our meetings are conducted.	Ask questions to clarify
At home	My little brother had trouble with math.	Visualize the problem
At home	My Mom was afraid to call my teacher. I told her, "You can do it!"	Self-talk

Conclusion

• •

The Expansion phase is an essential component of learning strategies instruction because the transfer of learning strategies to other tasks is a hallmark of the self-regulated learner. Students become independent strategy users only when they are able to apply a strategy learned for one type of task to other types of tasks and to identify appropriate learning strategies for solving many different types of problems. Once the expansion process is underway, teachers and students alike may find themselves applying strategies to a surprising variety of new situations.

PART THREE

From Theory through Practice

Chapter 9

THEORETICAL BACKGROUND AND RESEARCH ON LEARNING STRATEGIES

We believe that theory is vital for teachers because it provides insight into why students respond to instruction in certain ways. While learning theory may not allow us to predict or explain all of the variations in learners, it can provide a framework for understanding commonalities among students and possible reasons for individual variations. Different instructional approaches are based on explicit or implicit beliefs about human learning. For example, cooperative learning is based on a belief in the social nature of learning. Many systems of classroom management are based on a behavioral theory that emphasizes the pairing of appropriate stimuli and rewards to desired responses. Approaches that call for higher-level thinking and student autonomy, such as the model outlined in this book, are based in large part on cognitive learning theory.

Instructional Objectives

This chapter will help you to:

- Identify contemporary learning theories that have the greatest explanatory power for the concept of a strategic learner.
- Analyze examples of strategies research in first language contexts that have applications to second language learning and teaching.
- Learn about major research studies on language learning strategies.
- Examine the relationship between motivation and learning strategies.

Learning Theories Supporting the Use and Development of Learning Strategies

Two major domains of current learning theory and research provide a rationale for learning strategies instruction. These are cognitive learning models, which focus on learners' mental processes, and social or social-cognitive models, which investigate the roles of interaction between individuals and group processes in learning.

Cognitive Models of Learning

Cognitive models view learning as an active, dynamic process in which learners select from incoming information, encode it into long-term memory, and retrieve it when needed. Cognitive theorists generally postulate two types of knowledge stores in long-term memory:

 Declarative knowledge, which consists of information that we know about, such as facts, beliefs, and events; and

 Procedural knowledge, which is knowledge of how to perform skills and processes, such as reading, writing, math computation, and conducting science experiments.

This distinction is important because declarative knowledge and procedural knowledge are learned differently and should therefore be taught in different ways.

Three cognitive learning models shed light on how learning strategies work: information processing, schema theory, and Constructivism. These models support both the importance of learning strategies and the goal of helping students become independent learners. O'Malley and Chamot (1990) applied cognitive learning theory to second language acquisition as a theoretical foundation for understanding and applying language learning strategies.

Information Processing

Information processing theory examines the thinking processes associated with learning and remembering. These processes involve routing information from a person's immediate awareness into that person's long-term memory. The theory suggests that learning requires processing new information by organizing it, elaborating on it, and connecting it with existing knowledge. This is precisely the purpose of cognitive strategies such as *summarizing, inferencing,* and *predicting.* (For descriptions of the theoretical constructs and supporting research in information processing, see J. R. Anderson, 1983, 1990; and Schunk,

1996. For applications of information processing theory and research to learning in school, see Gagné, Yekovich, & Yekovich, 1993.)

Another critical component in information processing is metacognition, the "executive control" over thinking processes. The components of metacognition include both declarative knowledge about one's own thinking processes and learning strategies as well as procedural knowledge about how to monitor and direct learning and thinking. Explicit introduction to strategies, including when and why they are useful, helps support this metacognitive executive control.

In addition to the work of O'Malley and Chamot (1990) and O'Malley, Chamot, and Walker (1987), McLaughlin (1987) has applied information processing theory to second language learning. He describes a continuum from controlled processing, in which the learner must pay careful attention to linguistic features, to automatic processing, in which the learner, through practice, has built up the ability to process language with less conscious attention. The importance of metacognition in second language and foreign language learning has been further documented in the work of Wenden (1986, 1987a, 1991, 1998).

Schema Theory

Schema theory suggests that learning occurs as we try to organize and understand life experiences according to our pre-existing knowledge (Bartlett, 1932; R. C. Anderson, 1984). This pre-existing knowledge is stored in organized structures called schemata, which can be thought of as "concept maps" of a central concept and its associated ideas. Schemata can also be "scripts" for specific situations. For example, most of us have a schema for what will happen when we go to a fast-food restaurant. Having a schema, or relevant prior knowledge, allows us to *make predictions, visualize events, draw inferences, monitor comprehension,* and *create summaries*. Learning strategies such as these are critical to understanding new information in light of existing knowledge.

Schema theory has been applied to second language learning most extensively in the area of reading comprehension. In this area, the background knowledge (schemata) of a learner may differ conceptually and culturally from that of a native speaker of the language, thus introducing comprehension problems over and above any linguistic difficulties encountered (Carrell & Eisterhold, 1983).

The transferability of first language schemata to the second language has been identified as critical to successful school achievement for second language learners. Cummins (1996) has argued persuasively that strategies for activating prior knowledge are of particular importance for second language learners. Not only does the use of students' prior knowledge assist in learning new information, but perhaps even more importantly, "teachers can validate culturally diverse students' background experiences and affirm their cultural knowledge." (Cummins, 1996, p. 78)

Constructivism

Constructivism goes a step beyond schema theory by suggesting a more interactive relationship between new information and existing knowledge. According to this theory, learners actively construct meaning as they encounter new information (Bransford, Barclay, & Franks, 1972; Spiro, 1980). Learners use their background knowledge of the world as an initial frame for relating to new information. They then use cognitive strategies as tools to help build meaning from the new information and from their background knowledge. The role of metacognitive strategies is also critical in helping the learner update interpretations as the information unfolds.

Social-Cognitive Models of Learning

Because learning does not take place in a vacuum, factors other than the learner's thoughts, or cognitions, can affect learning. Social-cognitive models focus not only on the individual learner, but also on the social nature of learning and other factors. Such models offer explanations not only for why strategies work, but also for how strategies can be taught.

Bandura's Social-Cognitive Theory

According to Bandura's (1986) social-cognitive theory, learning is based on complex, reciprocal interactions among behavior, environment, and personal factors. Social-cognitive theory places special emphasis on the role of personal motivation—When a learner experiences success at a valued task, he or she develops a sense of self-efficacy—a belief that one has the capability to succeed at that kind of task. Self-efficacy can, in turn, affect whether the student is willing to try a task, as well as the student's persistence at the task, thoughts during the task, and eventual performance (Bandura, 1997). Using appropriate strategies can help build self-efficacy by creating success experiences and by giving students the tools for future successes. Social-affective strategies, such as *self-talk*, can also help students work through tasks by providing direct self-motivation. In our own research, we found that foreign language students with high self-efficacy also report using more learning strategies than do foreign language students with low self-efficacy (Chamot, Barnhardt, El-Dinary, Carbonaro, & Robbins, 1993). During strategies instruction, it is critical that teachers ensure that students see how each strategy helps them experience success. This success will, in turn, develop their feelings of self-efficacy.

Self-Regulated Learning

Bandura's complex social-cognitive theory inspired others to build more comprehensive views of learning. In self-regulated learning theories, cognitive, metacognitive, and motivational strategies interact to create effective learning (Borkowski, Carr, Rellinger, & Pressley, 1990; Schunk & Zimmerman, 1994; Zimmerman, 1990; Zimmerman & Schunk, 1989). Self-regulated learners have coordinated the use of several cognitive strategies, such as *predicting, visualizing,* and *summarizing.* They also have metacognitive understanding of when and where to use their strategies, as well as how to adapt them to new situations. They use metacognitive strategies—such as **planning, monitoring,** and **evaluating**—to guide their learning. The role of metacognition in second language acquisition has been investigated most extensively by Wenden (1987a, 1991). She provides a theoretical examination based on research in first language contexts of how metacognition and self-regulation can function in second language learning (Wenden, 1998).

Finally, self-regulated learners are motivated, and a great source of their motivation is that they know that they can succeed when they use the other strategies they have learned. Affective strategies such as *self-talk* help support motivation because they serve as reminders to students that they can succeed.

Vygotsky's Social-Cognitive Theory

Vygotsky's (1962, 1978) social learning theory suggests that students develop mature thinking by observing how teachers and other experts approach learning tasks and by practicing expert processes with coaching from the teacher. (See supporting research by A. Collins, Brown, & Newman, 1989; Rogoff, 1990; Wood, Bruner, & Ross, 1976.) Learners can operate in their Zone of Proximal Development when teachers and others more proficient provide the support needed for completing the learning task. Eventually, teachers provide less support and students begin to internalize the kinds of thought processes (such as strategies) that they have observed and practiced. Vygotsky's theory supports the critical roles of modeling how to use strategies and of scaffolding guidance as students become more independent learners.

Thus several cognitive and social-cognitive models of learning support the need for learning strategies and provide insights into why strategies use is instrumental to learning. Furthermore, such learning theories pave the way for learning strategies instruction, suggesting ways in which strategies might be taught. Specifically, these learning theories support explicit instruction that emphasizes metacognitive awareness of one's learning. They emphasize the importance of both connections to students' existing strategies and construction of individual understanding of strategies. They also highlight the critical role of modeling and practice, as well as the need for students to directly experience the benefits of strategies.

Insights from Learning Strategies Research

We turn now to research that has focused specifically on learning strategies. Our focus is on strategies instruction research, rather than the considerable body of research that describes only the strategies that students report using on different tasks. First, we discuss examples of research in first language contexts that appear to have applications to second language learning strategies instruction. Then, we provide an overview of some of the research, including our own, that has been conducted on language learning strategies instruction.

Research across Content Areas in Native English-Speaking Contexts

Cognitive and social-cognitive learning theories such as those described previously in this chapter inspired several instructional innovations that have had a significant impact on student achievement in mainstream education (see Pressley, El-Dinary, Gaskins, Schuder, Bergman, Almasi, & Brown, 1992). Furthermore, a substantial body of research supports the explicit teaching of learning strategies for academic achievement in a variety of content areas (Pressley, Woloshyn, & Associates, 1995; Weinstein & Mayer, 1986).

For example, teaching students to use problem-solving strategies has had a positive effect on their mathematics achievement (Carpenter, Fennema, Peterson, Chiang, & Loef, 1989; Pressley, Woloshyn, & Associates, 1995; Silver & Marshall, 1990). Instruction in reading strategies has significantly improved students' comprehension, with striking results for poor readers (Brown, Pressley, Van Meter, & Schuder, 1996; Bereiter & Bird, 1985; C. Collins, 1991; Duffy, Roehler, Sivan, Rackliffe, Book, Meloth, Vevrus, Wesselman, Putnam, & Bassiri, 1987; Gagné, 1985; Gagné et al., 1993; Garner, 1987; Palincsar & Brown, 1986). Reading strategies that have been successful in these first language settings include *activating background knowledge, predicting, inferencing, visualizing, self-questioning, verifying one's understanding,* and *summarizing.* Similarly, improvements in writing performance have been reported in several studies in which learning-disabled students were explicitly taught strategies for planning, composing, and revising their writing (Englert, Raphael, Anderson, Anthony, & Stevens, 1991; Harris & Graham, 1992; Schumaker & Deshler, 1992). Across content areas, mnemonic strategies for improving memory have shown great success (see Willoughby & Wood, 1995, for a review). Successful memory strategies include:

- rhymes

- the keyword method (described in Chapter 2)

- first-letter mnemonics (such as "HOMES" for the names of the Great Lakes)

- loci (taking an imaginative tour of your house and in each room, picturing an item on your shopping list)

- the pegword method (remembering a list in sequence by imagining an interactive visual image that rhymes with each number; for example, "one" rhymes with "bun," so imagine the first person on your calling list sitting on a bun, and so on)

Early strategies instruction studies verified that under the right conditions, students could learn to use strategies and that the use of the instructed strategies resulted in more effective learning and school achievement. (See Pressley, Johnson, Symons, McGoldrick, & Kurita, 1989, for a review.) Such validations of learning strategies instruction inspired the development of instructional models that incorporate learning strategies for content instruction for native English-speaking students (Bergman, 1992; C. Collins, 1991; Duffy et al., 1987; Englert et al., 1991; Gaskins & Elliot, 1991; Harris & Graham, 1992; Jones & Idol, 1990; Jones, Palincsar, Ogle, & Carr, 1987; Palincsar & Brown, 1986; Schumaker & Deshler, 1992; Snyder & Pressley, 1990). Further research examined how these instructional models were implemented in the classroom. (See, for example, Derry, 1990; Dole, Duffy, Roehler, & Pearson, 1991; El-Dinary 1993; El-Dinary, Brown, & Van Meter, 1995; Harris & Graham, 1992; Idol & Jones, 1991; Palincsar & Klenk, 1992; Pogrow, 1992; Pressley et al., 1995; and Wood, Woloshyn, & Willoughby, 1995.) This body of literature both extended the scope of learning strategies instruction and revealed the seemingly infinite complexities involved in trying to understand how learners process information and skills.

Research on teaching learning strategies to students who were studying school subjects in their native language has made it possible to identify effective approaches to strategies instruction. Pressley, Harris, and Marks (1992), for example, suggest guidelines for strategies instruction that include the following:

- Teaching only a few new strategies at a time

- Providing strategies practice with different types of tasks

- Teacher modeling of the strategies

- Telling students why strategies are important

- Identifying ways in which students can transfer strategies to new tasks

- Maintaining students' motivation to learn

- Encouraging students to reflect on their own learning

We have found that these suggestions are as important in the language classroom as in the content classroom. In Chapters 3 through 8, we incorporated these and other teaching suggestions based on empirical research into our instructional framework.

Research on Learning Strategies in Second Language Acquisition

Research on language learning strategies has focused mainly on descriptive studies that have identified characteristics of "the good language learner" and compared the strategies of more effective and less effective language learners. These studies have been critically important in laying the groundwork for understanding how language learners use learning strategies. They also have provided important information to guide experimental studies to identify the effects of learning strategies instruction on students.

Descriptive Studies of Language Learning Strategies

Descriptive studies of language learning strategies have taken several forms. This line of research began with studies of the characteristics of effective language learners. As the role of strategies became clear, researchers began developing instruments for measuring students' strategies use. Other studies have used individual, group, or think-aloud interviews to characterize how students apply strategies while working on language learning tasks. These descriptive studies include comparisons of learning strategies used by more and less effective language learners and, more recently, studies of how the use of strategies develops over time.

Studies of Characteristics of the Good Language Learner In 1975, Rubin suggested that a model of "the good language learner" could be identified by looking at the special strategies used by students who were

successful in their second language learning. Stern (1975) also identified a number of learner characteristics and strategic techniques associated with good language learners. Hosenfeld (1976) fleshed out these characteristics, by using verbal reports, or think-aloud protocols, to investigate students' mental processes while they worked on language tasks. These studies were followed by the work of Naiman, Fröhlich, Stern, and Todesco (1978, 1996), which further pursued the notion that second language learning ability resides at least in part in the strategies one uses for learning. Taken together, these studies identified the good language learner as one who has the following characteristics:

- Is an active learner
- Monitors language production
- Practices communicating in the language
- Uses prior linguistic knowledge
- Uses various memorization techniques
- Asks questions for clarification

Development and Application of Measures of Strategies Use The cataloging of characteristics of the good language learner in the literature made it possible to create instruments for measuring strategies use. Oxford (1986) used more than 60 strategies identified from the literature on second language learning to develop the Strategy Inventory for Language Learning (SILL). The SILL is a 121-item Likert-type instrument that classifies strategies as cognitive, compensation, metacognitive, social, or affective. It has versions in a number of languages and has been administered to a large number of language learners both in the United States and internationally in mainly foreign language contexts (for example, French or Spanish in the United States and English in Japan).

The SILL studies have revealed correlations between learning strategies and other variables such as learning styles, gender, and culture (Bedell & Oxford, 1996; Green & Oxford, 1995; Oxford & Burry-Stock, 1995). In one such study, the SILL was administered to 1,200 university students who were studying various foreign languages (Nyikos & Oxford, 1993). The analysis of responses revealed that language students might not use the strategies that research indicates would be most effective, such as strategies that promote self-regulated learning and those that provide meaningful practice in communication. This and other SILL studies have yielded important information about the reported language learning strategies use of a large number of language learners around the world. They also provide useful insights about learning strategies that might help students become better language learners.

Studies of Strategies Used During Language Tasks While
questionnaires such as the SILL are useful for gathering information
from large numbers of subjects for quantitative comparisons, in-depth
interview studies have elicited rich descriptions of students' use of
learning strategies. For example, in a longitudinal EFL study, Robbins
(1996a) investigated the learning strategies of Japanese college students
as they developed their ability to carry on conversations in English.
Paired with native speakers of English, the Japanese students were
videotaped before and after an eight-month period of language exchange.
The students watched videotapes of their conversations and provided
verbal reports on their thoughts during them. Despite their reputation for
reticence, the students reported their thought processes, and therefore
their learning strategies, in great detail. It was found that fewer learning
strategies were reported as the students progressed toward being more at
ease with conversation in English, probably because of fewer challenges
and pauses to recall the problem when reviewing the conversation. Some
students mentioned that the experience of watching themselves converse
on video made them more aware of what aspects of their speaking ability
they needed to improve.

An early study of 70 high school ESL students identified the range and
variety of learning strategies used for different tasks by successful
students. The study revealed that these good students were active and
strategic language learners who could focus on the requirements of a
task, reflect on their own learning processes, and transfer previously
learned concepts and learning strategies to the demands of the English
as a second language (ESL) or general education content classroom
(Chamot, 1987; O'Malley, Chamot, Stewner-Manzanares, Küpper, &
Russo, 1985a).

Studies Comparing More Effective and Less Effective Learners A
follow-up investigation to O'Malley, Chamot, et al. (1985a) compared
the learning strategy profiles of more successful and less successful
students in ESL classrooms and discovered significant differences in
the listening approaches of the two groups (O'Malley, Chamot, &
Küpper, 1989). The more effective students monitored their
comprehension by *asking themselves if what they were hearing made
sense,* they related new information to their own *prior knowledge,* and
they made *inferences* about possible meanings when encountering
unfamiliar words. In addition, the more successful students were able to
transfer their prior academic knowledge in Spanish to the requirements
of the English-language classroom. Thus these more effective ESL
listeners were displaying a number of learning strategies that are typical
of good readers in native English-speaking contexts (see Pressley,
Woloshyn, & Associates, 1995).

The body of research on second language reading and writing processes also includes descriptions and comparisons of strategies use by more effective and less effective readers and writers (see, for example, Barnett, 1988; Carrell, 1989; Cohen & Cavalcanti, 1990; Devine, 1993; Krapels, 1990). This research indicates that good second language readers are able to monitor their comprehension and take action when comprehension falters and that composing strategies are more important than language proficiency in good second language writing (Devine, 1993; Krapels, 1990).

In our own research with high school foreign language students, we conducted individual, group, and think-aloud interviews in which students identified the learning strategies they used for a variety of language tasks, including listening, reading, grammar cloze, role playing, and writing (Chamot, Barnhardt, El-Dinary, Carbonaro, & Robbins, 1993; Chamot, Küpper, & Impink-Hernandez, 1988a). Differences between more effective and less effective learners were found in the number and range of strategies used, in how the strategies were applied to the task, and in whether they were appropriate for the task. In these studies, students' understanding of the task's requirements and whether they could match a strategy to meet those requirements seemed to be a major determinant of effective use of learning strategies.

Other studies comparing more effective and less effective language students have repeatedly revealed that less successful learners do use learning strategies, sometimes even as frequently as their more successful peers, but they use the strategies differently (Abraham & Vann, 1987; Chamot, Barnhardt, El-Dinary, & Robbins, 1993; Chamot & El-Dinary, 1998; Chamot, Küpper, & Impink-Hernandez, 1988a, 1998b; Keatley & Chamot, in preparation; Padron & Waxman, 1988; Vandergrift, 1997a, 1997b; Vann & Abraham, 1990). These studies confirmed that good language learners demonstrated adeptness at matching strategies to the task they were working on, while the less successful language learners seemed to lack the metacognitive knowledge about task requirements needed to select appropriate strategies. This trend was apparent with children in foreign language immersion classrooms, high school ESL and foreign language students, and adult language learners.

Longitudinal Studies of the Development of Strategies Use More recently, longitudinal think-aloud research has been used to understand the development of language learning strategies. An ongoing longitudinal study of elementary school language immersion students is documenting differences between more able and less able second language readers and writers at various ages (Chamot, forthcoming; Chamot, 1996; Chamot

& El-Dinary, 1996; Chamot & Keatley, in preparation; Chamot, Keatley, Barnhardt, El-Dinary, Nagano, & Newman, 1996). This study has revealed a developmental sequence in the acquisition of learning strategies for reading and writing tasks, in that younger language learners resemble older, less effective learners.

In fact, these young readers and writers in immersion programs develop reading and writing abilities in much the same way that children do in nonimmersion native language programs. Many children (even some first graders) were able to describe their thinking processes, thereby demonstrating metacognitive awareness in their ability to describe their own thinking, usually in the second language. As further evidence of metacognition, students often had thoughtful responses about when and why they think in L2 or in L1.

In summary, the descriptive studies of language learning strategies (only a sampling of which we have presented here) have revealed suggestive differences between more successful and less successful learners. Can less successful students be taught to use the learning strategies that contribute to the achievements of more successful students? This is the basic question that guides intervention studies of language learning strategies.

Intervention Studies of Learning Strategies Instruction

While most learning strategies research conducted with language learners has been descriptive, a number of intervention studies have also been conducted. Intervention studies have sought to teach language learning strategies and to measure their effects on students. These experimental and quasi-experimental studies have taken place in classroom settings in which teachers and/or researchers have provided more or less direct strategies instruction to students to help them become better language learners. The effects investigated include performance on language tests, increase in reported use of learning strategies, attitudes, and self-efficacy.

A number of researchers have also suggested approaches and developed models for teaching language learning strategies and for helping teachers teach learning strategies. (See, for example, Brown, 1989; Chamot, Barnhardt, El-Dinary, & Robbins, 1996; Chamot & O'Malley, 1994; Ellis & Sinclair, 1989; Hosenfeld, Cavour, & Bonk, 1996; Kidd & Marquardson, 1996; Mendelsohn & Rubin, 1995; Nyikos, 1996; Oxford, 1990; Oxford, 1996; Oxford & Leaver, 1996; Rubin, 1996; Rubin & Thompson, 1994; Thompson & Rubin, 1998; Weaver & Cohen, 1997; Wenden, 1991; Wenden & Rubin, 1987; and Willing, 1985.) (For a review of the state of the art in teaching language learners how to learn, see Wenden, 1998.) In this section, we briefly review examples of intervention research in which students were taught to use learning strategies for various types of language learning tasks, including vocabulary learning, listening comprehension, reading comprehension, speaking, writing, and learning content subjects.

Vocabulary Strategies Instruction Studies Techniques abound for learning vocabulary, both in one's native language and in a second language. For instance, the effectiveness of the keyword method (see Chapter 2, p. 30), in which learners pair the word to be learned with a similar-sounding word in their native language and then link the two with a visual image, has been investigated in a series of nearly fifty experimental studies (reviewed by Pressley, Levin, & Delaney, 1982). This body of research has revealed that the keyword method is particularly effective for vocabulary recognition, especially of easily visualized words but it is less effective in helping students learn accurate pronunciation or spelling (Ellis & Beaton, 1993).

Other strategies, although less prolific than the keyword method, have also proven to be quite useful for vocabulary learning. Cohen and Aphek (1981) taught students of Hebrew to remember vocabulary words by making paired mnemonic associations. They found that students who made associations remembered vocabulary words more effectively than those who did not make associations. In the first experimental study of language learning strategies instruction, O'Malley, Chamot, Stewner-Manzanares, Russo, and Küpper (1985b) taught high school ESL students how to apply learning strategies to three different types of tasks, and compared the students' performance to that of students in a nonstrategies control group. In the vocabulary task, students had to make their own groupings of words to be learned and then make a mental image of each group of related words. These strategies (*grouping/classification* and *imagery/visualization*) were effective for students who had not developed alternative strategies but were not for those who already used strong memorization strategies.

A similarly designed study was conducted with Arabic-speaking students at a university intensive-English program, in which students received different types of strategies instruction for vocabulary learning. On posttest, a significantly higher rate of recall was attained by the group that received a combination of strategies designed to provide depth of processing through visual, auditory, and semantic associations (Brown & Perry, 1991).

In his review of vocabulary intervention studies, Ellis (1994) concluded that the most effective strategies for vocabulary learning are "inferring word meanings from context, semantic or imagery mediation between the FL word (or a keyword approximation) and the L1 translation, and deep processing for elaboration of the new word with existing knowledge" (p. 263).

Listening Strategies Instruction Studies Instruction in learning strategies for listening comprehension has been the focus of a number of language learning studies (for a review, see Chamot, 1995). In many of the studies on listening, the task was to listen to and view a video. In the O'Malley et al. (1985b) study described above, another of the three tasks was to listen to and view a video and then answer comprehension questions. Students in the intervention group were taught to *use selective attention, take notes,* and *cooperate* with a classmate to review their notes after listening. Results showed that the strategies were helpful for the videos that students found personally interesting but not for those that were less interesting or for which students lacked appropriate prior knowledge.

Additional studies have revealed other boundaries of strategies instruction, suggesting implications for teaching. Rubin and her colleagues (Rubin, Quinn, & Enos, 1988) taught high school students of Spanish to use learning strategies while listening to and viewing a video, and compared groups with three different types of strategies instruction to the control group, which had no strategies instruction. This study documented many of the problems associated with classroom-based experimental studies. For example, teachers often had difficulty implementing the learning strategies lessons, and students used the instructed strategies only when the video was challenging. For us, the implications of these problems are clear. That is, teachers need to design their own learning strategies lessons, and they need to teach students to use strategies for tasks that cannot be accomplished otherwise.

Ross and Rost (1991) used a ground-up approach to developing instruction in their listening comprehension study of communication strategies used by Japanese college students learning English. Researchers first identified differences in clarification strategies used by higher and lower proficiency-level students. Then students were randomly assigned for learning strategies training to one of three different videos and taught strategies previously identified for higher proficiency students. The results showed that less proficient students could successfully learn to use the same questioning strategies that were used by more proficient students to increase listening comprehension.

Another study of listening comprehension measured the transfer of the strategies taught (Thompson & Rubin, 1996). Third-year college students of Russian viewed a variety of authentic Russian video clips over the course of an academic year. One class was taught metacognitive and cognitive strategies for improving comprehension of the video material, and the other class viewed the same videos but had no strategies instruction. Students receiving strategies instruction showed significant improvement on the video comprehension posttest compared to the students in the control group. A standardized audio-only listening comprehension test was also administered to participating students. On this measure (which did not test what had been taught), the improvement of the experimental group approached, but did not reach, significance. In addition, students in the strategies group demonstrated metacognitive awareness through their ability to select and manage the strategies that would help them comprehend the videos.

Reading Strategies Instruction Studies Reading comprehension strategies have been the focus of several instructional studies in foreign language learning. In an early study, high school students of French were taught explicit reading strategies that improved their reading comprehension (Hosenfeld, Arnold, Kirchofer, Laciura, & Wilson, 1981). In an experimental study of metacognitive reading strategies instruction for college-level ESL, students in two experimental groups were taught to use either semantic mapping or an explicit technique for relating prior knowledge to the text (Carrell, Pharis, & Liberto, 1989). Students in both experimental groups showed significant comprehension gains over the control group when answering open-ended questions. However, this gain did not apply to multiple-choice questions.

Another experimental study of metacognitive strategies instruction involved third-grade Spanish-speaking children who were taught reading strategies in Spanish. The children improved in reading performance on standardized tests in both Spanish and English. They also were able to transfer the instructed metacognitive strategies to their second language (Muñiz-Swicegood, 1994).

A recent study with seventh-grade native Spanish-speaking low-level readers involved a number of strategic interventions (Jiménez & Gámez, 1998). First, students' metacognitive awareness of their own thinking was developed by teaching them to think aloud (in either Spanish or English or a mixture) about a Spanish text. Next, the researchers provided culturally relevant stories in English and taught students how to use strategies for unknown vocabulary, how to *ask themselves questions* about the text, and how to *make inferences*. Statements by students after the intervention indicated that they had more metacognitive understanding of their own reading processes and were aware of strategies they could use to assist comprehension.

Speaking and Writing Strategies Instruction Studies Learning strategies intervention studies for speaking and writing are few in number. This is because much of the research in these areas has been descriptive and has tended to focus on communication strategies or composing processes. (See, for example, Abraham & Vann, 1987; Chamot, 1987; Cohen, 1987; Cohen & Cavalcanti, 1990; Cohen & Olshtain, 1993; Faerch & Kasper, 1983; Leki, 1995; Raimes, 1985; Robbins, 1996a; Tarone, 1980, 1983; and Zamel, 1983.)

In the first experimental study, described earlier, on the effects of language learning strategies instruction on student achievement, the task on which strategies-trained students performed significantly better than students in the control group was a transactional speaking task (O'Malley, 1987; O'Malley & Chamot, 1990; O'Malley, Chamot, Stewner-Manzanares, Russo, & Küpper, 1985b). This study was conducted with 75 high school ESL students who were randomly assigned to experimental or control groups. For two weeks, the students in the experimental group were taught various strategies for academic tasks (vocabulary, listening, and speaking). For the transactional speaking task, in which students had to prepare a brief oral report on a topic of their choice and present it to a small group of classmates, significant differences in oral proficiency favored the strategies-trained groups. All practice sessions, as well as pretests and posttests, were tape-recorded and evaluated on pre-established criteria by outside judges. The experimental groups were taught *organizational planning* for their reports and techniques for *cooperating* with classmates to elicit feedback. The students in experimental groups were judged to be significantly more comprehensible and organized in their reports than the students in the control group. Almost all students wrote out their reports before presenting them orally, so it is likely that instruction in these same strategies would be equally helpful for written reports.

The effectiveness of learning strategies instruction for speaking was also investigated in EFL settings in Egypt and Japan (Dadour & Robbins, 1996). Learning strategies were explicitly taught to college-level EFL students in both countries. The study in Egypt was experimental, with students randomly assigned to intervention or control groups. The intervention groups participated in a special strategies instruction course. The results on the posttest showed that their speaking skills and use of the strategies were significantly superior to those of students in the control groups. The intervention study in Japan taught students a variety of strategies for speaking during three months and then assessed the value of the instruction through a student questionnaire. The results showed that most students understood the value of strategies instruction and wanted to learn more strategies for speaking.

Cohen and his associates (Cohen, Weaver, & Li, 1996; Cohen, 1998) investigated the impact of strategies-based instruction on college students of French and Norwegian during ten weeks of instruction. The intervention groups received instruction in learning strategies, while the comparison groups received language instruction only. Students were pretested and posttested on three different speaking tasks in the target language: a self-description, a retelling of a fairy tale they had read, and a description of a favorite city. After each task, students completed a checklist reporting the strategies they used. Students were also pretested and posttested with the Strategy Inventory for Language Learning (SILL). In addition, a sample of students at various proficiency levels were asked to complete learning strategies checklists explaining why they chose specific strategies, thus providing think-aloud data as they were completing the checklists.

The results indicated that integrating strategies instruction into the language course was beneficial to students, although the relationship of reported strategies use to performance was complex. For example, some students in the comparison group reported using strategies, even though they had not received strategies instruction, and in some instances, the increase in reported strategies use by comparison students seemed to be detrimental to their performance. Findings suggested that some students are able to acquire effective learning strategies without instruction while other students require systematic instruction and practice with learning strategies in order to learn to use them effectively.

An experimental study involving writing in conjunction with reading comprehension investigated the effects of learning strategies instruction on third- and fourth-grade limited English proficient children (Bermudez & Prater, 1990). Strategies taught to the experimental group were *brainstorming* and *clustering*. Before children read an expository text, such as a story, they used the title and illustrations to brainstorm what it might be about (in Chapter 2, this strategy is identified as *predicting*), and the teacher recorded the results on a graphic organizer. After reading, children in the experimental group were taught to cluster connected ideas in the text by color-coding similar ideas (we identify this type of strategy as *selective attention*). Finally, all students wrote a paragraph about the text. The results showed that the strategies group produced significantly more elaborations in their essays and that their paragraphs tended to be better organized than those of the control group.

Content-Based Strategies Instruction Studies Learning strategies instruction in content-based ESL has been investigated in a number of studies on the Cognitive Academic Language Learning Approach (CALLA), described in Chapter 1. Evaluations of the CALLA model were conducted for five different CALLA programs. Although all reported successful use of learning strategies by students, reliable assessment of the effect of learning strategies instruction was provided in only two of the programs (O'Malley & Chamot, 1998). In the first of these, teachers in ESL-mathematics classrooms implemented learning strategies instruction to assist students in solving word problems (Chamot, Dale, O'Malley, & Spanos, 1993). Students were taught to use **planning, monitoring, problem-solving,** and **evaluating** strategies in a sequential order for solving word problems. Students in high-implementation classrooms (in which teachers had provided explicit and frequent strategies instruction) performed significantly better on a word problem think-aloud interview than students in low-implementation classrooms (in which the instruction was mainly implicit and infrequent).

In the second study, Varela (1997) investigated the effects of CALLA learning strategies instruction in a middle school ESL-science classroom compared with a similar classroom that received equivalent instruction without the learning strategies component. This study was based on the transactional speaking component of O'Malley et al. (1985b; see also O'Malley & Chamot, 1990). In the Varela (1997) study, students in the intervention classroom were taught strategies to assist them in presenting an oral report on their science fair projects. The strategies included *using graphic organizers, selective attention, self-assessment,* and *self-talk.* After two weeks of instruction, students in the strategies group reported using significantly more strategies than control group students did. Also, their videotaped performances of their science fair reports showed significant improvement over their performances prior to the strategies instruction.

To conclude our summary of research on language learning strategies, we describe our studies of classroom-based learning strategies instruction. These studies reflect a long-standing interest in helping teachers incorporate learning strategies instruction into their language classrooms.

A course development study was designed to involve teachers in selecting and integrating strategies instruction into their high school/university Russian or Spanish classrooms (Chamot & Küpper, 1989, 1990; Chamot, Küpper, & Impink-Hernández, 1988a, 1988b; Chamot, Küpper, & Barrueta, 1990; Chamot, Küpper, Thompson, & Barnhardt, 1990; Chamot, Küpper, & Toth, 1990; O'Malley & Chamot, 1990). Researchers and teachers participated in developing instructional modules for teaching learning strategies for listening, reading, speaking, and writing. The modules were field-tested by participating teachers and then revised according to the teachers' suggestions. In a follow-up study, the modules were implemented by different teachers and for different languages. For example, the listening strategies module in Spanish was adapted for French, the reading strategies module for Russian was also adapted for French, and the writing strategies module for French was adapted for Spanish (Chamot & Küpper, 1990). Findings from these two studies indicated that learning strategies instruction calls for a special type of teaching and that teachers may need support in its implementation (which is the major purpose of this book). In addition, students' responses to the instruction indicated that they enjoyed learning strategies activities and had individual preferences for different strategies. Those responses also showed that the students were confused when too many strategies were introduced at once. These insights into some of the practical realities of learning strategies instruction have guided our recent research.

Thirteen high school teachers and four college teachers participated in two parallel studies that investigated the implementation of learning strategies instruction in Japanese, Russian, and Spanish foreign classrooms (Chamot, 1993, 1994; Chamot, Barnhardt, El-Dinary, & Robbins, 1996; Chamot, Barnhardt, El-Dinary, Carbonaro, & Robbins, 1993; Chamot & O'Malley, 1994b). Researchers developed resource guides for teaching learning strategies (the prototypes for this book) and provided ongoing professional development workshops and conferences to help teachers implement the instruction. Over the three years of the two studies, 722 high school students of Japanese, Russian, and Spanish and 50 college students of Japanese received instruction in language learning strategies from their teachers. Important outcomes of these studies were the development of the Metacognitive Model of Strategic Learning (see Chapter 2) and the Framework for Learning Strategies Instruction (see Chapter 3). The strategies instruction was evaluated through interviews and questionnaires with teachers and students. We discovered that once we provided scaffolding and sample lesson plans, teachers could go on to develop creative and effective learning strategies lessons that were seamlessly integrated into their course structure. Most students reported that the strategies instruction had a positive effect on their language learning, and some (but not all) students indicated that they also used the strategies outside of class. Students' metacognitive awareness of their own approaches to learning was reflected in their comments on the strategies they used or did not use and their reasons for using or not using them.

We continued this research direction in an instructional study of learning strategies conducted from 1993 to 1996 (Chamot, Barnhardt, & El-Dinary, 1996). The objective of this study was to investigate how to best support foreign language instructors of Chinese, French, German, Japanese, Russian, and Spanish so they could effectively teach language learning strategies in classes of different levels ranging from elementary immersion through higher education. Researchers worked with participant teachers for three years (1993–96), providing many types of professional support for teaching learning strategies. The methods of evaluation used were classroom observations, student group interviews, and teacher interviews and questionnaires. We learned that while workshops motivated teachers to try strategies instruction, follow-up support such as model lessons, one-to-one coaching, and peer discussions were invaluable to their integrating learning strategies into language instruction. One of the greatest challenges for teachers was shifting from implicitly applying strategies in activities to explicitly teaching students to apply strategies for themselves. Another critical shift was from teaching strategies as a separate entity to integrating strategies into the language curriculum. Teachers also struggled with determining an appropriate scope and sequence of strategies to teach at various levels, and they wanted guidance in how to scaffold strategies effectively at upper levels and for high achievers. Overall, however, teachers, when given coaching, were able to adapt instruction to their own languages and levels. This reinforced our long-held view that the Metacognitive Model of Strategic Learning (Chapter 2) and the Instructional Framework (Chapter 3) are applicable across languages and levels. Teachers in this study cited a variety of positive impacts that strategies instruction was having on their students, including:

- Improving students' understanding of the target language

- Helping students become more responsible and active learners

- Improving students' motivation for language learning

- Building students' independent use of strategies

Several teachers also said that strategies instruction had improved their teaching in general.

This handbook was developed, in part, in reaction to teachers' overwhelming positive response to the written materials provided in our workshops. We have also included a variety of sample lesson plans (Chapter 10) because feedback from teachers we have worked with indicates that teaching from such lessons provides both an opportunity to get accustomed to strategies teaching and a model for developing lessons independently. Through teacher tips, we also have attempted to integrate the kinds of suggestions we have found useful in individual coaching settings.

In summary, the effectiveness of learning strategies instruction has been well established in first language contexts. Research in those contexts has moved from validating instruction in individual strategies to identifying elements of effective strategies instruction integrated into a curriculum. Many of the same learning strategies used in first language contexts have also proven useful in second language learning. Studies in second language learning began by focusing on the strategies that distinguish effective language learners. Research is now moving toward an understanding of strategies development, validations of language learning strategies instruction in the classroom, and an understanding of the professional support that teachers need in order to develop effective strategies instruction.

Motivation and Learning Strategies

Learner motivation, though complex and multifaceted, is critical for all types of learning, including language learning. Motivation affects how hard students are willing to work on a task, how much they will persevere when they are challenged, and how much satisfaction they feel when they accomplish a learning task. When teachers teach learning strategies, it is critical that they develop students' motivation to use the strategies. In return, the use of learning strategies can increase student motivation for language learning tasks.

Several critical components play a role in student motivation, including how much students value the task (value), how much they expect to succeed in the domain (expectancy), how much they believe that they possess what it takes to succeed at the task (self-efficacy), and what factors they believe are responsible for success or failure at the task (attributions). Each of these components has implications for language learning strategies instruction.

Value

Students are more motivated on tasks that they value. Students may value a task because they find it intrinsically interesting, because they find it applicable to their lives, or both. Teachers try many ways to gain students' intrinsic interest in academic tasks, including using authentic literature, choosing activities that might be fun for students, and focusing on content that has cultural relevance. Learning materials are authentic when they contain content that applies to students' lives, when they connect with students' previous experiences, when they can be immediately applied to new experiences, and when they relate to other information students are learning (Chamot & O'Malley, 1994).

Expectancy

Over years of exposure to learning experiences, students develop overall expectations for success or failure in school. Thus students often have an overall feeling of being a "good student" or "bad student." As they grow older and have experiences in several content areas, they begin to differentiate their expectations for success. For example, a student may say he has "an ear for languages" or she "can't do math." Most high school students can identify areas that they think they are "good at" and "bad at." Each day in a classroom can reinforce a student's expectations of success or failure in that field. In turn, these deep-rooted expectations influence each future encounter in that field. Thus it is critical to ensure that students experience successes in the classroom. It is important to have tasks that are appropriately challenging—not so difficult that students cannot experience success and yet not so easy that success is not valued. Having access to appropriate strategies can help students experience success on challenging and meaningful tasks and can eventually lead to higher expectations of learning success.

Self-Efficacy

Self-efficacy is the specific confidence that one is capable of successfully completing a particular task. It is knowing that you have what it takes to do the task right (Zimmerman & Pons, 1986). Self-efficacy is at the core of motivation, self-esteem, and self-regulation (Bandura, 1993). The development of self-efficacy is tied closely with effective use of learning strategies (Zimmerman, 1990). Students with high self-efficacy have confidence that they can solve a problem because they have developed strategies for the task that have worked for them in the past. They believe that the more they learn and practice, the more their capabilities will improve, and they understand that mistakes are just a part of learning. In contrast, students with low self-efficacy think that they have inherent low ability. They believe that effort will reveal their own inability, and they choose easy tasks to try to avoid making mistakes (Bandura, 1993). Building students' strategic awareness can help them see that they are capable of solving problems when they use the correct tools. In second language learning research, correlations have been found between students' reported learning strategies use and their self-efficacy, in particular their beliefs about their own effectiveness as language learners (see Chamot et al., 1993; Chamot & O'Malley, 1993, 1994b; Robbins, 1993).

Attributions

Students' approach to school tasks can depend on the factors to which they attribute their success or failure. Learners often attribute performance to natural ability, luck, and outside influences such as a good or poor teacher. These are factors that are largely perceived as out of the learner's control. Less often, students may attribute school success to effort or, even more appropriately, to effective strategies. As with other motivational beliefs, students' attributions for success or failure evolve over a long time and are difficult to change. Strategies instruction helps to alter students' attributions by showing them that they can succeed if they use appropriate strategies and, conversely, that their failures can be attributed to the lack of effective strategies use rather than the lack of ability.

In sum, one goal of strategies instruction is to build student motivation, both for language learning and for strategies learning, by showing students their own success with strategies. Effective strategies use can help build students' self-efficacy for language tasks and their expectations for success in language learning. As students learn to attribute their success to effective strategies use, they will come to value and rely on strategies even more. On the road to these goals, teachers must ensure that students experience meaningful successes with strategies by providing authentic, appropriately challenging tasks and by teaching strategies explicitly so that students know how to apply them.

Conclusion

A variety of cognitive and social-cognitive theories inspired the development of learning strategies in native English-speaking contexts. Instructional models have shed light on how strategies instruction can be successfully integrated into content instruction to support learning in many domains. Research in ESL, foreign language, and bilingual education has verified that strategies can have a powerful impact on language learning.

Theories of learning continue to shed light on the importance of learning strategies instruction and to guide its implementation. For example, student motivation is an important consideration when presenting learning strategies instruction, and, in turn, strategies instruction can be quite powerful in building student motivation for language learning.

As teachers apply learning strategies instruction, their own classroom research also can inform their strategies instruction. Teachers can identify the strategies that best meet their students' immediate needs, they can explore students' reactions to their instructional approaches, and they can use classroom research as a tool for showing students that strategies really work.

LANGUAGE LEARNING STRATEGIES LESSONS

This chapter presents sample lessons that demonstrate how learning strategies can be integrated with a variety of language and content topics and tasks. Our experience has shown that many language teachers hesitate to add learning strategies instruction to their teaching because of an already crowded curriculum. We have heard many teachers say, "It sounds wonderful, but I don't have time to teach anything extra!" We wanted to show how strategies can be woven into the language curriculum as an integral part rather than as an add-on component that takes time away from language activities. So we invited a number of ESL, EFL, and foreign language teachers to contribute learning strategies lessons that they had taught successfully. We selected lessons to cover a range of learning strategies, different languages, and various proficiency and grade levels. We also selected lessons that could be adapted to languages and levels other than the ones for which they were originally designed. Instead of a series of learning strategies activities, these are language lessons to which learning strategies instruction has been added. These authentic lessons have actually been used in real language classrooms, and we hope that they will provide useful examples of how learning strategies can be taught in the second or foreign language classroom.

Organization of the Lessons

Each lesson is organized in the CALLA instructional framework, beginning with a Preparation phase and moving through the Presentation, Practice, Evaluation, and Expansion phases. The recursive nature of this framework is illustrated in lessons that return to a previous phase as needed. (See Chapter 3 for a description of the instructional framework.)

First is a descriptive title for each lesson. Next is the language level (beginning, intermediate, or advanced), language (ESL, EFL, Content-based ESL, or FL), and grade level (Elementary, Middle School, High School, or Adult). A plus (+) sign after the grade level indicates that the lesson also is appropriate for higher grade levels. Also indicated is whether lessons are adaptable to language contexts other than the one for which the lesson was originally designed.

Next, each lesson lists the Focus Language Learning Strategy or Strategies (LLS) and any Review Language Learning Strategies (LLS). The Focus LLS receives explicit instruction in the lesson. The Review LLS are either implicit in the lesson, or students are merely reminded to use them.

Language Objectives and Strategy Objectives are provided in the next part of each lesson. The objectives identify what students will know and be able to do as a result of the lesson. The language objectives identify the modes of communication that students will practice during the lesson. The learning strategy objectives describe how students will use both Focus and Review LLSs with the content of the lesson.

The next section of each lesson plan provides a Strategy Rationale that explains how the strategy or strategies will help students for specific learning tasks. This rationale is addressed to the teacher to help the teacher understand the purpose and benefits of the strategy or strategies. Suggestions for sharing this rationale with students are provided in the Procedures section of the lesson.

A list of materials needed for the lesson is given next. Either student worksheets are described, or examples of them are provided at the end of the lesson.

The Procedures section of each lesson describes what the teacher does and what students do during the five phases of instruction (Preparation, Presentation, Practice, Evaluation, and Expansion). The procedures are fairly detailed and include sample questions and think-alouds for teachers to model the strategies taught.

How to Use the Lessons

We hope these sample lessons will provide teachers with ideas on how strategies can be used in their own classrooms. The lessons originate from specific contexts and curricula, and thus some elements may be more or less appropriate for a particular teacher's situation. Although the language and level are listed as they occurred in the initial classroom, many of the lessons can be adapted for different languages and grade levels.

The lessons have been drawn from a variety of contexts: ESL-language arts and content classes, beginning through advanced foreign language classes, EFL in various countries, and elementary- through adult-level language classes. The lessons also vary in length of time, as some represent just one activity in a class, while others would be taught as a unit spanning several days.

We chose lessons that provide examples for almost all of the strategies described in Chapter 2. Although the strategies are presented according to the levels in which the sample lesson occurred, this does not mean that the strategies are tied to a specific level. Remember, it is the tasks, curriculum, and students' abilities which should determine the appropriate strategies to teach. Many of the lessons illustrate how strategies can be taught in combinations. For example, an ESL middle school lesson combines *personalization* and *note-taking*. A lesson on writing folk tales combines *organizational planning* and *self-management*. These combinations were effective for the particular language and context. Other strategy combinations are possible—we encourage teachers to experiment. When reading the lessons, teachers should focus on how the strategies were chosen to match the lesson's language content. Teachers should think about whether they would have chosen to teach similar or different strategies for the learning tasks presented. The choices are not limited to those we have identified. Teachers can modify the lessons to fit their curricula.

Teachers should pay attention to how other teachers make strategies instruction explicit for their students by naming and defining the strategies. They should notice how the teachers follow the instructional sequence of preparing their students for strategies, presenting new strategies, giving students the opportunity to practice the strategies immediately, reminding students to evaluate the effectiveness of the strategies, and encouraging transfer of the strategies in the Expansion phase. Finally, teachers should think about which strategies are appropriate for them to teach and how they can incorporate the strategies model presented here into their own classroom situation.

Conclusion

The sample language learning strategies lessons in this chapter are provided to help teachers get started with learning strategies instruction. The lessons are authentic lessons developed by language teachers and have been successfully implemented in their classrooms. We realize that every teacher has an individual teaching style, and we do not expect that a teacher will follow these lesson plans as if they were recipes. The teacher should take the ideas and adapt them to the way that he or she teaches while remembering that explicit instruction (naming the learning strategy, explaining its rationale, modeling it, and telling when and how to use it) is needed if students are to become independent strategies users.

Finally, we would like to express our sincere appreciation to the teachers who so generously shared their learning strategies lessons for this book. Their contributions made it possible to demonstrate how learning strategies instruction can be integrated into the language classroom.

Writing about Family

LANGUAGE LEVEL: Intermediate **LANGUAGE:** ESL/FL

GRADE LEVEL: Any **FOCUS LLS:** Using Background Knowledge

LANGUAGE OBJECTIVE: Write a composition about family

STRATEGY OBJECTIVE: *Use background knowledge* to prepare for writing an essay

STRATEGY RATIONALE: Writing a composition can seem like a very difficult task. Often, however, students do not think about all of the knowledge they have on the subject before they begin writing. *Using background knowledge* gets the students ready for the task by helping them familiarize themselves with the topic before they begin to write.

MATERIALS: Pictures of family that students bring from home; a picture of family that the teacher brings; markers; paper

PROCEDURES

Preparation

1. Go around the room asking general questions about the students' families, for example:

- Is your family big or small?
- How many brothers and sisters do you have?
- Do you have a dog?
- What is your dog's name?
- Where do you live?
- How old is your sister?
- What do you like to do with your family?

You may wish to make a class chart about students' family information.

2. Ask students how they come up with topics and ideas for writing. Record their ideas on an overhead and save.

Presentation

3. Introduce the writing task and the strategy of *using background knowledge.*

"Wow! You can talk a lot about your family! Today, you are going to write an essay about your family, but first, we are going to review everything that you already know. This is a strategy to prepare you to write. It is called *using background knowledge.*"

4. Show your own family picture to the class, and model using background knowledge.

"Look! It's a picture of my family. I am going to write a composition about my family, but first, I am going to think about everything I know in English about my family. This will help me to organize and write my composition. On the board, I am going to draw a circle for each person in my family. [Draw circles, and say aloud each person you are thinking of.] I am going to draw a circle for my mother, Carol Ann. I am also going to write her name in the circle. I ask myself, 'What else do I know about my mother, in English?' I am going to put the ideas about my mom in the circle. For example, she is 55 years old. I only want to write the ideas that I have, not the whole sentence. What else? My mother has brown hair. I am going to write 'brown hair' in the circle. My mother likes to read. I am going to write 'read' in the circle."

5. Continue this process with other ideas about your mother. Then, move on to other family members, pets, and so on, using the picture to show the students your family members. When you are finished, explain to students that you have surprised yourself with how much you know about your family.

"Using your background knowledge is an excellent strategy for planning a composition."

Practice
6. Have students draw circles for each member of their families on big sheets of paper with different colored markers. They can use their pictures to help them think. While they are working, walk around the room to help with questions and offer positive feedback.

7. When students have finished activating their background knowledge, explain that now they are going to use what they activated to write a composition. Explain that students can write a paragraph about each circle they made. They can also draw a picture or include the photo. (This whole process could take several days.)

Evaluation
8. After they have finished their first drafts, have students present the first drafts with their pictures to each other in pairs or small groups.

9. Have students seek suggestions for improving their drafts, and then revise them. Continue the revision process as needed until the final editing and sharing of compositions with others.

Ask students, "What was the strategy you used to plan your composition? Was it useful? Could you do the same thing to plan other compositions or oral descriptions?"

Expansion
10. Give students another topic related to their lives (or brainstorm ideas with students). Ask them to interview one or more members of their families to gather information and then use this background knowledge to write another composition, following the process writing procedures described previously. Check how they activated their background knowledge before they began to write.

Contributed by Suzanne Tapia and Anna Uhl Chamot

Setting Language Learning Goals

LANGUAGE LEVEL: Intermediate+   **LANGUAGE:** ESL/FL

GRADE LEVEL: Adult   **FOCUS LLS:** Setting Goals

LANGUAGE OBJECTIVE: Identify and discuss language learning goals and responsibility in reaching those goals

STRATEGY OBJECTIVE: Use the strategy *goal setting* to prepare actively for progress in language learning and in taking responsibility for this learning

STRATEGY RATIONALE: Laying the foundations for a learner-responsible classroom begins with helping students understand the meaning and importance of setting their own language learning goals.

MATERIALS: Worksheet, "Set Goals" (page 187)

PROCEDURES

Preparation

1. Ask students what types of goals they set for themselves in their everyday lives, perhaps in sports or saving money. Elicit answers, and write them on the board.

"What kinds of goals do you set for yourselves in your life? Do you set goals for yourself when you are preparing for a sports competition, for example, trying to beat a certain time in a 100-meter race? Do you set goals for yourself at work, for example, 'I want to be shift supervisor by the end of this year'?"

2. Ask students if they set goals for themselves in language learning. Record their responses on the blackboard. Steer students toward realistic goals.

"What sorts of goals do you set for yourselves when you are learning English? Try to be specific and realistic when setting your goals."

Presentation

3. Tell students that setting goals is useful every time they start a new language learning task, whether it is reading, writing, listening, or speaking, because in this way they have direction for their efforts and they can plan appropriate and effective strategies. They can use the strategy of *goal setting* in class, for homework, and in their everyday lives—every time they have to do something in English.

4. Model setting a goal for two listening tasks. Tell students that they will practice setting goals next.

"I'm going to practice setting a goal for my listening task. I'm going to think aloud and make notes as I do it, so you can follow my thinking. Well, I want to find out when the Museum of

Science downtown is open. So, I can get the phone number from the telephone book and call. Probably, they will have a recording—those are hard to understand, and they have a lot of information. But my goal is to understand the days and times that the museum is open. I won't pay attention to the other words, just the days and times. Okay, now I have a goal for my task and I can start planning what strategies to use to meet that goal."

5. Work with students to set goals for another task. There will be more than one possible goal, depending on a student's purpose. Elicit and write the students' goals on the board.

"Okay, now we are going to work together to set goals. Our next task is watching the news. Do you watch the news at home? It's difficult to understand everything, isn't it? But if we set a goal, then we can focus on what we want to do and plan some strategies. Hmm, tonight when I watch the news, I want to understand the topics of the top three stories on the news. They are the most important, and I'd like to be informed on important issues. So, my goal is to understand the topics of those stories. What are some other goals that you could have? What are you interested in when you watch the news?

Practice
6. Hand out the worksheet, "Set Goals." Ask students to select and write a goal for each task on the worksheet. Assure them that there can be more than one goal for each task, depending on their purpose, but that they should choose only one goal. Monitor as they work.

Evaluation
7. Divide students into groups of five. Have them share their goals with other members in their group and then report to the class. Monitor to ensure that each goal is limited and related to the task.

8. For homework, have students perform one of the practice tasks. In the next class, lead students in a discussion about setting goals. Ask them if setting a goal helped them in performing their task.

Expansion
9. Have students do one of the following activities.

- For intermediate to advanced students, have them write paragraphs or essays about their goals and what they do to reach them.
- Have students record progress toward their goals by completing a personal language goals chart for weekly, biweekly, or monthly use.

Contributed by Jennifer Kevorkian

Set Goals

Directions For each of the following tasks, set one goal for yourself. Then, circle the task that you will do for homework.

Sample Task: Talking to your child's teacher
Goal A: Ask and learn what your child is doing in math class.
Goal B: Ask and learn where the class is going for the class trip.

Task One: Writing a letter to your landlord

Goal: _____

_____

Task Two: Having a conversation with your neighbor

Goal: _____

_____

Task Three: Talking to customers at your job

Goal: _____

_____

Task Four: Reading the newspaper

Goal: _____

_____

Task Five: Listening to the traffic report on the way home from work

Goal: _____

_____

Evaluating Progress toward Goals

LANGUAGE LEVEL: Intermediate   **LANGUAGE:** ESL

GRADE LEVEL: High School+   **FOCUS LLS:** Checking Goals

                                                      REVIEW LLS: Setting Goals

LANGUAGE OBJECTIVE: Discuss language learning goals and progress toward them, evaluating the effectiveness of the activities that are being used to reach them

STRATEGY OBJECTIVE: Check progress toward goals

STRATEGY RATIONALE: Having students *set goals* is a good way to encourage them to take responsibility for charting their own language learning journey. Having set the goals, students then need to refer back to those goals periodically to make sure that they are on track. Note: This lesson assumes that students have set goals for one or more activities.

MATERIALS: Student goals from the worksheet, "Personal Language Goals and Self-Assessment" (page 61); record of activities, including homework and class work; worksheet, "Check Goals" (page 190)

PROCEDURES

Preparation

1. Ask students how they know whether they have reached goals that they have set in their lives. Give an example, and then elicit students' responses and write them on the board.

"We already talked about setting goals for tasks in our lives, for example, wanting to run the 100-meter dash in a certain amount of time at a track meet. How do you know if you have met your goal? Well, in this case, you'd probably run the race and then see what your time was. If your time met or exceeded your goal, then you would have met your goal. If you didn't meet your goal, then you would need to keep working on that goal. You might want to think of new ways to reach your goal. Can you give us any examples of goals you have set and how you checked to see if you reached them?"

2. Ask students if and how they check the goals they set for their language learning tasks. Elicit and write responses.

Presentation

3. Tell students that *checking goals* for language learning tasks can be a very useful strategy, especially if the tasks are very challenging. If they check their goals, they can decide whether they have reached the goals or need to keep trying.

"When you are learning another language, *setting* and *checking goals* is also very useful. One example is taking a test. If your goal is to pass the test, and you do, then you have met your goal. If you didn't pass the test, you need to study the material that was on the test."

4. Tell students that they are going to practice evaluating progress toward their goals. Model the evaluation activity that you want students to carry out. Using a think-aloud activity to model can be very effective in eliciting student contributions and questions. Keep notes on a transparency of the worksheet.

"Now I'm going to think through a task and goal that I set for myself last week when I was trying to use Russian in my community. I am studying Russian, and I want to practice. One of my tasks was using Russian at the deli. My goal was to ask for half a kilo of Swiss cheese at the counter. Well, I did get the Swiss cheese, but the woman gave me a whole kilo instead of half a kilo! I didn't meet my goal. I need to review and practice my Russian numbers at home! Next week, I will try again."

Practice

5. Tell students that they will now check their progress toward one of their language learning goals. They will use the worksheets that you distribute to log their tasks, goals, and goal checking. Assure students that this is not a test and that they will have the opportunity to keep working toward their goals.

"Now I want you to check one of the goals that you set for yourself last week. You have had time to work toward your goal. Check if you reached it or not. If you didn't, don't be discouraged. You can figure out what the problem is and keep working! This is not a test."

Evaluation

6. Monitor students as they fill out their worksheets. Have them report about their progress either to a small group or to the class.

7. Discuss with students how checking progress toward goals helps them keep track of their learning. Discuss if and how it is helpful as they learn a language.

Expansion

8. Students create a portfolio of goals and the progress they make toward meeting them.

9. Group students according to goals and let them work together to brainstorm ways they can reach those goals.

Contributed by Jennifer Kevorkian

Check Goals

Directions Complete the following worksheet.

1 Language learning task:

_____

2 Goal:

_____

_____

_____

3 Circle the statement that is true for your task.
I reached my goal!
I need to work more to reach my goal.

4 If you reached your goal, how do you know that you reached it?

_____

_____

_____

_____

_____

5 If you did not reach your goal, what can you do to help yourself reach it?

_____

_____

_____

_____

_____

Circle Step

LANGUAGE LEVEL: Beginning
GRADE LEVEL: Kindergarten–Grade 1

LANGUAGE: EFL
FOCUS LLS: Selective Attention
REVIEW LLS: Cooperation

LANGUAGE OBJECTIVE: Listen to and remember words describing emotions or physical states
STRATEGY OBJECTIVE: Use *selective attention* to zoom in on and remember important words

STRATEGY RATIONALE: Even very young students use strategies to help them learn. The strategy *selective attention* (called "zooming in") helps young children ignore distractions and focus on the important information they must remember to successfully complete the task.

MATERIALS: None

PROCEDURES

Preparation

1. Review the words that students have learned that relate to how they feel: fine, hungry, happy, sad, and so on. Ask students to tell you the feeling words they remember and to repeat them.

"How do you remember these words?"

Presentation

2. Explain the strategy *selective attention*.

"When we listen, we sometimes need to pay attention only to part of what is said. Just as a camera 'zooms in' on one part of a scene, our mind can zoom in on part of what someone says."

3. Model the strategy by holding a cupped hand before one eye like a telescope and moving toward a student or an object while looking through the "lens." Ask students to repeat the expression "zoom in" and to use the gesture.

4. Model the use of "zooming in" by mumbling a sentence with the word "candy" said clearly in the middle or at the end of the sentence: "My mumble mumble me some **candy** mumble mumble." Ask students to tell you what you were talking about in the sentence. The students will probably respond that you were talking about candy.

"Like a camera, you can pick out, or 'zoom in,' on one word even though you did not hear the whole sentence clearly. This practice can help you do some of the work in your language class."

5. Write these phrases on a chalkboard: "My name's _____. I feel _____." Model listening for what is in the blanks by saying the phrases with nonsense words: "Blah-blah Hiro. Blah-blah fine." Tells students to listen for the words in the blanks as they do the "circle step" activity.

Practice

6. Ask students to stand in a circle, and hold hands. You join the circle then take one step forward, and say, "My name's Alice. I feel happy." Ask students to repeat your sentences. If some students have difficulty repeating them, encourage other students to help them by cooperating or working together.

7. Play some cheerful background music to make the activity more like a dance. The students step forward into the circle and repeat your words, "My name's Alice. I feel happy." (More advanced learners can change this to the third-person forms, "Her name's Alice. She feels happy.") Then, they take turns, one at a time stepping forward, giving their name, and saying how they feel. The other students in the circle either repeat what each student said or rephrase it.

Evaluation

8. Ask students if they could do the "Circle Step" easily when they didn't worry about anything but the new words each person said. Ask students to raise their hands if they used "zooming in."

9. Point out times when students helped each other and made the activity more fun by working together. Ask students to raise their hands if they helped another student, and praise them if they did.

"You used *cooperation* today, good for you!"

Expansion

10. Give examples of other times when it can be helpful to use "zooming in." For example, it can be used when someone is talking too fast for another person to catch every word, when there is static on the radio or TV, or in a noisy room. Point out how students use *cooperation* in school clubs or sports. Ask students to tell about times that they have helped each other in class by using the strategy *cooperation*.

Contributed by Larry Chin

Answering Comprehension Questions

LANGUAGE LEVEL: Beginning   **LANGUAGE:** ESL

GRADE LEVEL: Middle School+   **FOCUS LLS:** Using Background Knowledge;
                       Ask If It Makes Sense

                             REVIEW LLS: Selective Attention

LANGUAGE OBJECTIVE: Understand a reading text

STRATEGY OBJECTIVE: *Use background knowledge* of question words to understand the question, and then *ask if it makes sense* to check answers to comprehension questions

STRATEGY RATIONALE: Answering comprehension questions is one of the most common classroom tasks. However, beginning students often rush to find the answer before fully understanding the question. Students can selectively attend to and use what they know about question words to help them understand and answer questions. They can use the strategy *ask if it makes sense* to check their response and identify problems.

MATERIALS: Copies of text and comprehension questions; worksheet, "Guidelines for Answering Comprehension Questions" (page 195)

PROCEDURES

Preparation

1. Prior to this lesson, have students read a text and complete comprehension questions. At the beginning of class, ask students what they do when they answer a comprehension question. Make a list of students' ideas on the board. Review and comment on the students' list. Note: Students should have knowledge of question words before doing this lesson.

Presentation

2. Add to the list *use what you know* about question words to understand the question and *ask yourself if it makes sense* to check your answer. Explain how students can use what they know to check if their answers make sense and to successfully answer comprehension questions.

"Using the two strategies together can help you accurately answer comprehension questions. First, you can use what you know about the question word to help you understand the question. Use *selective attention,* a strategy you already know, to locate the question word. Then ask yourself, 'What does the word mean? What information am I looking for?' Once you understand the question, you can use the text to answer it. After you write your answer, use the strategy *ask yourself if it makes sense* to check your answer."

3. Model the strategy by thinking aloud.

"Let me show you what I mean with an example. Let's see, the first question asks, 'Who did Kate meet on the bridge?' Let me think . . . what do I know about the question? I will use *selective attention* or *focusing* and circle the question word, 'who,' because 'who' tells me that I will answer with a person or a name. Let's continue. Kate met with someone on the bridge.

Who was it? Maybe there were several people. Now that I think I understand the question, I can go to the text to find the answer. I am going to look for the names of people. Reading: *'On her way to the station, Kate met her father and uncle on the bridge.'* Now that I have found an answer in the text, I will check to see that my answer is really answering the question. I will do this by reminding myself of the question word. 'Who did Kate meet? Kate met her father and uncle.' Yes, that answer makes sense because it asks for a person and I answered with a person."

4. Ask students to tell you the steps you took to answer the question. Elicit the strategies: *using what you already know* to understand the question, *scanning* the text for the answer, and checking the answer against what you know to determine *if the answer makes sense.*

Practice

5. In pairs, students can review their work on the comprehension questions and revise any answers that are incorrect. They should not erase old work, but rather write the new answer beside it. Students should use the process you demonstrated. Have them follow the guidelines and complete the worksheet, "Guidelines for Answering Comprehension Questions," noting why they changed their answer. (Having students work in pairs will encourage them to discuss their answers and verbalize their thinking processes.)

Evaluation

6. Review students' work. Ask students to give their first and second answers and to explain why they changed their answers.

7. Ask students if and how the strategies of *using what you know* and *asking yourself if it makes sense* helped them and if they would use them again. Ask them to discuss difficulties they had using the strategies or suggestions for using it.

Expansion

8. For homework, assign another short text to read. Have students write comprehension questions and answer them on a separate piece of paper. In class the next day, have students exchange questions with a classmate and practice the strategies by completing the chart.

Contributed by Jennifer Delett

Guidelines for Answering Comprehension Questions

1 Find the question word in the question (who, what, where, when, why, or how) and write it here.

2 Identify what type of information you will need to find to answer the question (person, place, event, time, reason, or procedure), and write it down.

3 Scan the text for the answer to the question, and write it down.

4 Check your answer by comparing it to the question and asking if it makes sense.

QUESTION	QUESTION WORD	TYPE OF INFORMATION	ANSWER
Who did Kate meet on the bridge?	Who	person, name(s)	She met her uncle and father.

Preparing to Read

LANGUAGE LEVEL: Intermediate
GRADE LEVEL: High School

LANGUAGE: ESL
FOCUS LLS: Cooperation
REVIEW LLS: Using Background Knowledge

LANGUAGE OBJECTIVE: Discuss experiences with classmates to increase prior knowledge about a topic before reading

STRATEGY OBJECTIVE: Use the strategy of *cooperation* to share prior knowledge and prepare for a reading task

STRATEGY RATIONALE: Students who think about what they already know are better prepared for and more successful in their second language reading. Sharing prior experiences with classmates increases all students' background knowledge about a topic and therefore better prepares them for reading.

MATERIALS: Colored markers; graphic organizer consisting of a center circle and four smaller circles around the center circle (one for each student); student copies of the text; worksheet, "Group Report" (page 199)

PROCEDURES

Preparation 1

1. Ask students to consider what they do to prepare for a sporting event, such as a soccer match, or for a musical performance. Write all of their ideas on the board.

2. Ask students what they do to prepare for reading, and list those activities in a column next to the preparation strategies for sports or music. Encourage students to use the first list for ideas and to identify similarities.

"It is helpful to prepare before a race or a match to put forth your best effort. Preparing for reading in language is just as helpful."

Presentation 1

3. Review the strategy of *using background knowledge*. Tell students that they are going to practice the strategy for preparing to read in cooperative groups.

"How do you use the strategy *using background knowledge?* Why do you use this strategy?" (Thinking about what we already know about a topic helps us connect new ideas to what we know and to understand what we read.)

4. Demonstrate *using background knowledge* by displaying a graphic organizer consisting of a center circle and four smaller circles around the center circle. Write in the center circle the name of the story or book that your class has previously read. In each of the outer circles, write one of the four key concepts.

"I am going to demonstrate the strategy you are going to practice in groups. I am going to think aloud so you can hear what I am thinking as well as see what I am writing. I am going to think about one of the four important ideas and write what I am thinking about that idea. Let's see . . . wolf. Well, they look like dogs, but they are scary. I think they live in forests, and they eat rabbits. Wolves are often in fairy tales and folk tales. What else . . . they have long noses, whiskers. . . ."

5. After you think aloud, stop and ask students what you thought/wrote about. Then have students think about what they know about the second idea. Ask them to jot it down and share it with the class.

6. Explain that after they brainstorm alone, they will share their ideas with their groups. Emphasize the importance of discussing their ideas with their team members. (Model the discussion process for lower-level students.)

Preparation 2
7. Explain to students that they are going to practice *using background knowledge* in cooperative groups. Review the strategy of *cooperation*. Have students make a T-list on their papers and on the left side write "What I like about cooperative group work" and on the right side write "What is difficult about working in cooperative groups." Students write their comments individually and then share them with the class as you write them on the board.

Presentation 2
8. To make the activity cooperative, each person in the group has an essential role. This ensures that all students contribute to the success of the activity and that all students practice speaking and listening, and reading and writing. Before students form groups, review the roles:

- The timekeeper keeps time during the one-minute brainstorming sessions.
- The task master leads the discussion and directs the completion of the report.
- The note-taker fills in the report.
- The reporter reports the findings to the class.

"By working in groups, we learn about more ideas and add to our prior knowledge by sharing our ideas with others. You will evaluate your use of *cooperation* after the activity."

Practice
9. Divide students into groups of four. Give each student a colored marker and graphic organizer for the book the class is going to read. Students have one minute to think about and write down what they know about one of the four words. When the minute is over, students write about the second word. Each student writes about each of the four words. After four minutes, students discuss what they know in the group by completing the worksheet, "Group Report." After another four or five minutes, students report to the whole class.

Evaluation

10. After students have read the text, lead them in a discussion of the strategies they used.

"How did thinking about what you know about the topics help you read? Did it help you make predictions about the story? Would you use this strategy again?"

"How did your group work? Did you learn anything from your teammates? Did you find any other benefits of working together? What will you do differently next time?"

Expansion

11. Have students use *cooperation* again for another task, keeping in mind the suggestions and recommendations from the Evaluation phase. Have students keep a list of tasks for which they use *cooperation* and note how successful the strategy was for each task.

Suggestions for applications to other languages and levels:

- Have students identify the four concepts to brainstorm about by looking at the book's cover, title, chapter title, author, or any other readily available information, instead of having the teacher provide this information. This will give students more control and further develop their independent use of the strategies. For example, before reading the book *The Secret Soldier,* students might look at the title and select "soldier" as one idea to think about. They might see a picture of a war and select "war" as another idea.

- Have students complete a group report to evaluate their use of the strategy.

Contributed by Jennifer Delett

Group Report

Name of Book: _____

Author: _____

Group Members: _____

_____

_____

Background knowledge is what you already know about a topic. Talking about what you know about a topic will help you understand what you read. Work with your group to share what each of you already know about the topics we will read about in the book.

1 Compare what group members wrote for each topic.

_____

_____

_____

2 Choose one topic. What do all group members have in common about the topic? (For example, all group members have seen an elephant in the zoo.)

_____

_____

_____

3 What has one member learned or experienced that the others have not? (For example, one member did a report about elephants in school or one member learned to feed an elephant.)

_____

_____

_____

4 What was the most interesting thing your group talked about as you discussed each topic?

_____

_____

_____

Applying Rules When Reading

LANGUAGE LEVEL: Intermediate   **LANGUAGE:** Russian (can be adapted to any language)
GRADE LEVEL: High School   **FOCUS LLS:** Deduction

LANGUAGE OBJECTIVE: Read and understand a text

STRATEGY OBJECTIVE: Use *deduction* to apply language rules when reading to figure out what is being said in the text

STRATEGY RATIONALE: *Deduction* helps in comprehension of reading materials. Using rules already known increases self-reliance and confidence for completing the task.

MATERIALS: Excerpt on an overhead transparency from a student think-aloud interview illustrating *deduction;* any challenging reading text; one copy of Figure 4.8, "Learning Strategies Think-Aloud Record," (page 69) for each student

PROCEDURES

Preparation

1. Give students a sentence either in English or in the target language. The sentence should contain an invented word that could possibly occur in the language or a word that is new to students. Some example sentences in English could be: "The nitgak ate its meal quickly and then looked around for more." or "The birdiful chicken was browned to a nice honey color." Ask students how they might figure out the unknown words. In the examples given here, the words would be "nitgak" and "birdiful."

Presentation

2. Present the strategy *deduction* by asking for student responses to the unknown words.

"You didn't know the word in this sentence, but you were able to figure out "nitgak" was a noun and that it could be some kind of animal. How did you know "nitgak" was a noun?" (Students may respond that the article "the" gave them a clue and that "nitgak" was the subject of the sentence and came before the verb. The context might also have helped. Focus on the linguistic, grammatical clues that students give.)

3. Give an explicit presentation of the strategy.

"When you apply language rules to help you understand, you are using the strategy *deduction. Deduction* helps because you can use what you already know about the language to figure something out. We all know some grammar in our own language, and of course we study grammar when we learn another language. These rules can be of use to you."

4. Model using *deduction* by giving an example of how a student uses the strategy.

"I am going to give you an example of how a student just like you—same age group and studying Russian—uses *deduction* to understand what she is reading in Russian. This student is reading a sentence in Russian. [You write the sentence on the board.] This student did a think-aloud in which she recorded her thought processes on tape while she was reading. This is what she said about this sentence:

[Put the following tape transcript on an overhead transparency.]

It said something about her at the store. I'm not completely sure, but it says "store." I remember that's "buy." I looked at the end of the word "-la," and I remembered that that's like a form of the past tense. So I took that off and thought maybe I could figure out what the word is without it. And then you know all Russian verbs end with the same two letters, so I put that on, and it came out to be "buy."

5. Ask the students how the student in the think-aloud figured out the word "buy." Students may respond that she used the context because she recognized the word "store" and that she recognized the word was a verb because of its ending. She then used her knowledge of Russian verbs to figure out it was in the past tense. She took off the past tense marker and added the infinitive marker that all verbs have and was able to come up with the correct meaning.

Practice

6. Give students a reading passage in the target language and a think-aloud record. Divide them into groups of two, and have them do pair think-alouds. (See Chapters 4 and 5 for more information on how to conduct student think-alouds.)

"One student will say his or her thoughts aloud; in other words, how he or she is understanding while reading. The other student will write down any use of rules that he or she observes. After five minutes, you will switch roles. Be prepared to share your record sheets with the class."

Evaluation

7. Go over segments of the reading text as a whole class. Have students share their notes on their record sheets for different parts of the text. Note where students used similar and different language rules. Ask students if thinking about their language knowledge helps them understand.

Expansion

8. Have students keep a learning log in which they record their strategies for certain tasks. Ask them when they have found *deduction* to be helpful.

9. Have students think about other situations, besides language learning, in which they have used *deduction*. Point out that *deduction* can be applying any rule, not just linguistic rules. For example, mention how Sherlock Holmes might have used *deduction* to solve a mystery.

Contributed by Sarah Barnhardt

Learning Vocabulary

LANGUAGE LEVEL: Intermediate   **LANGUAGE:** ESL

GRADE LEVEL: High School+   **FOCUS LLS:** Grouping

LANGUAGE OBJECTIVE: Learn technical English vocabulary for computer applications (This lesson assumes that students have been taught and have been using a word processing application on a computer. Students are now learning an e-mail application.)

STRATEGY OBJECTIVE: Use *grouping* to facilitate learning and remembering new vocabulary

STRATEGY RATIONALE: Manipulating words in groups, mentally and on paper, provides memory links and maps the words onto students' background knowledge. Thinking about the words that are similar across computer applications and those that are unique to each application gives logical organizational structure to learning the vocabulary.

MATERIALS: Strategies questionnaire; worksheet, "English Vocabulary for Technology" (page 204); access to a computer lab

PROCEDURES

Preparation

1. Give students a strategies questionnaire that asks them to think about how they like to learn vocabulary for the technology part of the class.

"Today we are going to talk about the similarities and differences between e-mail and word processing. We are going to start by focusing on how we can learn the technical vocabulary associated with computers. Here's a questionnaire that will help you think about how you learn new words in English. Complete the questionnaire by numbering the strategies from 1 to 5, with 1 being your favorite strategy and 5 being your least favorite. Please write down any other strategies that you like to use. When you finish, share your answers with 2 or 3 of your classmates."

Sample items for the strategies questionnaire:

_____ I work together with a friend, and we sit at the computer to learn the new words.

_____ I put the new words on flash cards.

_____ I group the words by thinking about computer programs I already know.

_____ I think about the words while I work on the computer by myself.

_____ I draw pictures of the words.

Presentation

2. Present the strategy *grouping* by telling students why and when it is useful.

"Today we are going to look at the strategy *grouping*. *Grouping* helps you remember because you organize the vocabulary, and you have to think about how you organize it. *Grouping* can be especially useful with technology vocabulary. Here's an example of how I use *grouping*. I have been using computers for a while, and I know many types of programs. I notice that many of the words are the same in the different programs. For example, "print" is "print" in any program. If I had to learn these words in another language, I would try to group words that are the same across programs and those that are different or specific to each program. In this way, when I learn a new program I will know which words are new and which I need to study."

3. Demonstrate how you use *grouping* when learning new computer applications. Draw a table on the board using the same format as the worksheet, "English Vocabulary for Technology." Write "Word Processing" and "Spreadsheet" in the first column, under "Application."

"Let's say I know word processing well, but I am just learning spreadsheets. Some of the words that are the same for both programs are filename, print, scroll bars, save, open, copy, and paste. [Write these words in the chart in the third column, under "Similar Vocabulary."] Words that I have found in spreadsheets that are new are cell, formula, function, and range. [Write these words in the second column, under "Specific Vocabulary."] If I already remember and know a word from word processing, then I don't need to spend time studying it again. This makes me feel good because I already know something, and I can focus my attention on the new words."

Practice
4. Give students the worksheet, "English Vocabulary for Technology." Tell them that they are going to use the strategy, *grouping*, to sort the vocabulary that they learned a couple of weeks ago for word processing and the vocabulary they learned the day before for e-mail. Have them work in pairs. In the "Similar Vocabulary" column of the chart, have them list words that are found in both word processing and e-mail. Then have them write, in the column marked "Specific Vocabulary," those words that are found only in word processing and those that are found only in e-mail.

Evaluation
5. When students have finished, ask the pairs to share their charts with other pairs.

"When you have finished, share your chart with another pair to see if they have any words in addition to those you have. Did the other students put the words in the same groups as you did? Do you think organizing the vocabulary like this will help you study and learn it? Why? Can you think of other ways you could group the words?"

6. Give students time to study the words in the lab or at home. After a specified amount of time, give students a quiz on the vocabulary. After the quiz, ask students if they would use the strategy of *grouping* again.

Expansion
7. Enlarge the grouping chart by adding another row for the Internet. Have students fill in vocabulary that is similar and different for the Internet. Any other computer application can be used in place of the Internet.

Contributed by Sarah Barnhardt

English Vocabulary for Technology

WORD PROCESSING AND E-MAIL

STRATEGY Grouping—Organize the vocabulary for learning

Remember that many words will be the same across applications. If you already know and remember words from a previous application, then you can focus on learning the new vocabulary.

Directions Work with a partner. Fill in the chart with the vocabulary from word processing and e-mail applications.

APPLICATION	SPECIFIC VOCABULARY	SIMILAR VOCABULARY
Word Processing	Example: Bold	Example: Print
E-mail	Example: Send	

Identifying and Evaluating Strategies to Unlock the Meanings of New Words

LANGUAGE LEVEL: Intermediate
GRADE LEVEL: Middle School+

LANGUAGE: Any
FOCUS LLS: Evaluating Strategies

LANGUAGE OBJECTIVE: Read and understand a text selection
STRATEGY OBJECTIVE: Identify and *evaluate the strategies* that students are currently using to unlock the meanings of new words

STRATEGY RATIONALE: Students have knowledge about language and learning that they use to help them learn and remember new words. Teachers can help students improve their learning by encouraging them to identify and *evaluate the strategies* they are using to unlock the meanings of new words.

MATERIALS: An appropriate level reading; worksheet, "What Strategies Are You Using to Figure Out the Meanings of New Words?" (page 208)

PROCEDURES

Preparation

1. Students may be familiar with taking specific steps to solve a math or science problem, whereas they are less likely to be aware of steps for learning a language. Having students analyze these steps prompts them to think about their learning and to transfer the awareness of the process to language learning. Give the students a math problem to solve. Ask them to think about how they would solve the problem and to write down the procedure.

2. Discuss the steps as a class, and connect them to language learning.

"Do you ever think or talk about how you figure out the meanings of new words when you are reading? You are going to practice finding the meanings of new words in a reading passage, and you are going to think about the steps you take to find those meanings."

Presentation 1

3. Tell students that there are many ways to use what they already know about language and reading in order to understand the meanings of new words.

"You know about language and learning, and you can use what you know to learn and remember new words. I am sure that you are currently using one or more strategies to do this. Now you are going to read the passage in your text and underline the words that you do not know. Afterwards, you are going to work with a partner to find the meanings of the words that you underlined by using the text and what you already know."

4. Demonstrate the process. Put a section of the text that students will read on an overhead projector. Then, ask students to listen and watch as you think aloud how you would try to figure out the meanings of new words. (See Chapters 4 and 5 for information on thinking aloud.) Your think-aloud might sound like this:

"Okay, I am going to begin reading this text. *Kate crossed the bridge after midnight. She did not think she would see anyone.* Hmm, I do not know what this word is [underline *crossed*]. Let's see. Does it sound like any word in Spanish? Cross, *cruzar.* Maybe it means the same thing. Well, I know it is a verb because it ends in ed, so it's a past tense verb. So it could mean the same as *cruzar.* Kate crossed the bridge. Could it be the same as Kate walked over the bridge? . . ."

5. Ask students to explain what you did to figure out the meaning of the word "crossed." Discuss with the class the different strategies you used: *transfer/cognates, prior knowledge* of the language, and rereading the sentences and *making inferences* from the context. (This presentation focuses on identifying strategies; later in this lesson, you will demonstrate the evaluation of strategies.) During the lesson, encourage students to focus on how they learn new words, not just on the new meanings.

Practice
6. Have students read part or all of the text and underline new words. Pair students, and ask them to use the strategies they know to find the meanings of the new words. Have students take turns using the think-aloud technique you modeled. While one student is working, the other takes notes on the student's thinking process. After the students have worked on several words, have the pairs review their strategies by using the worksheet, "What Strategies Are You Using to Figure Out the Meanings of New Words?" Ask each pair to complete their worksheet, listing the new word in the "New Word" column and what they did to find the meaning of the word in the "What Did You Do to Find Out the Meaning?" column.

Presentation 2
7. Model the *evaluating strategies* for the students.

"When I tried to find the meaning of the word "crossed" in the story, I first tried to see if the word was a cognate because that was the easiest strategy for me to think of. Then I read and reread the word to see if I recognized any part of the word—the prefix or suffix—and tried to determine what part of speech it was. Finally, I reread the sentences around the word to see if I could get the meaning from context. I used several strategies to unlock the meaning of the word. I think I was successful because I got an idea of what the word meant and I could continue reading for comprehension."

Evaluation

8. After your modeling, ask the pairs to *evaluate the strategies* each used by indicating in the "Was It Successful?" column of the chart whether the strategy was successful, somewhat successful, or not too successful.

9. After students have reviewed their strategies in pairs, discuss the strategies as a group. Have the class discuss the strategies they used and evaluate their effectiveness. At this time, you can give names to the strategies that students used. (For example, *cognates, inferencing,* and *prior knowledge.* See the list of strategies in Chapter 2.) The following questions will get students to think more critically about what they learned and, more important, how they learn. (As you discuss different strategies, be clear and consistent about strategy names and definitions.)

"Did the strategy work? Why did it work? What new strategies did you learn? What, if anything, will you do differently when you encounter new words in a text? How do you know what strategy to use and when?"

Expansion

10. For homework, ask students to continue reading the text and keep a log of the strategies they use when they encounter new words. After they have done this, ask them to evaluate the strategies. Did the strategies help them understand the text and learn the meanings of new words? What other strategies might they use?

Contributed by Jennifer Delett

What Strategies Are You Using to Figure Out the Meanings of New Words?

Directions Use the think-aloud technique to find what strategies you are using to figure out the meanings of new words. Read a section of the story, and then think aloud. Your partner will write down what you are doing to learn the new word. Then you will do the same for your partner as he or she reads. Use the following space to take notes.

STUDENT 1 NOTES

_____
_____
_____
_____
_____
_____
_____
_____

STUDENT 2 NOTES

_____
_____
_____
_____
_____
_____
_____
_____

Directions Complete the chart. Write the new word in the first column and what you did in the second column. Use the third column to assess your strategies use.

NEW WORD	WHAT DID YOU DO TO FIND OUT THE MEANING?	WAS IT SUCCESSFUL?
Crossed	Used context	Successful

Reading a Russian Fairy Tale

LANGUAGE LEVEL: Advanced

GRADE LEVEL: High School

LANGUAGE: Russian (can be adapted to any language)

FOCUS LLS: Prediction/Verification through Summarizing

REVIEW LLS: Using Background Knowledge

LANGUAGE OBJECTIVE: Read a fairy tale in the target language and retell the main ideas

STRATEGY OBJECTIVE: Use *prediction* and *verification through summarizing* to prepare for and check understanding of a reading text

STRATEGY RATIONALE: *Prediction* helps the student prepare for the task because the student recalls relevant background knowledge about the topic. The student can then evaluate the accuracy of his or her expectations through verification. Both *verification* and *summarizing* help reinforce understanding of the information.

MATERIALS: A Russian fairy tale; vocabulary list; worksheet, "Prediction and Verification through Summarizing" (page 212)

PROCEDURES

Preparation

1. Begin the lesson by leading a discussion about reading different genres, such as social satire, horror, comedy, mystery, and romance. The discussion can be among the whole class or small groups/pairs who then share summaries of the discussion with the class. In the discussions, ask students to talk about what they do to help themselves read different genres. Ask students to focus on what they do to help themselves understand before, during, and after reading. Encourage students to discuss their approaches to reading different genres in their native languages.

2. As students share their strategy techniques, you can make a list of strategies on the board for each of the genres. Add an evaluative component by asking students why they feel a strategy is useful for a particular genre or for all genres. Discuss how genres and students' knowledge of them influences their expectations when reading. Conclude by telling students that they have come up with a lot of useful strategies.

"Today, the class is going to look at a Russian fairy tale and practice a few strategies that are very useful when reading this and other genres."

Presentation 1

3. Present and demonstrate the strategy *prediction* by modeling it in a reading context. Provide information necessary for explicit instruction by naming and defining the strategy and explaining why and when *prediction* is useful.

"When I read, I try to think about what I am going to be reading before I start. So, for example, if I know I am going to be reading a mystery, I think about what kinds of characters and ideas might be in the story. There are going to be good guys and bad guys. The good guy may be a detective. There is going to be some kind of problem—the bad guy has probably caused some sort of trouble. The good guy is going to spend most of the story trying to solve the mystery, and in the end, he will succeed. The bad guy will eventually get just punishment. Usually, there is some romantic involvement with the "good guy" that also has a happy ending."

4. Ask students to comment on your think-aloud of using the strategy *prediction.*

"Do you think my predictions were good? Would you make different predictions? Do you think it's possible that the genre could have another structure in a different culture? *Prediction* is a strategy we use before we start reading so that we can think about what we are going to read. I think it's useful because it helps me get ready. It also makes me feel like I am part of the story, and that helps me read. Why do you think this is a useful strategy? What do you think you need to think about in order to make appropriate predictions?"

Practice 1
5. Give students practice using *prediction* by asking them to predict when reading a fairy tale. Ask students to use their knowledge of all fairy tales to make general predictions about the Russian fairy tale.

"Now we are going to read a Russian fairy tale. I want you to use *prediction* so you think about what is going to happen in this tale before we actually read it. First, we will make general predictions because we don't have any information about the tale yet. Think of all of the fairy tales you have read so you can think about what you know about fairy tales. This will help you make good predictions. Let's predict the kinds of characters we might find in the fairy tale." (Students might respond with any of the following: kings, princes, princesses, witches, fairies, animals, children, and so on.)

6. Give students a worksheet or write on the board the title of the fairy tale, a list of characters, and any key vocabulary in the story. Ask them to predict the beginning, middle, and end of the fairy tale based on the information they have. Depending on students' language level, they can write their predictions in the target language or their native language.

"You now have more information about the tale. Why do you think this additional information will help you make better predictions about the story? You probably have some ideas as to what the story will be about. In the worksheet, "Prediction and Verification through Summarizing," under the column, "Predictions Before Reading," write your predictions about what you expect will happen in the beginning, middle, and end of the tale."

Presentation 2
7. Hand out the fairy tale to students. Before students begin reading, introduce the strategy *verification through summarizing* so students can follow through on their predictions and evaluate their comprehension.

"It's not enough to just make predictions. You also need to think about the accuracy of your predictions. *Verifying your predictions* helps you think about how well your knowledge matches the information in the text. This is useful because if your predictions are correct, then you have evidence that you understood what you read. However, if your predictions are not correct, then you might want to check your understanding and think about why your predictions are inaccurate so that you can make better predictions next time. *Verifying predictions* can be done by *summarizing* what you have read. By restating the main ideas of what you read, you can decide how well you understood and can help yourself remember the information." (Assure students that inaccurate predictions are not "wrong answers." They are just a way of helping them think about and understand a story.)

Practice 2
8. Have students practice *verification of their predictions by summarizing* events in the story.

"Read the fairy tale. After you have finished reading, complete the column in the chart labeled "Summaries After Reading" by writing summaries of what actually happened in the beginning, middle, and end of the story."

Evaluation
9. Ask students to share their predictions and summaries for the beginning, middle, and end of the tale.

"Did your predictions match your summaries? How were they similar? How were they different? If there were differences, why do you think this happened? Were your predictions and summaries similar or different from other classmates' predictions and summaries? How do you think you could improve the accuracy of your predictions next time? Do you feel you understood the story? Could you summarize the story for yourself or someone else? Do you think *prediction* and *verification through summarizing* helped your comprehension of the story? What role did the genre of fairy tales play in the ease and success with which you made predictions? Would you use the strategy differently with another genre?"

Expansion
10. As a homework assignment or in the next class, have students apply the strategies *prediction* and *verification through summarizing* to another fairy tale. This will help them to increase their accuracy of predicting for fairy tales. If you want them to broaden their use of *prediction* and *verification,* have them apply the strategies to a story of a different genre. The strategy can also be used with a listening activity.

Contributed by Sarah Barnhardt

Prediction and Verification through Summarizing

DIrections Before reading the fairy tale, write, in the "Predictions Before Reading" column, predictions of what you think will happen in the beginning, middle, and end of the tale based on the information your teacher gives you.

After reading the fairy tale, verify your predictions by writing in the "Summaries After Reading" column, summaries of events in the beginning, middle, and end of the tale. How do your summaries compare with your predictions? Note the accuracy in the last column.

GENRE: FAIRY TALE TITLE OF STORY:	PREDICTIONS BEFORE READING	SUMMARIES AFTER READING	VERIFICATION OF PREDICTIONS (HOW ACCURATE WERE THEY?)
IN THE BEGINNING			
IN THE MIDDLE			
IN THE END			

Using Storytelling to Teach Imagery

LANGUAGE LEVEL: Beginning   **LANGUAGE:** ESL

GRADE LEVEL: Elementary   **FOCUS LLS:** Imagery

LANGUAGE OBJECTIVE: Listen to and recall the story in preparation to retell it

STRATEGY OBJECTIVE: Use imagery to understand and recall the story

STRATEGY RATIONALE: Forming mental images or drawing pictures helps one remember the information or story plot. Linking pictures to events is a natural and fun way to learn. Even as early as elementary school, students can use and discuss the strategy of *imagery*.

MATERIALS: None

PROCEDURES

Preparation

1. Gather students in a circle on the floor, and introduce the story you are going to tell. Make sure to tap into students' *background knowledge,* and encourage *predictions* about the story. Before you begin, ask students what they will do to remember the story. Write ideas on the board, and comment positively about them.

Presentation 1

2. As you begin to tell the story, ask students to close their eyes and listen. Stop at an appropriate spot in the story, and ask students what they imagine the characters are doing in the scene. For example, you might ask, "Does anyone see a picture of the scene? What do you think the characters look like? What do you see?" Ask volunteers to respond by describing what they see. Tell students that they are using a learning strategy called *imagery,* or making pictures.

"You are using a very good strategy to remember the story by making these pictures. It is called *imagery.* Can you say that word? Imagery. Imagery means making pictures. [Write "imagery" and "making pictures" on the board.] You all made pictures in your minds when I was telling you the story. Why did you do that? [Write down their comments, and respond positively to them.] I also use the strategy of making pictures because it helps me remember things that I hear, read, or study. The clearer I make the image, the better I remember."

3. Demonstrate the strategy. As you continue the story, describe what you are seeing in your mind.

Practice 1

4. As you continue the story, encourage students to practice using the strategy.

"As I tell the story, I want you to practice the strategy of *imagery.* I will stop to ask you what pictures you have made in your head."

5. At another appropriate place in the story, stop and ask students for their images. Finish the story in this fashion, asking students for their images when the opportunity allows it.

"What images do you have in your mind? Has anything changed from the first time?"

Presentation 2

6. After reading the story, draw a quick sketch of your mental image to demonstrate how drawing is also part of the strategy.

"I can also make my images on paper to help me remember the story. I am going to draw a few pictures to remind me of the most important things that happened in the story."

Practice 2

7. Have students work in groups to draw pictures that will help them remember the story. Later that day, or the next day, have students retell the story again, using their drawings.

Evaluation

8. Once you have finished reading the story, begin your discussion by asking several students to retell the story. (Focusing on the *imagery* should help students to report more detailed accounts of the story.) During or after your discussion of the story, hold a discussion about strategy use. Ask students to raise their hands if making the pictures helped them remember the story. Ask them to raise their hands if they would use the strategy again.

Expansion

9. Discuss with the students other contexts in which they can use the strategy. For example, if students are reading in English or their first language, tell them that they can use this strategy when they read on their own. They can also use the strategy when learning vocabulary.

10. Ask students to use the strategy of *imagery* at home as they have a family member tell them a story. Tell them that they can make pictures in their minds or on paper. The next day, they will share their stories with their classmates.

Suggestions for applications to other languages and levels:

This strategy can be used with any language or level. For older and more advanced students, focus on how to transfer the strategy from a storytelling situation to a reading or listening situation.

Contributed by Jennifer Delett

Finding the Meaning from the Text

LANGUAGE LEVEL: Intermediate
LANGUAGE: Any
GRADE LEVEL: Middle School+
FOCUS LLS: Inferencing; Using Resources

LANGUAGE OBJECTIVE: Read and comprehend a text
STRATEGY OBJECTIVE: Use the strategy of *inferencing* to unlock the meanings of new words while reading, and apply the strategy of *using resources* to verify guesses

STRATEGY RATIONALE: Students often become dependent on dictionaries for looking up new words as they read. This strategy, used alone, can slow them down and lead them to incorrect definitions. Often, the information that students need is available if they look at other parts of the task and at their own resources. Guessing the meaning of unfamiliar words can help them quickly solve problems without their having to go to other people or reference material. Students can use resources to verify their guesses.

MATERIALS: Sample text on an overhead

PROCEDURES

Preparation

1. Give students a text, and have them scan through and jot down all new words.

2. Then, ask them how they would normally find the meanings of these words, and list their strategies on the board.

Presentation

3. Introduce students to the strategy *inferencing*.

"You have come up with a lot of different ways that you can find the meanings of new words while you are reading. It is important to begin to use strategies that rely on your own resources. One strategy that I like to use is called *inferencing*, or using the context. I like this strategy because it makes learning new words seem like a puzzle. While I am reading, I use all of the information, such as other sentences, pictures, and captions to help me unlock the meaning of the new word. I usually can guess at the meaning by using what I know about the word, the pictures, or the context of the story. Then, if necessary, I *use my resources,* such as the dictionary or asking someone else to check my guess."

4. Put a page from the text on the overhead projector and model the strategy *inferencing*.

"I am going to show you how to use the strategy *inferencing*. One word that I underlined was 'ducked.' Let's see if I can figure out what that word means. First, I read the whole sentence: 'Allen ducked behind the wood pile so that the men would not see him.' I also look at the picture. In the picture, Allen is hiding behind a pile of wood. Men are on the other side. I guess that 'duck' might mean 'hide.' That would make sense in the sentence: 'Allen hid behind the wood pile so that the men would not see him'."

5. Review with the students the strategy you used.

"I use the strategy *inferencing* by relying on the information I understood in the story, the picture and the other words and sentence, to guess the meaning of the word. I was pretty sure that I was correct, but if I was not sure, I could ask someone or look for the word in the dictionary to check the meaning. But, it's best to try to understand the context first before looking up the word so that you can locate the correct meaning."

Practice

6. Have students work in pairs to use *inferencing* to find the meanings of the words on their list of new words from the text. Students fill in a chart. In column one, "New Word," students write the word. In column two, "What Do You Think the Word Means?", they write their guess. In column three, "How Did You Guess the Meaning?", they write how they made the guess. In column four, "What Resources Did You Use to Check the Meaning?", they write the resource they used to check the meaning, if it was necessary.

Evaluation

7. Have students share answers from the worksheet as a class and discuss how they made their guesses.

"Did *inferencing* help you while reading? Would you use *inferencing* in the future before asking the teacher or using the dictionary? When did you decide to *use resources* and how did that help you check the meaning?

Expansion

8. Assign additional reading from the text for homework. Students should use *inferencing* on their own while reading and then write a reflection to evaluate their success with the strategy. Have students answer some or all of the following questions in the reflection.

- How often did you use *inferencing* while you were reading? (Write the words you used *inferencing* with.)
- What did you use to make your inferences? (pictures, other sentences)
- How successful was the strategy for you?
- What other strategies did you use? (using resources, asking someone else)
- Was the strategy helpful?
- Will you use the strategy again?

Contributed by Jennifer Delett

Writing Folk Tales

LANGUAGE LEVEL: Intermediate+   **LANGUAGE:** ESL

GRADE LEVEL: High School   **FOCUS LLS:** Organizational Planning; Self-Management

LANGUAGE OBJECTIVE: Identify the components of a folk tale (theme, characters, events) and understand and use the four stages of writing (planning, composing, revising, editing)

STRATEGY OBJECTIVE: Use *organizational planning* to identify and group the components of a folk tale and prepare to write, and use *self-management* to plan and manage your time as you write

MATERIALS: Poster of self-management strategies; worksheet, "Are You Your Own Boss?" (page 220)

PROCEDURES

Preparation

1. Elicit students' current procedures and strategies for planning before writing. Write a list of ideas on the board.

"You have been reading many folk tales. Now, you are going to write your own folk tale. What ideas do you have for how you will prepare to write your story? What will you do before you write? [List student's ideas.] How did you come up with the ideas? What makes you think that?" (In this way, focus is on students' thought processes and reflection is encouraged.)

Presentation 1

2. Explain the four stages of writing: planning, composing, revising, and editing. Tell students that they are going to focus on planning and that you are going to share another strategy with them to help them plan their writing.

"Before we write our folk tales, we are going to use a strategy called *organizational planning* to prepare to write. Planning before writing gives you direction for the task and helps you make sure you will complete the task. It also builds your confidence because you have control of the process. *Organizational planning* can be, for example, brainstorming and grouping your ideas to use in the task."

3. Introduce the story map as a graphic organizer for planning to write.

"We have used story maps to understand folk tales. Now we are going to use a story map as an organizer to help us plan to write folk tales. A graphic organizer helps us organize our thoughts and organize our writing."

4. Demonstrate the strategy by partially completing a story map like the one on page 218 for your own story.

"I'm going to demonstrate how to use the strategy as I plan for my own folk tale. Let's see . . . I want to begin with the theme, or the message to the reader. My theme will be 'the good person always wins.' I am going to write this in the center circle of the story map, where it says theme. The theme is the guide for the rest of my planning. Next, I will think of my characters. I think there will be a wolf and a rabbit. Now I need to fill in some of the main events—what will happen at the beginning, middle, and end of the story. Now that I have completed the organizer, I have a map of where my story will go. I have a plan for writing."

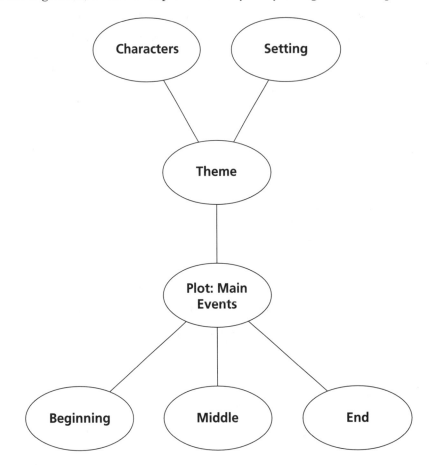

Practice 1

5. Have students complete a story map for their folk tales. Students may work in groups to share ideas and help each other. When students are finished, have pairs exchange their story maps and check that they are complete.

Presentation 2

6. When students are ready to write, introduce the next stage of the process—writing—and another strategy to use during the writing stage—*self-management*. Have students brainstorm about *self-management,* and list their ideas on the board.

"What do you think *self-management* means? What does a manager of a store or business do?" (Examples: hires people, helps workers, oversees or checks on people's work, makes sure people come to work on time and that they get paid, supports workers) "You might do some of these things for yourself. Do you ever manage yourself? For example, you might have to manage your time: getting up on time for school, getting to class on time, getting to work on time, and making time for your homework."

7. Define and explain *self-management*. Display the self-management strategies poster.

"*Self-management* means arranging conditions to help yourself learn. This includes managing and monitoring yourself during a learning task or assignment. Looking out for yourself and managing your learning will help you perform best. Here are some self-management strategies you can use when writing."

- Check on yourself—Watch the time. Know that you need to get the job done, so you should not spend too much time on any single part of it.

- Get right to the job—Go right to work and right to English without translating.

- Limit your breaks—Stay focused and limit distractions that could keep you from getting your work done.

- Support yourself—Tell yourself that you have great ideas and that you know a lot of English. Use what you know and write as much as you can. Then revise and edit later.

Practice 2
8. Have students begin to write their stories. Remind them to use their story maps to guide them as they write. Pass out the worksheet, "Are You Your Own Boss?", and instruct students to make a check mark each time they use one of the strategies.

Evaluation
9. After students have written their first draft, have them review their self-management checklist and their story maps. Have students evaluate their strategies use by answering some questions.

"Do you think the strategies of *organizational planning* and *self-management* helped you get the job done on time? Were you able to stay focused? Were you able to work in English? Do you think you will use these strategies the next time you write?"

Expansion
10. Have students develop a list of other tasks for which they can use either *self-management* or *organizational planning*. Write the list on the board. Ask each student to try each strategy in one of the suggested areas.

11. As students revise their stories, ask them how they will use the two strategies. (For example, for *organizational planning* they might come up with a plan for how they will revise their stories or they might revise their story maps. Then they might use the *self-management* strategies to help them finish their final drafts.)

Contributed by Allison Copeland and Jennifer Delett

Are You Your Own Boss?

USING SELF-MANAGEMENT IN WRITING

Directions Make a check mark in the appropriate box each time you use one of the self-management strategies.

SELF-MANAGEMENT STRATEGIES	1	2	3	4	EVALUATE: DID IT HELP YOU?
Check on yourself Manage your time.					
Get right to the job Work and write in English without translating.					
Limit your breaks Stay focused and eliminate distractions.					
Support yourself Tell yourself that you have great ideas. Write as much as you can, and edit later.					

A Person You'll Never Forget

LANGUAGE LEVEL: Intermediate
GRADE LEVEL: Middle School+

LANGUAGE: ESL
FOCUS LLS: Personalization; Note-Taking

LANGUAGE OBJECTIVE: Understand and remember a story and organize information
STRATEGY OBJECTIVE: Use the strategy of *personalization* to understand and remember a story and to remember and use new descriptive vocabulary

STRATEGY RATIONALE: Connecting information to your experiences makes it more meaningful to you and thus more memorable.

MATERIALS: Graphic organizer, "The Person I Will Never Forget" (page 223)

PROCEDURES

Preparation

1. Ask students what strategies they use to remember when they read, both in their native language and in the target language. Write those strategies on the board.

"When you listen to or read a story, what things do you do to help you understand the story?"

Presentation

2. Introduce and discuss the strategy of *personalization* for remembering new information.

"I want to share with you a new strategy for remembering information from a story. I like to use a strategy called *personalization. Personalization* means connecting the new information to your own experience. Doing this makes the information more meaningful to you and therefore more memorable. Use this strategy any time you want to remember new information that seems difficult to remember."

3. Model the strategy of *personalization* using the characters from a story that students have read.

"I will demonstrate the strategy *personalization* using an example from the story we just read, 'Grandma and Me.' We will use a graphic organizer to organize our ideas. First I will fill out the graphic organizer about Grandma, then I will do the same for my grandmother. I will begin by writing 'Grandma' in the center circle. Then I will brainstorm Grandma's qualities in the upper left corner box. Let's see, I am going to look back through the book for some ideas. She was kind, old, forgiving, small, quiet, liked dogs, liked strawberries. . . . Next, I will list reasons why the boy won't forget her in the bottom left corner box. Well, she forgave the boy even when he made a mistake. She was never angry with him, and she always loved him. She gave him a special gift."

"Now, to remember the story, I will use the strategy *personalization*. I will make a personal connection between the story and my life by completing another organizer about my grandmother, someone whom I will never forget. Well, first I will write 'My Grandmother' in the center circle. Then I will write her qualities in the upper left box. She is old, strong, healthy, hard-working, funny, and fun to be with. Next, I will list the reasons why I will never forget her. Well, she taught me about cooking and baking; she told me stories about her family; and she gave me her wedding dress."

Practice

4. Have students use the graphic organizer to practice *personalization.*

"I want you to use the same organizer to brainstorm about someone you will never forget. It could be your grandmother or someone else special to you. Doing this will help you make a connection between the story and your life and will help you remember the story."

Evaluation

5. A few days later, ask students to recall and retell the story. Afterwards, ask students if they thought that making a personal connection to the story helped them remember it.

Expansion

6. Students can also use *personalization* to remember new vocabulary. They can brainstorm a list of adjectives to describe people. Students then use some of the words to describe the person they will never forget. By making a personal connection with the word to a person they know, they will be more likely to remember the word.

Contributed by Karisa Tashjian and Jennifer Delett

The Person I Will Never Forget

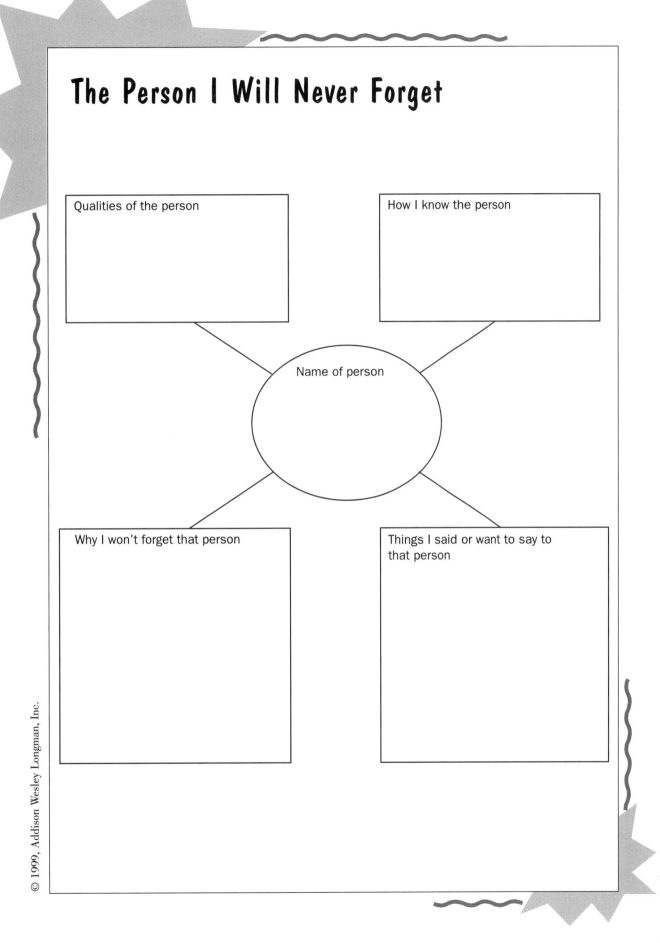

Qualities of the person

How I know the person

Name of person

Why I won't forget that person

Things I said or want to say to that person

Predicting with Storytelling

LANGUAGE LEVEL: Any

GRADE LEVEL: Elementary+

LANGUAGE: ESL/FL

FOCUS LLS: Prediction

LANGUAGE OBJECTIVE: Recall and retell a story

STRATEGY OBJECTIVE: Use the strategy *prediction* to focus on and recall the events in a story

STRATEGY RATIONALE: Anticipating what might happen next helps readers focus on the important events in a story to see if their predictions were correct. Revising predictions based on what actually happens in a story keeps readers engaged in thoughtful reading.

MATERIALS: Story script of "The Tailor" (page 226)

PROCEDURES

Preparation 1

1. Ask students what strategies they use to comprehend when they read, both in their native language and in the target language. Encourage students to share their strategies, and write those strategies on the board.

"When you listen to or read a story, what things do you do to help yourself understand the story?"

2. Present typical story scenarios to students, and ask them to predict what will happen. Wait for responses after each scenario, and write ideas on the board.

"We are going to listen to and retell a story, and while we retell the story, we are going to practice a strategy that you can use while you are reading folk tales on your own. Think for a minute . . . if you are reading a story about a young girl and a prince, what do you think will happen in the story? If you are reading a story about a boy who goes fishing and catches a small fish and eats it, then catches a bigger fish and eats it, and then catches an even bigger fish, what do you think the boy will do?"

Presentation

3. Discuss the strategy of *prediction,* which will be illustrated and practiced during the storytelling.

"What are you doing when you answer my questions? You predict based on what you know about the story or other stories like it. *Prediction* is an effective strategy you can use before and during reading to help you look for and remember information you are expecting. For example, you expected the young girl to marry the prince. So, when you read the story, you would be reading to see if she did. Predicting based on the patterns in the story helps you check to see if the story makes sense. It also makes the story more meaningful and easier to remember because you connect it to something you already know, like a similar story." (You may also want to demonstrate how to predict, if you feel it is necessary.)

Preparation 2

4. Activate students' *background knowledge* about tailors.

"We are going to tell a story about a man who makes clothing for other people. He is called a tailor. Do you sew, or do you know someone who sews? Is there a tailor in your neighborhood?"

Practice 1

5. Conduct the storytelling session, having students practice the strategy of *prediction*. Tell students that they will practice retelling the story when you are finished.

"We are going to listen to and retell a story called "The Tailor." Before and during the story, I am going to remind you to make predictions and check your predictions. I am also going to ask you to tell me why you made the predictions and what information in the story helped you make the predictions."

(During the story, give students time to predict where there are predictable actions or language. Encourage predictions by providing long pauses, using proper intonation, and acknowledging predictions.)

Practice 2

6. Have students retell the story in groups of three or four. Encourage students to focus on their predictions to help them remember the events in the story.

Evaluation

7. Help students evaluate their use of the strategy *prediction*. Lead students in a discussion about how they used the strategy during storytelling and how they could use the same strategy during reading.

"While listening to the story, did you make predictions? When did you make predictions? Why did you make predictions? Many of you naturally made predictions based on what you knew or what you heard. The story had a pattern, and you used the pattern to help you understand the story. What were some of the patterns? (For example, language: old and worn, cut and sew; actions: went back to his shop and came out with something smaller.) Did the strategy help you to understand and retell the story?"

Expansion

8. Have students apply *prediction* to a reading text and then report on their experiences.

"Do you ever predict when you read on your own? When you read a story tonight, predict what you think will happen. Use what has happened in the story, but also use your knowledge of other stories. Write down what you predicted and why so that we can discuss it tomorrow. Think about how this helped you to understand the story."

Contributed by Jennifer Delett

The Tailor

The tailor is a very poor man who is always busy making beautiful clothes for his customers. He never has time or money to make clothes for himself, although he really wants to. One evening, he goes to the back of his shop and he finds just enough material to make himself a beautiful coat. He wears the coat proudly all over town. One day, he realizes that the coat is getting old and worn. He is sad to part with the special gift he has given himself. So, he decides to make it into a fine jacket. So he cuts and sews and makes himself a beautiful little jacket. He wears his jacket proudly all over town. But, one day the tailor realizes that his jacket, too, is getting old and worn. Again, he feels sad to get rid of his special gift. Only the sleeves are frayed, so he decides to make it into a vest. So he cuts and sews and makes himself a beautiful vest. He wears the vest proudly all over town. Every time he wears it, it reminds him of his coat and his jacket. However, as time passes he realizes the vest, too, is getting old and worn. Once more, reluctant to part with the vest, the clever and creative tailor goes into his shop and cuts and sews. Soon he emerges with a hat made of the same material as the coat, the jacket, and the vest. Again, he wears the hat proudly all over town. In time, the hat too gets old and worn. Now the tailor is really sad, but being the resourceful person that he is, and being reluctant to part with his gift, once more he returns to his shop. When he finally emerges for the last time, he is holding something very small in his hand. It is a button, but it is not just a button. It is a whole lot more. Whenever he looks at the button, he sees the hat, the vest, the jacket, and the coat, and he thinks of all the wonderful memories of that special gift he gave himself so long ago.

Presenting Oral Reports on Science Projects

LANGUAGE LEVEL: Intermediate
GRADE LEVEL: Middle School+

LANGUAGE: Content-Based ESL (Science)
FOCUS LLS: Evaluate Yourself (Self-Assessment),
Take Notes, Selective Attention,
Talk Yourself Through It

LANGUAGE OBJECTIVES: Name and listen for important elements in an oral report. Identify and summarize essential information and vocabulary from an oral report. Attend to essential information and vocabulary when presenting an oral report

STRATEGY OBJECTIVES: Self- and peer-assess oral reports, identify and attend to keywords, summarize information on note cards, and self-talk to allay presentation anxiety

STRATEGY RATIONALE: These lessons exemplify multi-strategy applications. Combining several strategies over three days shows students how strategies can help accomplish a complex task.

MATERIALS: Student science boards describing projects they have completed; ruled index cards; highlighters in three colors; sample index cards

PROCEDURES

Day 1: Introduction of Self-Assessment

Preparation

1. Ask students the following questions.

"What experiences have you had with oral reports in other classes? Why is it important to be able to give a good oral report? What might be difficult about giving an oral report? What do you like about giving an oral report?"

2. Have two volunteers from mainstream classes (considered to be good presenters) present their science projects.

"What did each student do well? How might he or she improve?"

3. Brainstorm the elements of a good oral report (an introduction, a loud and clear voice, eye contact, saying the steps in order, a closing, and so on). Write ideas on the board.

4. Create an assessment checklist that contains the criteria that students (and you) deem important to remember in an oral presentation. Following is a sample checklist.

- Did the student say his or her name and the name of the project?
- Did the student speak loudly and clearly?
- Did the student look (mostly) at the audience?

- Did the student say the steps of the scientific process (Problem, Hypothesis, Materials, Procedure, Results, Conclusion)?
- Did the student say "Thank you" and "Any questions?"
- What could the presenter do to improve his or her oral report?

Presentation

5. Tell the students that they are going to learn the strategy *self-assessment*.

"Being able to review your work to see what you did well is an important part of learning. It is important to know what you did well so that you can repeat your good work in the future. It is also important to be able to determine what you might improve. This strategy is called *self-assessment*. Today we are going to practice *self-assessment* by first assessing me when I give an oral presentation, and then by assessing your classmates. Then you will assess your own presentations when you practice in groups and at home."

6. Model a good oral report on a science project. Think aloud about the elements (criteria) the students brainstormed to determine if you did them in your presentation.

7. Pass out the assessment checklist you created, and check the criteria together.

Practice

8. Have students work in groups of three to present their oral reports. Have them use the assessment checklist to assess each other.

Evaluation

9. Ask students to present their reports in front of a mirror at home for practice. Tell them to complete a checklist about themselves when they finish.

Day 2: Introduction of Note-Taking and Selective Attention

Preparation

10. Ask students to tell you the criteria they used to assess the oral presentations. Have volunteers share a review of the presentations they did for homework and their checklists, discussing any elements they wish to improve. Discuss possible solutions with the class.

Presentation

11. Model an oral report that misses some of the elements. In particular, omit and mix up some of the steps in the science experiment.

12. Have students complete the checklist. When you get to the last question (What could the presenter do to improve his or her oral report?), help students identify the problem you had including all of the steps in order. Ask students if they noticed the same problem in the presentations of some of their classmates or in their own oral presentations.

13. Brainstorm ways to help get organized and remember the project. Suggest that in order to help them remember, students could take notes on the important ideas and vocabulary they will use when presenting their reports. Tell students that they will be practicing two strategies now: *selective attention* and *note-taking*.

"With the strategy *selective attention,* you attend to keywords. By attending to special information, you limit the number of things you write down on your index cards so you don't end up reading your report. Writing down these words is called *note-taking.* You take notes in many ways for many purposes. (Have students offer instances of note-taking). In this case, you write down select words to help spark your memory when you present your oral report."

14. Provide students with sample index cards containing notes about their project. Model how to determine important information and words as you complete these cards.

"On my note cards I might include such things as transitional words (for example, first, second, then, example, finally), science vocabulary (such as milliliters, graduated cylinder, subtracted, hypothesis, results, procedures), or important phrases (such as 'My hypothesis was supported.' 'Thank you. Any questions?')."

15. Model how to glance at your index cards for information as you present an oral report. Ask why it is important not to look at the index cards during the entire report.

Practice

16. Give each student two index cards. Have them copy the information from the sample cards. Help them identify the important information for their project.

17. When they have completed their index cards, give students different colored highlighters. Have them highlight different parts of their project in colors (for example, Steps in pink; Procedure in yellow; Science words/keywords in red). Tell students that this will help draw their attention to the important information when they glance at their cards while presenting.

18. Have students work in their groups again, this time, using their newly created index cards to help them remember their procedures. Ask them to complete checklists about their peers.

Evaluation

19. Ask students the following questions. Remind them of the two strategies they used.

"Did the index cards help you? Did the members of your group do better with or without the index cards?"

20. Have students present their reports at home and complete a checklist about themselves.

Day 3: Introduction of Self-Talk

Preparation

21. Ask students to recall the lessons and strategies from the previous two days.

22. Have volunteers describe their assessment of the oral reports they conducted at home the night before.

Presentation

23. Have students discuss their feelings about giving an oral report. When some describe feeling nervous, ask, "Do you feel less nervous now that you have practiced and created note cards?" Explain that most people feel less nervous when they feel well prepared.

24. Brainstorm ways in which the students can feel less nervous. (Imagine you are at home in front of your mirror, use an internal voice to tell yourself that you are doing a good job, think of a friend in the audience who is supporting you, and so on.) Write student suggestions for alleviating nervousness on the board.

25. Introduce students to the strategy *talk yourself through it* or *self-talk.*

"Making positive statements such as 'I can do it' can help you complete a difficult task. Reassuring yourself during a difficult task, like a presentation, can help you be less nervous."

26. Have students select the tactic they will use to help them feel less nervous when they present their reports. Have them write it down in their science journal or notebook.

Practice

27. Have volunteers present their oral reports to the whole class. Have the class complete a checklist for each oral report.

Evaluation

28. Ask the volunteers which tactic they used.

"Did it help you feel less nervous?"

Expansion

29. Do a class experiment and have students go through the steps of conducting an oral report about that experiment. Encourage them to use the learning strategies they used for the science project.

30. Suggest that another teacher assign an oral presentation in his or her class. Have that teacher ask students to recall and use the same strategies they used for their science reports.

Contributed by Elizabeth Varela

Applying Positive Self-Talk to Speaking Tasks

LANGUAGE LEVEL: Beginning+

GRADE LEVEL: High School+

LANGUAGE: ESL

FOCUS LLS: Self-Talk (Talk Yourself Through It)

LANGUAGE OBJECTIVE: Prepare and present a one-minute presentation to the class

STRATEGY OBJECTIVE: Use positive *self-talk* to complete language learning tasks and increase feelings of self-efficacy, and identify and limit the use of negative self-talk

STRATEGY RATIONALE: *Self-talk* is a strategy that all people use when they are faced with new situations and as they carry out known tasks and routines. Negative self-talk can lead to feelings of low self-efficacy and can discourage the student from completing, or even attempting, new tasks. Positive self-talk empowers the student because reassuring oneself may enable the student to do more than he or she thought possible.

MATERIALS: Poster paper and markers; worksheet, "Using Self-Talk" (page 233)

PROCEDURES

Preparation

1. Ask students if they talk to themselves as they prepare to do and do something new, such as driving to a new location. Elicit and identify examples of positive and negative self-talk. Write all examples on the board in "Positive" and "Negative" columns as appropriate. If the self-talk is in students' native language, use translation.

"Talking to yourself can be very helpful if you are going to try something new or as you are trying to get something done. When do you talk to yourselves? Do you say positive or negative things to yourself?"

2. Ask students whether they use *self-talk* when they are preparing for a language learning task. Elicit and write all of the examples on the board, identifying each as positive or negative. Note the similarities to the self-talk for nonlanguage tasks.

"Talking to yourself can also be helpful when you are learning English. What do you say to yourself when you are preparing to use English? Do you think it is more helpful to use positive or negative self-talk?"

Presentation

3. Tell students that they are going to practice using *self-talk* as they prepare for and carry out a speaking task in English.

"We have a lot of strategies for preparing to speak in English. For example, we have practiced rehearsing. Today, we are going to practice the strategy *self-talk* to help us with a speaking task. You can use *self-talk* when you prepare to speak and also as you speak."

4. Model the strategy for a speaking task. Tell students that they will later practice the same strategy with another task. Emphasize the conscious use of positive self-talk.

"Okay, now I am going to show you how I can use *self-talk* to help me with a speaking task in a language I am learning, Spanish. My speaking task is to call the local Spanish grocery store and ask if they have coconut milk because I want to make a special dessert. Listen, this is my thinking: Before I call, I will use *self-talk* because I am a little bit nervous. I will tell myself, 'It's okay, I have a lot of strategies I can use. If they don't understand me at first, I will try again. I can do this. I am confident that I can talk about this.' While I am talking to the grocer, I can tell myself, 'Be calm and speak slowly. If I don't understand, I can ask the grocer to repeat what she said.' When I finish talking to the grocer, I will ask myself if my strategy of *self-talk* helped me."

5. Have students work with you to apply the *self-talk* strategy to another speaking task.

Practice

6. Tell students that they will now practice using the *self-talk* strategy for a speaking task. (The speaking task should be challenging enough to students so that they will need to use the strategy, but it should not be too difficult.)

"Okay, now it's your turn. Your speaking task is to give a one-minute presentation to the class about what you did last weekend. To prepare, write down on your worksheet, 'Using Self-Talk,' the kinds of self-talk you can use to help you and when you will use *self-talk*. When you are finished, you will give the presentation and then evaluate whether using *self-talk* helped you."

Evaluation

7. After students complete the worksheet and give their presentations, discuss as a class the role of *self-talk* as students prepared for and carried out the speaking task. Then have students fill out the final part of the worksheet.

"Did using *self-talk* help you at all? What kinds of *self-talk* did you use before you started? What kinds of *self-talk* did you do during the presentation?"

Expansion

8. Teach students positive self-talk words and phrases of encouragement in the target language.

9. Have students create a poster of native and target language positive self-talk and hang it in the classroom.

Contributed by Jennifer Kevorkian

Using Self-Talk

Directions Your speaking task is to give a one-minute presentation to the class about your weekend. Complete this worksheet. Use *self-talk* to help you prepare for and carry out your speaking task.

1 What positive self-talk can you use to prepare for the presentation?

I can tell myself _____.

I can tell myself _____.

I can tell myself _____.

I can tell myself _____.

2 What positive self-talk can you use during the presentation?

I can tell myself _____.

I can tell myself _____.

I can tell myself _____.

I can tell myself _____.

3 Did using self-talk help you give your presentation? How?

_____

_____

_____

_____

Substituting for Unknown Descriptive Words

LANGUAGE LEVEL: Beginning

GRADE LEVEL: Middle School

LANGUAGE: French (can be adapted to any language)

FOCUS LLS: Substitution

LANGUAGE OBJECTIVE: Use adjectives to describe familiar people and objects

STRATEGY OBJECTIVE: Use substitution to practice finding alternative ways of describing things when the specific adjective is not known or recalled

STRATEGY RATIONALE: Students often feel "stuck" if they cannot think of a specific word. They need to realize that they have other vocabulary that they can use in place of the word they cannot think of. By developing the strategy of *substitution*, students can greatly enhance their abilities to communicate, both verbally and written.

MATERIALS: Pictures cut from magazines; paper

PROCEDURES

Preparation

1. Ask students if there are times when they cannot think of a word in French (or other target language). Ask them how they feel when that happens. Ask them if they want to give up? Does it stop them from trying to say what they wanted to say? Give them an example.

"Once when I was in France, I went into the store to buy a newspaper. Guess what! I could not remember how to say 'newspaper.' I was too embarrassed to ask, so I left without thinking about how I might have gotten my point across. How do you think I could have gotten my point across without knowing the word for 'newspaper'?" (Answers could include, just looked for it, spoken in English, or described the newspaper.)

2. Discuss what the result might have been if you had used any of those alternatives. Ask students how they think you would have felt when you left the store with a newspaper. Discuss why you might have felt proud or happy.

Presentation

3. Explain to students that they are going to learn how to use the strategy *substitution* to help them when they cannot remember a word in French.

"I want to help you speak French with as little frustration as possible. I know that sometimes, when you cannot remember a word in French, it can be very frustrating. Today, we are going to learn a strategy that might help you when you cannot remember a word in French. You are going to use the strategy *substitution*, which means you substitute another word or phrase to get your point across without having to use the word you cannot remember."

4. Present some examples to them. You can do these in French or English, depending on the level of the students.

"Let's do an example. You want to tell someone that you like her new haircut, but you cannot remember how to say 'haircut.' What are some alternatives to using the word? (They will probably come up with examples such as, 'I like your hair. You look nice today. Did you go to the beauty salon/barber today?') Isn't it amazing how you can find lots of ways to get your point across?"

Practice

5. Have students practice *substitution* by using any vocabulary unit that they are studying, for example, a unit on adjectives that describe people and objects. Begin by working as a whole class. Show students a picture of a person who is bald. Tell them that they are to describe the person, but they do not know the word for "bald." Give the students time to think. Some students might come up with an answer like "no hair" or "not much hair." If they have problems, give them an example to get the process started. Once the students do get started, they should be able to invent some creative alternatives, for example, "smooth head," "head like a baby," "does not need a comb," and so on. The substitutions can be written on the board or on a transparency, if the group is at the appropriate level.

6. Continue showing pictures, giving them one word that they are to use but that they do not know. Have them give alternatives.

7. Once students understand the strategy, divide them into groups of three or four. Give each group several pictures, with the word that they do not know written on an attached piece of paper. In their groups, have them brainstorm various substitutions for the unknown word in each picture. Have them write their substitutions on paper. When groups are finished with their pictures, reassemble the class.

Evaluation

8. Have each group present each picture, the word they do not know, and the list of substitutions they developed. By sharing their lists, they offer many creative substitutions to their classmates.

9. After the whole class has presented their materials, ask them how helpful the strategy was. In what other situations will this strategy be useful? Have them give specific examples.

Expansion

10. For homework, have students do one of the following activities.

- Give them a list of words for which they are to write substitutions.
- Have students describe situations in which they might use this strategy, including, for example, their own list of words that they make up and substitutions for those words.

Contributed by Suzanne Tapia

Summarizing a Story

LANGUAGE LEVEL: Beginning, Intermediate   **LANGUAGE:** Any

GRADE LEVEL: Elementary+   **FOCUS LLS:** Summarize

LANGUAGE OBJECTIVE: Create an oral story as a class

STRATEGY OBJECTIVE: Periodically *summarize* the oral class story to help remember it

STRATEGY RATIONALE: *Summarizing* helps the student decide how well he or she understood the story or text. It also reinforces the student's learning of the message.

MATERIALS: Interesting pictures that the students can use to create a class story (same number of pictures as students in the class); six pictures for the teacher to use for the Preparation activity; masking tape

PROCEDURES

Preparation

1. Use a variety of pictures to tell students a story. Use mostly vocabulary that they already know, but say it fairly quickly with some vocabulary they do not know. Do not stop to review the story.

2. When you have finished, ask them if they understood the story and all of its details. Ask them what they did to remember the story.

"How many of you understood the story I just told you? Did you understand every detail? Do you remember what happened in the beginning of the story? What did you do to remember the story?"

Presentation

3. Tell students that they are going to practice the strategy *summarize* to help them to better understand what they hear.

"There are many times when you hear a story, watch a television show, or read an article that is so long or has so much information that, by the end of it, you are not sure what happened, just like in the story I just told you. Today, we are going to learn a strategy to help us review periodically what is happening in a story so that by the end of the story, you will have a very good idea of what happened. We are not going to repeat exactly what we heard. We are going to tell in our own words what happened. This strategy is called *summarizing*. Use the strategy to check your understanding of the story and to help you remember it."

4. Tell students that you are going to tell them the story again and that you will use *summarizing* to restate the story in your own words to check your understanding.

5. Tell them several sentences about the first two pictures. Then stop and restate in an abbreviated manner what you just told them. Go on to the next two pictures. Continue the story with several more sentences, and then stop and retell it in your own words. Go on to the next two pictures, continue with several more sentences, and stop and summarize what happened.

6. At the end of the story, summarize in your own words what the whole story was about.

Practice

7. Tape pictures along the front of the room. (These can be taped along the bottom of the chalkboard or on the wall so that all students can see them.) The class will use the pictures to tell a story. Start the story by choosing a picture, taping it to the chalkboard, and saying two or three sentences about the picture. Students then take turns selecting a picture and saying a few sentences to continue the story. After every two or three pictures, students use the strategy *summarize* to review what has happened. Continue in this manner until everyone in the class has had a turn. (Expect the stories to be silly and to not make much sense!)

Evaluation

8. At the end of the story, have students work with a partner to review the story in summarized form. Walk around the room to make sure that everyone understands.

9. When students have finished, discuss the effectiveness of the strategy with them. Have students raise their hands in response to the following two questions.

"You have just proven how effective this strategy is because as I was walking around the room, I found out that everyone understood what happened in the story. Did the strategy *summarize* help you remember the story? Did it help you check to see if you understood?"

Expansion

10. Discuss with them how they can transfer this strategy to reading.

"Today, we used this strategy for an oral story. When will you use *summarizing* again? Could you use this strategy when you are reading?"

11. Give students a story to read for homework. Depending on the reading level of the students, have them write a one-sentence summary after every three sentences, after every paragraph, or after every page. The following day, have them compare their summaries with partners or in small groups.

Contributed by Suzanne Tapia

References

Abraham, R. G., & Vann, R. J. (1987). Strategies of two language learners: A case study. In A. Wenden & J. Rubin (Eds.), *Learner strategies in language learning* (pp. 85-102). Englewood Cliffs, NJ: Prentice-Hall.

Anderson, J. R. (1983). *The architecture of cognition.* Cambridge, MA: Harvard University Press.

Anderson, J. R. (1990). *Cognitive psychology and its implications* (3rd ed.). New York: Freeman.

Anderson, R. C. (1984). Role of the reader's schema in comprehension, learning, and memory. In R. C. Anderson, J. Osborn, & R. J. Tierney (Eds.), *Learning to read in American schools* (pp. 243-258). Hillsdale, NJ: Erlbaum.

Bandura, A. (1986). *Social foundations of thought and action: A social cognitive theory.* Englewood Cliffs, NJ: Prentice-Hall.

Bandura, A. (1992, April). *Self-efficacy mechanism in sociocognitive functioning.* Paper presented at the annual meeting of the American Educational Research Association, San Francisco, CA.

Bandura, A. (1993). Perceived self-efficacy in cognitive development and functioning. *Educational Psychologist, 28,* 117-148.

Bandura, A. (1997). Self-efficacy: *The exercise of control.* New York: Freeman.

Barnett, M. A. (1988). Teaching reading strategies: How methodology affects language course articulation. *Foreign Language Annals, 21*(2), 109-119.

Barnhardt, S., Kevorkian, J., & Delett, J. (1997). *Portfolio assessment in the foreign language classroom.* Washington, DC: National Capital Language Resource Center.

Bartlett, F. C. (1932). *Remembering.* Cambridge, England: Cambridge University Press.

Bedell, D. A., & Oxford, R. L. (1996). Cross-cultural comparisons of language learning strategies in the People's Republic of China and other countries.
In R. L. Oxford (Ed.), *Language learning strategies around the world: Cross-cultural perspectives* (pp. 47-60). Honolulu, HI: University of Hawaii Press.

Bereiter, C., & Bird, M. (1985). Use of thinking aloud in identification and teaching of reading comprehension strategies. *Cognition and Instruction, 2*(2), 131-156.

Bergman, J. L. (1992). SAIL—A way to success and independence for low-achieving readers. *Reading Teacher, 45*(8), 598-602.

Bermudez, A. B., & Prater, D. L. (1990). Using brainstorming and clustering with LEP writers to develop elaboration skills. *TESOL Quarterly, 24,* 523-528.

Borkowski, J. G., Carr, M., Rellinger, E. A., & Pressley, M. (1990). Self-regulated strategy use: Interdependence of metacognition, attributions, and self-esteem. In B. F. Jones (Ed.), *Dimensions of thinking: Review of research* (pp. 53-92). Hillsdale, NJ: Erlbaum & Associates.

Bransford, J. D., Barclay, J. R., & Franks, J. J. (1972). Sentence memory: A constructive versus interpretive approach. *Cognitive Psychology, 3,* 193-209.

Brown, H. D. (1989). *A practical guide to language learning: A fifteen-week program of strategies for success.* New York: McGraw-Hill.

Brown, T.S., & Perry, F. L., Jr. (1991). A comparison of three learning strategies for ESL vocabulary acquisition. *TESOL Quarterly, 25*(4), 655-670.

Brown, R., Pressley, M., Van Meter, P., & Schuder, T. (1996). A quasi-experimental validation of transactional strategies instruction with low-achieving second grade readers. *Journal of Educational Psychology, 88,* 18-37.

Cantoni-Harvey, G. (1987). *Content-area language instruction: Approaches and strategies.* Reading, MA: Addison-Wesley.

Carpenter, T., Fennema, E., Peterson, P. L., Chiang, C., & Loef, M. (1989). Using knowledge of children's mathematics thinking in classroom teaching: An experimental study. *American Educational Research Journal, 26,* 499-532.

Carrell, P. L. (1987). Content and formal schemata in ESL reading. *TESOL Quarterly, 21,* 461-482.

Carrell, P. L., & Eisterhold, J. (1983). Schema theory and ESL reading pedagogy. *TESOL Quarterly, 17,* 553-573.

Carrell, P. L., Pharis, B. G., & Liberto, J. C. (1989). Metacognitive strategy training for ESL reading. *TESOL Quarterly, 23*(4), 647-678.

Chamot. A. U. (1987). The learning strategies of ESL students. In A. Wenden & J. Rubin (Eds.), *Learner strategies in language learning* (pp. 71-83). Englewood Cliffs, NJ: Prentice Hall International.

Chamot, A. U. (1990). Cognitive instruction in the second language classroom: The role of learning strategies. In J. E. Alatis (Ed.), *Linguistics, language teaching and language acquisition: The interdependence of theory, practice and research.* Georgetown University Round Table on Languages and Linguistics 1990. Washington, DC: Georgetown University Press.

Chamot, A. U. (1993). Student responses to learning strategy instruction in the foreign language classroom. *Foreign Language Annals, 26*(3), 308-321.

Chamot, A. U. (1994). A model for learning strategy instruction in the foreign language classroom. In J. E. Alatis (Ed.), *Georgetown University Round Table on Languages and Linguistics 1994* (pp. 323-336). Washington, DC: Georgetown University Press.

Chamot, A. U. (1995). Learning strategies in listening comprehension: Theory and research. In D. Mendelsohn & J. Rubin (Eds.), *The theory and practice of listening comprehension for the second language learner* (pp. 13-26). San Diego, CA: Dominie Press.

Chamot, A. U. (1996). Learning strategies of elementary foreign-language-immersion students. In J. E. Alatis (Ed.), *Georgetown University Round Table on Languages and Linguistics 1995.* Washington, DC: Georgetown University Press.

Chamot, A. U. (in press). How children in language immersion programs use learning strategies. In M. A. Kassen (Ed.), *Language learners of tomorrow: Process and Promise!* Lincolnwood, IL: National Textbook Company.

Chamot, A. U., Barnhardt, S., & El-Dinary, P. B. (1996). *Teaching strategies to develop effective foreign language learners.* (Final Report). Unpublished manuscript.

Chamot, A. U., Barnhardt, S., El-Dinary, P. B., Carbonaro, G., & Robbins, J. (1993). *Methods for teaching learning strategies in the foreign language classroom and assessment of language skills for instruction.* (Final report). Washington, DC: Center for International Education, U.S. Department of Education. (ERIC Document Reproduction Service No. ED 365 157).

Chamot, A. U., Barnhardt, S., El-Dinary, P. B., & Robbins, J. (1996). Methods for teaching learning strategies in the foreign language classroom. In R. L. Oxford (Ed.), *Language learning strategies around the world: Cross-cultural perspectives* (pp. 175-187). Honolulu, HI: Second Language Teaching & Curriculum Center, University of Hawaii Press.

Chamot, A. U., Dale, M., O'Malley, J. M., Spanos, G. A. (1993). Learning and problem solving strategies of ESL students. *Bilingual Research Quarterly, 16* (3&4), 1-38.

Chamot, A. U., & El-Dinary, P. B. (1998). Children's learning strategies in immersion classrooms. Manuscript submitted for publication.

Chamot, A. U., Keatley, C., Barnhardt, S., El-Dinary, P. B., Nagano, K., & Newman, C. (1996). *Learning strategies in elementary language immersion programs.* (Final report). Washington, DC: Center for International Education, U.S. Department of Education. (ERIC Document Reproduction Service No. ED 404 878).

Chamot, A. U., & Küpper, L. (1989). Learning strategies in foreign language instruction. *Foreign Language Annals, 22,* 13-24.

Chamot, A. U., & Küpper, L. (1990). *Learning strategy instruction in the foreign language classroom: Speaking.* McLean, VA: Interstate Research Associates. (ERIC Document Reproduction Service No. ED 343 439).

Chamot, A. U., Küpper, L., & Barrueta, M. (1990). *Learning strategy instruction in the foreign language classroom: Listening.* McLean, VA: Interstate Research Associates. (ERIC Document Reproduction Service No. ED 343 441).

Chamot, A. U., Küpper, L., & Impink-Hernandez, M. V. (1988a). *A study of learning strategies in foreign language instruction: Findings of the longitudinal study.* McLean, VA: Interstate Research Associates. (ERIC Document Reproduction Service No. ED 352 823).

Chamot, A. U., Küpper, L., & Impink-Hernandez, M. V. (1988b). *A study of learning strategies in foreign language instruction: The third year and final report.* McLean, VA: Interstate Research Associates. (ERIC Document Reproduction Service No. ED 352 825).

Chamot, A. U., Küpper, L., Thompson, I., & Barnhardt, S. (1990). *Learning strategy instruction in the foreign language classroom: Reading.* McLean, VA: Interstate Research Associates. (ERIC Document Reproduction Service No. ED 343 438).

Chamot, A. U., Küpper, L., & Toth, S. (1990). *Learning strategy instruction in the foreign language classroom: Writing.* McLean, VA: Interstate Research Associates. (ERIC Document Reproduction Service No. ED 343 440).

Chamot, A. U., & O'Malley, J. M. (1993). Teaching for strategic learning: Theory and practice. In J. E. Alatis (Ed.), *Georgetown University Round Table on Languages and Linguistics 1993.* Washington, DC: Georgetown University Press.

Chamot, A. U., & O'Malley, J. M. (1994a). *The CALLA handbook: Implementing the Cognitive Academic Language Learning Approach.* White Plains, NY: Addison Wesley Longman.

Chamot, A. U., & O'Malley, J. M. (1994b). Language learner and learning strategies. In N. C. Ellis (Ed.) *Implicit and explicit learning of languages* (pp. 371-392). San Diego, CA: Academic Press.

Chamot, A. U., Robbins, J., and El-Dinary, P. B. (1993). *Learning strategies in Japanese foreign language instruction.* (Final report). Washington, DC: Center for International Education, U.S. Department of Education. (ERIC Document Reproduction Service No. ED 370 346).

Cohen, A. D. (1987). Student processing of feedback on their compositions. In A. Wenden & J. Rubin (Eds.),

Learner strategies in language learning (pp. 57-69). Englewood Cliffs, NJ: Prentice-Hall International.

Cohen, A.D. (1990). *Second language learning: Insights for learners, teachers, and researchers.* New York: Newbury House/Harper & Row.

Cohen, A. D. (1998). *Strategies in learning and using a second language.* London: Longman.

Cohen, A. D., & Aphek, E. (1981). Easifying second language learning. *Studies in Second Language Learning, 3,* 221-36.

Cohen, A. D., & Cavalcanti, M. C. (1990). Feedback on composition: Teacher and student verbal reports. In B. Kroll (Ed.) *Second language writing: Research insights for the classroom* (pp. 155-177). Cambridge, England: Cambridge University Press.

Cohen, A. D., & Olshtain, E. (1993). The production of speech acts by EFL learners. *TESOL Quarterly, 27*(1), 33-56.

Cohen, A. D., Weaver, S., & Li, T-Y. (1998). The impact of strategies-based instruction on speaking a foreign language. In A. D. Cohen, *Strategies in learning and using a second language* (pp. 107-156). London: Longman.

Collins, C. (1991). Reading instruction that increases thinking abilities. *Journal of Reading, 34,* 510-516.

Collins, A., Brown, J. S., & Newman, S. E. (1989). Cognitive apprenticeship: Teaching the craft of reading, writing, and mathematics. In L. B. Resnick (Ed.), *Knowing, learning, and instruction: Essays in honor of Robert Glaser* (pp. 453-494). Hillsdale, NJ: Erlbaum.

Cummins, J, (1996). *Negotiating identities: Education for empowerment in a diverse society.* Ontario, CA: California Association for Bilingual Education,

Dadour, E. S., & Robbins, J. (1996). University-level studies using strategy instruction to improve speaking ability in Egypt and Japan. In R. L. Oxford (Ed.), *Language learning strategies around the world: Cross-cultural perspectives* (pp. 157-166). Honolulu, HI: Second Language Teaching & Curriculum Center, University of Hawaii Press.

Derry, S. J. (1990). Learning strategies for acquiring useful knowledge. In B. F. Jones & L. Idol (Eds.),

Dimensions of thinking and cognitive instruction (pp. 347-379). Hillsdale, NJ: Lawrence Erlbaum.

Devine, J. (1993). The role of metacognition in second language reading and writing. In J. G. Carson & I. Leki (Eds.), *Reading in the composition classroom: Second language perspectives* (pp. 105-127). Boston, MA: Heinle & Heinle.

Dole, J., Duffy, G., Roehler, L., & Pearson, P. D. (1991). Moving from the old to the new: Research in reading comprehension instruction. *Review of Educational Research, 61*(2), 239-264.

Duffy, G. G., Roehler, L. R., Sivan, E., Rackliffe, G., Book, C., Meloth, M. S., Vavrus, L. G., Wesselman, R., Putnam, J., & Bassiri, D. (1987). Effects of explaining the reasoning associated with using reading strategies. *Reading Research Quarterly, 22*(3), 347-368.

El-Dinary, P. B. (1993). Teachers learning, adapting and implementing strategies-based instruction in reading. *Dissertation Abstracts International.* (University Microfilms No. 9407625).

El-Dinary, P. B., Brown, R., & Van Meter, P. (1995). Strategy instruction for improving writing. In E. Wood, V. E. Woloshyn, & T. Willoughby (Eds.). *Cognitive strategy instruction for middle and high schools* (pp. 88-116). Cambridge, MA: Brookline Books.

Ellis, G., & Sinclair, B. (1989). *Learning to learn English: A course in learner training. Teacher's book.* Cambridge, England: Cambridge University Press.

Ellis, N. C. (1994). Vocabulary acquisition: The implicit ins and outs of explicit cognitive mediation. In N. C. Ellis (Ed.) *Implicit and explicit learning of languages* (pp. 211-282). San Diego, CA: Academic Press.

Ellis, N. C., & Beaton, A. (1993). Psycholinguistic determinants of foreign language vocabulary learning. *Language Learning, 43*, 559-617.

Englert, C. S., Raphael, T. E., Anderson, L. M., Anthony, H. M., & Stevens, D. D. (1991). Making strategies and self-talk visible: Writing instruction in regular and special education classrooms. *American Educational Research Journal, 28*, 337-372.

Gagné, E. D. (1985). *The cognitive psychology of school learning.* Boston, MA: Little, Brown.

Gagné, E. D., Yekovich, C. W., & Yekovich, F. R. (1993). *The cognitive psychology of school learning* (2nd ed.). New York, NY: HarperCollins.

Garner, R. (1987). *Metacognition and reading comprehension.* Norwood, NJ: Heinemann.

Gaskins, I. W., & Elliot, T. T. (1991). *Implementing cognitive strategy instruction across the school: The Benchmark manual for teachers.* Cambridge, MA: Brookline Books.

Ghatala, E. S., Levin, J. R., Pressley, M., & Lodico, M. G. (1985). Training cognitive strategy monitoring in children. *American Educational Research Journal, 22*, 199-216.

Green, J. M., & Oxford, R. (1995). A closer look at learning strategies, L2 proficiency, and gender. *TESOL Quarterly, 29*(2), 261-297.

Faerch, C., & Kasper, G. (1984). Two ways of defining communication strategies. *Language Learning, 34*, 45-63.

Harris, K. R., & Graham, S. (1992). *Helping young writers master the craft: Strategy instruction and self-regulation in the writing process.* Cambridge, MA: Brookline Books.

Hosenfeld, C. (1976). Learning about learning: Discovering our students' strategies. *Foreign Language Annals, 9*, 117-129.

Hosenfeld, C., Cavour, I., & Bonk, D. (1996). Adapting a cognitive apprenticeship method in foreign language classrooms. *Foreign Language Annals, 29*(4), 588-596.

Hosenfeld, C., Arnold, V., Kirchofer, J., Laciura, J., & Wilson, L. (1981). Second language reading: A curricular sequence for teaching reading strategies. *Foreign Language Annals, 14*(5), 415-422.

Idol, L., & Jones, B. F. (1991). *Educational values and cognitive instruction: Implications for reform.* Hillsdale, NJ: Lawrence Erlbaum.

Jiménez, R. T., & Gámez, R. (1998). Literature-based cognitive strategy instruction for middle school Latino students. In R. M. Gersten & R. T. Jiménez (Eds.), *Promoting learning for culturally and linguistically diverse students.* Belmont, CA: Wadsworth.

Jones, B. F., & Idol, L. (1990) Introduction. In B. F. Jones & L. Idol (Eds.), *Dimensions of thinking and cognitive instruction* (pp. 1-13). Hillsdale, NJ: Lawrence Erlbaum.

Jones, B. F., Palincsar, A. S., Ogle, D. S., & Carr, E. G. (1987). *Strategic thinking and learning: Cognitive instruction in the content areas.* Alexandria, VA: Association for Supervision and Curriculum Development.

Keatley, C., & Chamot, A. U. (1998). *Learning strategy use by children in language immersion classrooms.* Manuscript in preparation.

Kidd, R., & Marquardson, B. (1996). The Foresee approach for ESL strategy instruction in an academic-proficiency context. In R. L. Oxford (Ed.), *Language learning strategies around the world: Cross-cultural perspectives* (pp. 189-204). Honolulu, HI: Second Language Teaching & Curriculum Center, University of Hawaii Press.

Krapels, A. R. (1990). An overview of second language writing process approach. In B. Kroll (Ed.), *Second language writing* (pp. 37-56). Cambridge, England: Cambridge University Press.

Leki, I. (1995). Coping strategies of ESL students in writing tasks across the curriculum. *TESOL Quarterly, 29*(2), 235-260.

Mendelsohn, D., & Rubin, J. (1995). *The theory and practice of listening comprehension for the second language learner.* San Diego, CA: Dominie Press.

McLaughlin, B. (1987). *Theories of second language learning.* London: Edward Arnold.

Mohan, B. A. (1986). *Language and content.* Reading, MA: Addison-Wesley.

Muñiz-Swicegood, M. (1994). The effects of metacognitive reading strategy training on the reading performance and student reading analysis strategies of third grade bilingual students. *Bilingual Research Journal, 18*(1&2), 83-97.

Naiman, N., Fröhlich, M., Stern, H. H., & Todesco, A. (1978). *The good language learner.* Toronto: Ontario Institute for Studies in Education. [New edition 1996. Clevedon, England: Multilingual Matters.]

National Standards in Foreign Language Education Project. (1996). *Standards for foreign language learning: Preparing for the 21st century.* Lawrence, KS: Allen Press.

Nyikos, M. (1996). The conceptual shift to learner-centered classrooms: Increasing teacher and student strategic awareness. In R. L. Oxford (Ed.), *Language learning strategies around the world: Cross-cultural perspectives* (pp. 109-117). Honolulu, HI: Second Language Teaching & Curriculum Center, University of Hawaii Press.

Nyikos, M., & Oxford, R. L. (1993) A factor analytic study of language learning strategy use: Interpretations from information-processing theory and social psychology. *Modern Language Journal, 7,* 11-22.

Ogle, D. (1986). The K-W-L: A teaching model that develops active reading of expository text. *The Reading Teacher, 39,* 564-70.

O'Malley, J. M. (1987). The effects of training in the use of learning strategies on acquiring English as a second language. In A. Wenden & J. Rubin (Eds.), *Learner strategies in language learning* (pp. 133-144). Englewood Cliffs, NJ: Prentice-Hall.

O'Malley, J. M., & Chamot, A. U. (1998). *Accelerating academic achievement of English language learners: A synthesis of five evaluations of the CALLA model.* Manuscript submitted for publication.

O'Malley, J. M., & Chamot, A. U. (1990). *Learning strategies in second language acquisition.* Cambridge, England: Cambridge University Press.

O'Malley, J. M., Chamot, A. U., & Küpper, L. (1989). Listening comprehension strategies in second language acquisition. *Applied Linguistics, 10*(4), 418-437.

O'Malley, J. M., Chamot, A. U., Stewner-Manzanares, G., Küpper, L., & Russo, R. P., (1985a). Learning strategies used by beginning and intermediate ESL students. *Language Learning, 35,* 21-46.

O'Malley, J. M., Chamot, A. U., Stewner-Manzanares, G., Russo, R. P., & Küpper, L. (1985b). Learning strategy applications with students of English as a second language. *TESOL Quarterly, 19,* 285-296.

O'Malley, J. M., Chamot, A. U., & Walker, C. (1987). Some applications of cognitive theory to second language acquisition. *Studies in Second Language Acquisition, 9*, 287-306.

Oxford, R. L. (1986). *Development and psychometric testing of the Strategy Inventory for Language Learning.* Alexandria, VA: U.S. Army Research Institute for the Behavioral and Social Sciences.

Oxford, R. L. (1990). *Language learning strategies: What every teacher should know.* New York: Newbury House.

Oxford, R. L. (1996). *Language learning strategies around the world: Cross-cultural perspectives.* Honolulu, HI: Second Language Teaching & Curriculum Center, University of Hawaii Press.

Oxford, R. L., & Burry-Stock, J. A. (1995). Assessing the use of language learning strategies worldwide with the ESL/EFL version of the *Strategy Inventory for Language Learning System, 23*(2) 153-175.

Oxford, R. L., & Leaver, B. L. (1996), A synthesis of strategy instruction for language learners. In R. L. Oxford (Ed.), *Language learning strategies around the world: Cross-cultural perspectives* (pp. 227-246). Honolulu, HI: Second Language Teaching & Curriculum Center, University of Hawaii Press.

Padron, Y. N., & Waxman, H. C. (1988). The effects of ESL students' perceptions of their cognitive strategies on reading achievement. *TESOL Quarterly, 22*, 146-150.

Palincsar, A. S., & Brown, A. L. (1984). Reciprocal teaching of comprehension-fostering and comprehension-monitoring activities. *Cognition and Instruction, 1*, 117-175.

Palincsar, A. S., & Brown, A. L. (1986). Interactive teaching to promote independent learning from text. *The Reading Teacher, 39*(2), 771-777.

Palincsar, A. S., & Klenk, L. (1992). Examining and influencing contexts for intentional literacy learning. In C. Collins & J. N. Mangieri (Eds.), *Teaching thinking: An agenda for the twenty-first century* (pp. 297-315). Hillsdale, NJ: Erlbaum.

Paris, S. G., & Winograd, P. (1990). How metacognition can promote academic learning and instruction. In B. F. Jones & L. Idol (Eds.), *Dimensions of thinking and cognitive instruction.* Hillsdale, NJ: Erlbaum, pp. 15-51.

Pearson, P. D. & Gallagher, M. C. (1983). The instruction of reading comprehension. *Contemporary Educational Psychology, 8*, 317-344.

Post, M. & Poss, S. (1991). Learner use of strategies in interaction: Typology and teachability. *Language Learning, 41* (2), 235-273.

Pressley, M., El-Dinary, P. B., Gaskins, I., Schuder, T., Bergman, J. L., Almasi, J., & Brown, R. (1992). Beyond direct explanation: Transactional instruction of reading comprehension strategies. *Elementary School Journal, 92*(5), 513-555.

Pressley, M., Harris, K. R., Marks, M. B. (1992). But good strategy instructors are constructivists! *Educational Psychology Review, 4*, 3-31.

Pressley, M., Johnson, C., Symons, S., McGoldrick, J., & Kurita, J. (1989). Strategies that improve memory and comprehension of what is read. *Elementary School Journal, 90*, 3-32.

Pressley, M., Levin, J. R., & Delaney, H. D. (1982). The mnemonic keyword method. *Review of Educational Research, 52*, 61-91.

Pressley, M., Woloshyn, V., & Associates (1995). *Cognitive strategy instruction that really improves children's academic performance* (2nd ed.). Cambridge, MA: Brookline Books.

Raimes, A. (1985). What unskilled writers do as they write: A classroom study of composing. *TESOL Quarterly, 19*, 229-258.

Robbins, J. (1993). *Report on the pilot study of 'Learning strategies for the Japanese language classroom.'* Paper presented at the Georgetown University Round Table on Languages and Linguistics, Washington, DC.

Robbins, J. (1996a). Between 'Hello' and 'See you Later:' Development of Strategies for Interpersonal Communication in English by Japanese EFL Students. *Dissertation Abstracts International.* (University Microfilms No. 9634593).

Robbins, J. (1996b, November). *Language learning strategies instruction in Asia: Cooperative autonomy?* Paper presented at Autonomy 2000 conference at King Mongut's Institute of Technology, Thonburi. Bangkok, Thailand. (ERIC Document Reproduction Service No. ED409728).

Rogoff, B. (1990). *Cognitive apprenticeship.* New York: Oxford University Press.

Ross, S., & Rost, M. (1991). Learner use of strategies in interaction: Typology and teachability. *Language Learning, 41*(2), 235-273.

Rubin, J. (1975). What the "good language learner" can teach us. *TESOL Quarterly, 9,* 41-51.

Rubin, J. (1981). Study of cognitive processes in second language learning. *Applied Linguistics, 11,* 117-31.

Rubin, J. (1996). Using multimedia for learner strategy instruction. In R. L. Oxford (Ed.), *Language learning strategies around the world: Cross-cultural perspectives* (pp. 151-156). Honolulu, HI: Second Language Teaching & Curriculum Center, University of Hawaii Press.

Rubin, J., Quinn, J., & Enos, J. (1988). *Improving foreign language listening comprehension.* Report to U.S. Department of Education, International Research and Studies Program.

Rubin, J., & Thompson, I. (1994). *How to be a more successful language learner* (2nd ed.). Boston, MA: Heinle & Heinle.

Schumaker, J. B., & Deshler, D. D. (1992). Validation of learning strategy interventions for students with learning disabilities: Results of a programmatic research effort. In B. Y. L. Wong (Ed.), *Contemporary intervention research in learning disabilities: An international perspective* (pp. 22-46). New York: Springer-Verlag.

Schunk, D. H. (1996). *Learning Theories* (2nd ed.). Englewood Cliffs, NJ: Prentice-Hall.

Schunk, D. H., & Zimmerman, B. J. (1994). *Self-regulation of learning and performance: Issues and educational applications.* Hillsdale, NJ: Lawrence Erlbaum.

Silver, E. A., & Marshall, S. P. (1990). Mathematical and scientific problem solving: Findings, issues, and instructional implications. In B. F. Jones & L. Idol (Eds.), *Dimensions of thinking and cognitive instruction* (pp. 265-290). Hillsdale, NJ: Lawrence Erlbaum.

Slavin, R. E., Karweit, N. L., & Madden, N. A. (1989). *Effective programs for students at risk.* Needham Heights, MA: Allyn and Bacon.

Snow, M. A., Met, M., & Genesee, F. (1989). A conceptual framework for the integration of language and content instruction. *TESOL Quarterly, 23,* 201-217.

Snyder, B., & Pressley, M. (1990). Introduction to cognitive strategy instruction. In M. Pressley, V. Woloshyn, & Associates, *Cognitive strategy instruction that really improves children's academic performance* (2nd ed., pp. 1-18). Cambridge, MA: Brookline Books.

Spiro, R. J. (1980). Constructive processes in prose comprehension and recall. In R. J. Spiro, B. C. Bruce, & W. F. Brewer (Eds.), *Theoretical issues in reading comprehension* (pp. 245-278). Hillsdale, NJ: Erlbaum.

Stern, H. H. (1975). What can we learn from the good language learner? *Canadian Modern Language Review, 31,* 304-318.

Tarone, E. (1980). Communication strategies, foreigner talk, and repair in interlanguage. *Language Learning, 30*(2), 417-431.

Teachers of English to Speakers of Other Languages. (1997). *ESL standards for pre-K-12 students.* Alexandria, VA: Author.

Thompson, I., & Rubin, J. (1996). Can strategy instruction improve listening comprehension? *Foreign Language Annals, 29*(3), 331-342.

Vandergrift, L. (1997a). The comprehension strategies of second language (French) listeners: A descriptive study. *Foreign Language Annals, 30*(3), 387-409.

Vandergrift, L. (1997b). The Cinderella of communication strategies: Reception strategies in interactive listening. *Modern Language Journal, 81*(4), 494-505.

Vann, R. J., & Abraham, R. G. (1990). Strategies of unsuccessful language learners. *TESOL Quarterly, 24*(2), 177-198.

Varela, E. E. (1997). *Speaking solo: Using learning strategy instruction to improve English language learners' oral presentation skills in content-based ESL.* Unpublished doctoral dissertation, Georgetown University, Washington, DC.

Vygotsky, L. S. (1962). *Thought and language.* Cambridge, MA: MIT Press.

Vygotsky, L. S. (1978). *Mind in society: The development of higher psychological processes.* Cambridge, MA: Harvard University Press.

Warschauer, M. (1995). *E-Mail for English teaching: Bringing the Internet and computer learning networks into the language classroom.* Alexandria, VA: TESOL.

Weaver, S. J., & Cohen, A. D. (1997). *Strategies-based instruction: A teacher-training manual.* Minneapolis, MN: Center for Advanced Research on Language Acquisition, University of Minnesota.

Weinstein, C. E., & Mayer, R. E. (1986). The teaching of learning strategies. In M. R. Wittrock (Ed.), *Handbook of research on teaching* (3rd ed., pp. 315-27). New York: Macmillan.

Wenden, A. L. (1986). Helping L2 learners think about learning. *English Language Teaching Journal, 40,* 3-12.

Wenden, A. L. (1987a). Incorporating learner training in the classroom. In A. Wenden & J. Rubin (Eds.), *Learner strategies in language learning* (pp. 159-168). Englewood Cliffs, NJ: Prentice-Hall.

Wenden, A. (1987b) Metacognition: An expanded view on the cognitive abilities of L2 learners. *Language Learning,* 37 (4): 573-597.

Wenden, A. L. (1991). *Learner strategies for learner autonomy.* London: Prentice-Hall International.

Wenden, A. L. (1998). *Learner training in foreign/second language learning: A curricular perspective for the 21st century.* New York. (ERIC Document Reproduction Service No. ED 416 673).

Wenden, A., & Rubin, J. (1987) *Learner strategies in language learning.* Englewood Cliffs, NJ: Prentice-Hall.

Willing, K. (1989). *Teaching how to learn: Learning strategies in ESL. A teacher's guide.* Sydney, Australia: National Centre for English Language Teaching and Research, Macquarie University.

Willoughby, T., & Wood, E. (1995). Mnemonic strategies. In E. Wood, V. E. Woloshyn, & T. Willoughby (Eds.), *Cognitive strategy instruction for middle and high schools* (pp. 5-17). Cambridge, MA: Brookline Books.

Wood, E., Woloshyn, V. E., & Willoughby, T. (1995). *Cognitive strategy instruction for middle and high schools.* Cambridge, MA: Brookline Books.

Wood, P., Bruner, J., & Ross, G. (1976). The role of tutoring in problem solving. *Journal of Child Psychology and Psychiatry, 17,* 89100.

Zamel, V. (1983). The composing processes of advanced ESL students: Six case studies. *TESOL Quarterly, 17,* 165-187.

Zimmerman, B. J. (1990). Self-regulated learning and academic achievement: An overview. *Educational Psychologist, 25*(1), 3-17.

Zimmerman, B. J., & Pons, M. M. (1986). Development of a structured interview for assessing student use of self-regulated learning strategies. *American Educational Research Journal, 23*(4), 614-628.

Zimmerman, B. J., & Schunk, D. H. (Eds.). (1989). *Self-regulated learning and academic achievement: Theory, research, and practice.* New York: Springer-Verlag

Index